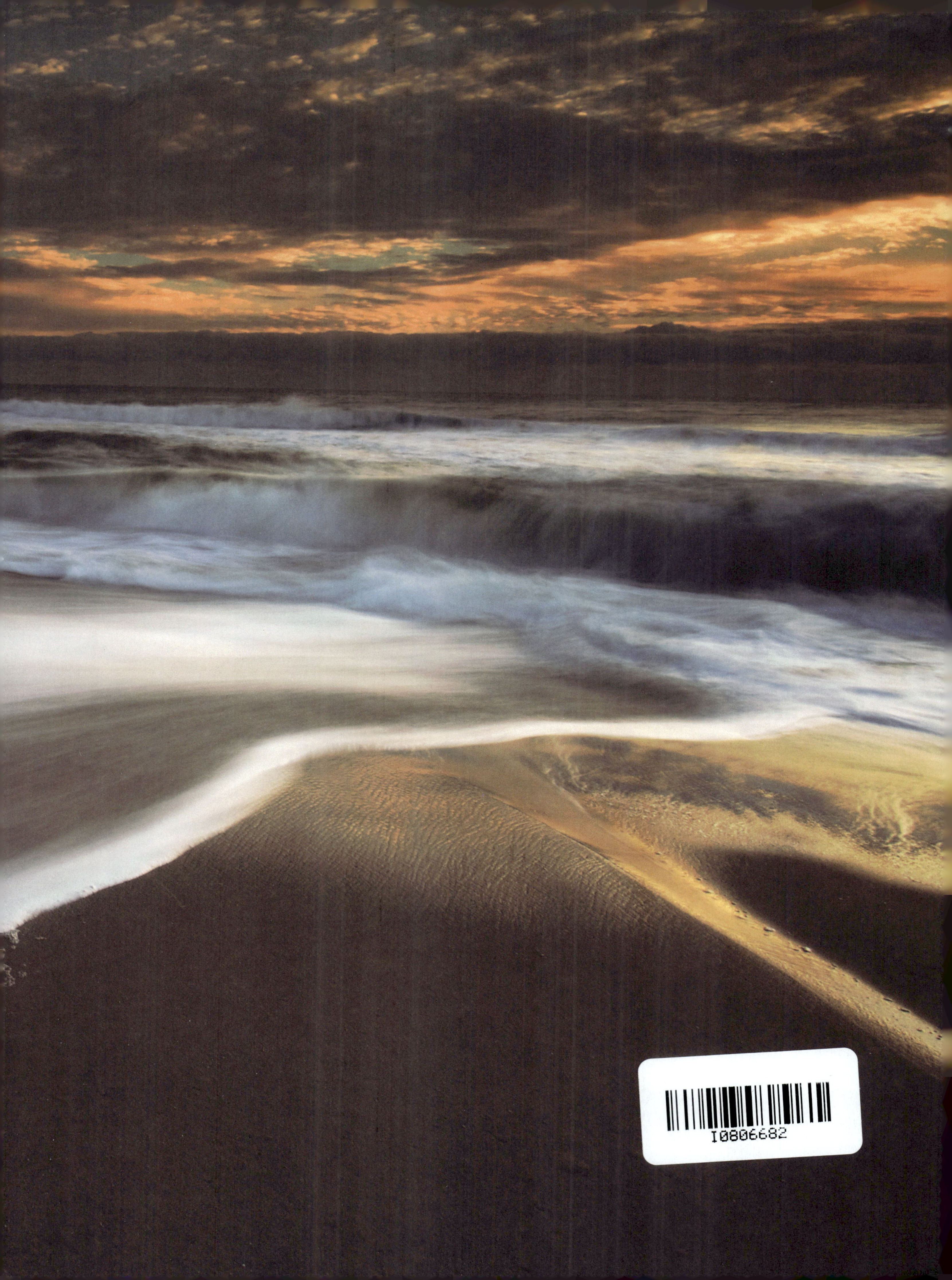

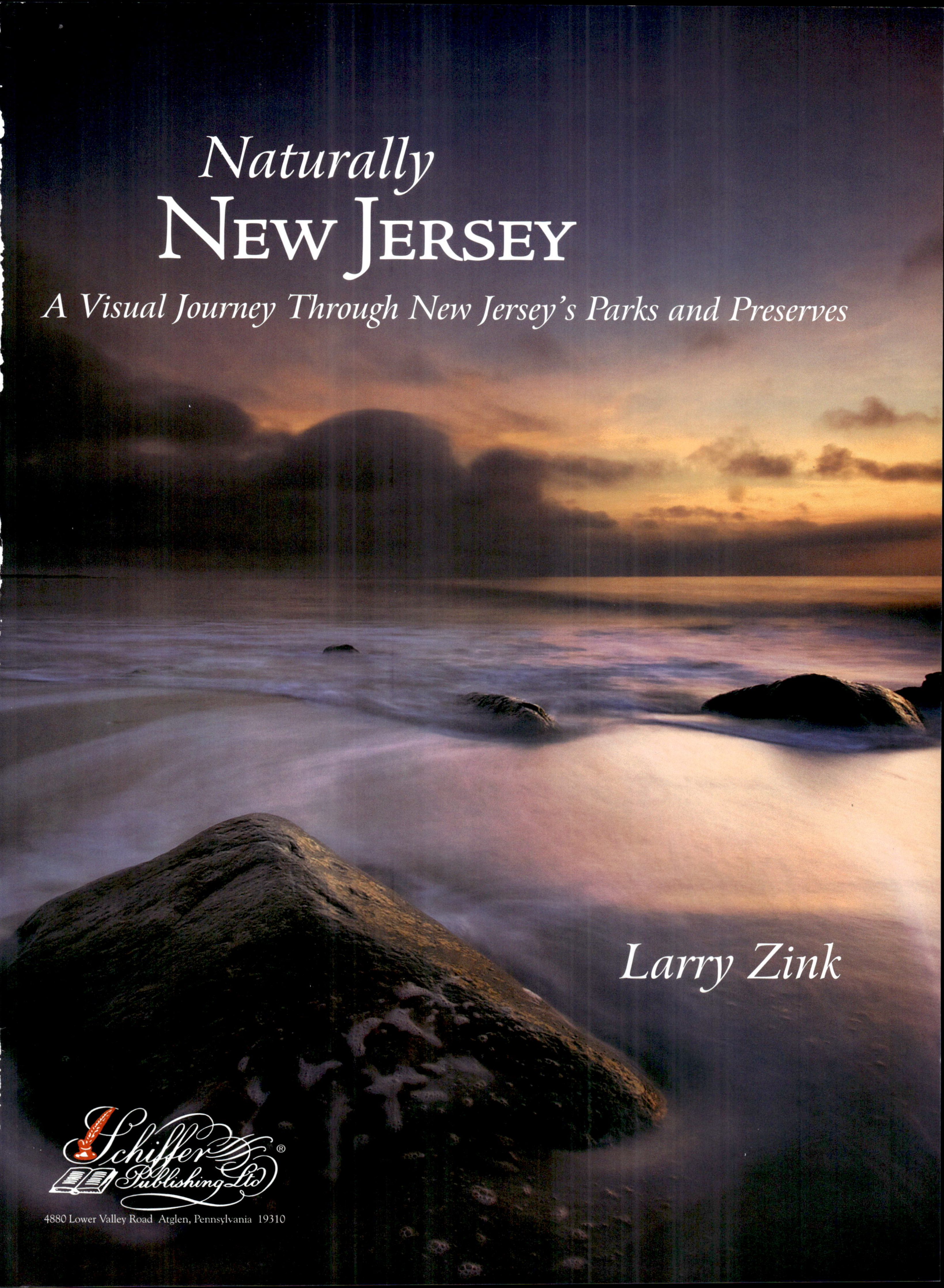

Naturally New Jersey

A Visual Journey Through New Jersey's Parks and Preserves

Larry Zink

Schiffer Publishing Ltd®
4880 Lower Valley Road Atglen, Pennsylvania 19310

Schiffer Books are available at special discounts for bulk purchases for sales promotions or premiums. Special editions, including personalized covers, corporate imprints, and excerpts can be created in large quantities for special needs. For more information contact the publisher:

Library of Congress Control Number: 2012930943

Covers and book designed by: Bruce Waters
Type set in Arrus BT Itakic-Zurich BT light

ISBN: 978-0-7643-3997-4
Printed in Hong Kong

Published by Schiffer Publishing Ltd.
4880 Lower Valley Road
Atglen, PA 19310
Phone: (610) 593-1777; Fax: (610) 593-2002
E-mail: Info@schifferbooks.com

For the largest selection of fine reference books on this and related subjects, please visit our website at
www.schifferbooks.com
We are always looking for people to write books on new and related subjects. If you have an idea for a book, please contact us at
proposals@schifferbooks.com

This book may be purchased from the publisher.
Please try your bookstore first.

You may write for a free catalog.

In Europe, Schiffer books are distributed by
Bushwood Books
6 Marksbury Ave.
Kew Gardens
Surrey TW9 4JF England
Phone: 44 (0) 20 8392 8585; Fax: 44 (0) 20 8392 9876
E-mail: info@bushwoodbooks.co.uk
Website: www.bushwoodbooks.co.uk

Leigh, Dylan, Hannah, and Karen, and, of course, Mom and Dad.

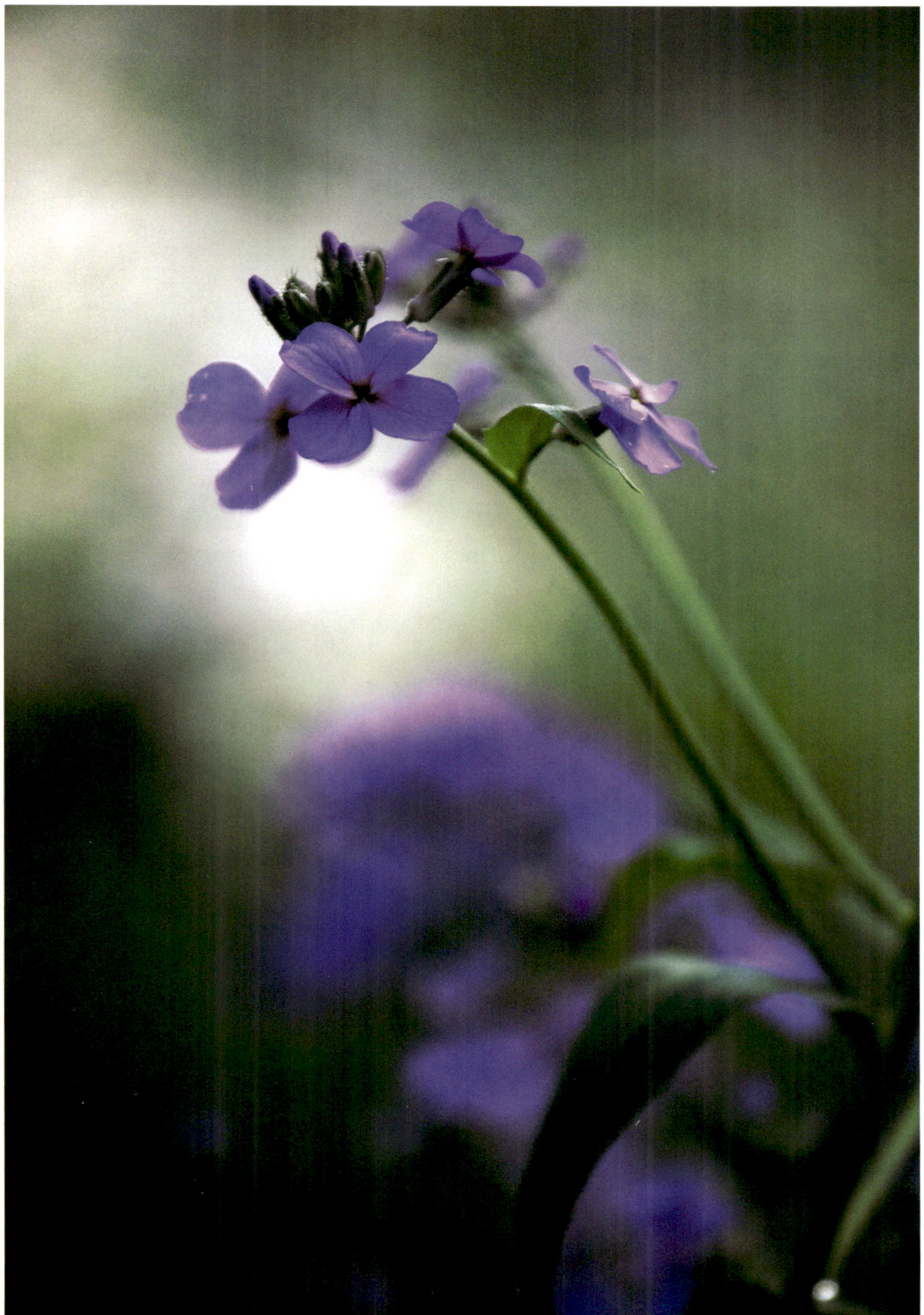

Acknowledgments

There are many people who have contributed to making this book a reality. This project was born out of many subway ride conversations with Michael Bailey. If it weren't for those conversations, this book may have never happened. I'd like to thank everyone at Macy's and at the Brooklyn Photo Studio who has ever taken an interest in my work. I appreciated your advice, conversation, and support. To all of my family and friends who gave me ideas and direction over the past couple of years, thank you. I would be remiss if I didn't thank Marc Staccioli who accompanied me on hikes and shot my portrait for this book. Also, Rose Inguanti helped me make valuable connections that greatly enhanced this project. Finally a special thank you goes to Schiffer Publishing for giving me this extraordinary opportunity.

Contents

Foreword

The Treasures of New Jersey

For most people, when they travel through New Jersey they have a limited view, you might even call it tunnel vision. But when you look closely at New Jersey's natural places, you realize New Jersey is really the light at the end of the tunnel. Even though New Jersey is the most densely populated state and has more superfund sites than any other state, we have some of the most remarkable natural areas and scenic vistas in the United States. Whether it is the one million acres Pinelands, an United Nations Biosphere Preserve, the scenic beauty and pristine waters of the Highlands, the migratory birds in Delaware Bay Shore, or the rugged rocks and mountains of the Skylands, the most important part of New Jersey's open space legacy is all our state parks. This book celebrates the beauty of New Jersey's state parks and many natural areas.

New Jersey is unique. It has one of the most diverse ecosystems anywhere in the country, going from sand dunes to marshes, field and forest, all the way up to granite mountains. In New Jersey, you can go kayaking around a salt marsh then turn the corner to see the New York City skyline. You can go hiking in the mountains and not see a house for miles, then climb a ridge and see a metropolitan area lying in front of you. You can climb a craggy hill in the Pinelands and see the Atlantic City casinos far in the distance. That is what makes New Jersey such a unique and special state naturally.

We are also one of the most bio-diverse states. New Jersey is the northern-most range of many southern species and the southern-most range of northern species, making it one of the best places in the country to view a wide mix of flora and fauna. New Jersey is a vibrant landscape with a beautiful spectrum of colors, from waterfalls to fall foliage, from the sunset over the Kittatiny Ridge to the sunrise over the Ken Lockwood Gorge.

Many of the wonderful places that are showcased in the book were threatened with development at one time or another and the public outcry against the loss of these treasured places led to their preservation. Whether it is Terrace Pond being under the runway of a jet port, the Pinelands becoming a giant Levittown, the Meadowlands being inundated by a mall, or the Tocks Island Dam flooding areas above the Delaware Water Gap, all of these environmental battles have made the appreciation of these open spaces even more enjoyable.

New Jersey has the highest property taxes in the country, yet citizens have voted to raise property taxes for open space in 266 towns and all 21 counties. All thirteen ballot questions for open space funding have passed over the last 50 years. The people of New Jersey are very supportive of open space and have permanently preserved 1.3 million acres of it. When you live in the most densely populated state in the nation, you get a much deeper appreciation for the value of open spaces.

Our state parks are the backbone of our open space system. With 19 million visitors a year, more people visit New Jersey's state parks than visit any one national park. People enjoy our parks through hiking, birding, swimming, or just sitting by a pine tree on a rock outcrop reading a book.

Our parks and natural areas are, in some ways, even more important to us New Jerseyans than National Parks. The Highlands are a train or bike ride away, but we cannot bike from Hackensack to Yellowstone in an hour. 5.5 million people don't get their drinking water from Yosemite, but do from the Highlands. Our state parks and opens spaces are the treasures of New Jersey and our legacy to future generations.

—Jeff Tittle, New Jersey Director of Sierra Club

Naturally New Jersey

As a photographer, I've been surprised and amazed at the natural diversity of New Jersey. This project started out as a simple exercise in creativity for myself, but as I began shooting New Jersey's landscapes and getting exciting results, my motivation to create became an obsession. My obsession became this book.

There are two basic elements in creating beautiful landscape photography: an interesting composition and the quality of light. The crucial combination of these two elements, working hand in hand, make the photograph truly stand out.

Good photographic composition involves the arrangement and balance of objects within an image that create visual interest. I'm always aware of the foreground as it relates to the background, elements that can lead the viewer's eyes through the image, and how the light affects those elements. Without that combination, the image usually will be aesthetically unsatisfying.

The second main element in an image is the quality of the light. In nature photography, the quality of light refers to the angle and color of the sun. The best light and color is either pre-dawn to early morning or late day to twilight. At those times, the light produces an interesting depth due to shadows and textures. Shooting before the sun is above the horizon or right after it sets takes advantage of amazing light that bounces off the existing sky. The ambient glow is wonderful and mysterious, especially in the right landscape. Many photographers refer to this time as "the magic hour." At times the light can be fleeting or it is a grand show that unfolds before your eyes; to me, that is the inherent challenge and excitement of shooting landscapes.

The images in this book are meant to show a different side of New Jersey. I didn't want to shoot the normal icons of the state: the boardwalks along the shore, the beautiful red mill in Clinton, or the stunning buildings scattered throughout. Instead, my intention is to show the natural wilderness of New Jersey in an exciting manner. I also wanted to shoot in areas that were open to the public. Therefore, the criteria for the photographs were that they had to be in parks, preserves or wildlife management areas. I thought it was important that people who want to explore some of these beautiful areas on their own have the ability to do so. Many of these spots can be reached rather easily, involving, at most, a 5-mile hike to an isolated spot, but usually much less effort.

I have traveled to over thirty different parks, logged a couple thousand miles on my car, gotten up at four in the morning far too often to remember, and met so many nice people along the way. As a landscape photographer in New Jersey, one is blessed. From beautiful sunsets at the state's highest peak at High Point State Park to the soft muted shades of sunrises at Sandy Hook Recreation Area, there are boundless opportunities. From the incredible uniqueness of the Pinelands to clear running trout streams and cascades, natural New Jersey provides a welcome respite from a busy and connected world that is the state. It may not have 6000-foot snow-covered mountain vistas or open spaces as far as the eye can see, but within the most densely populated state in the union lies a particular beauty waiting to be seen and enjoyed.

Many of the parks in the state have had to be saved from destruction or neglect, or have required a fight against suburban sprawl simply to exist. As a result, they are precious resources that the residents of New Jersey own and enjoy.

We live in a busy and hurried existence today and we're always connected to something or someone via our electronic devices. As I hiked to many of the locations that are in this book, I became more connected with the environment and the need to save and preserve it. It is an amazing experience to sit on top of a mountain and watch the sunrise and it is exhilarating to stand in a clear mountain stream as a bear walks by. So, I hope that you are motivated to visit the state's natural resources, to spend time in its parks, and to enjoy their beauty. Whether examined up close or from a mountain top vista, it is distinctly and naturally New Jersey.

—Larry Zink

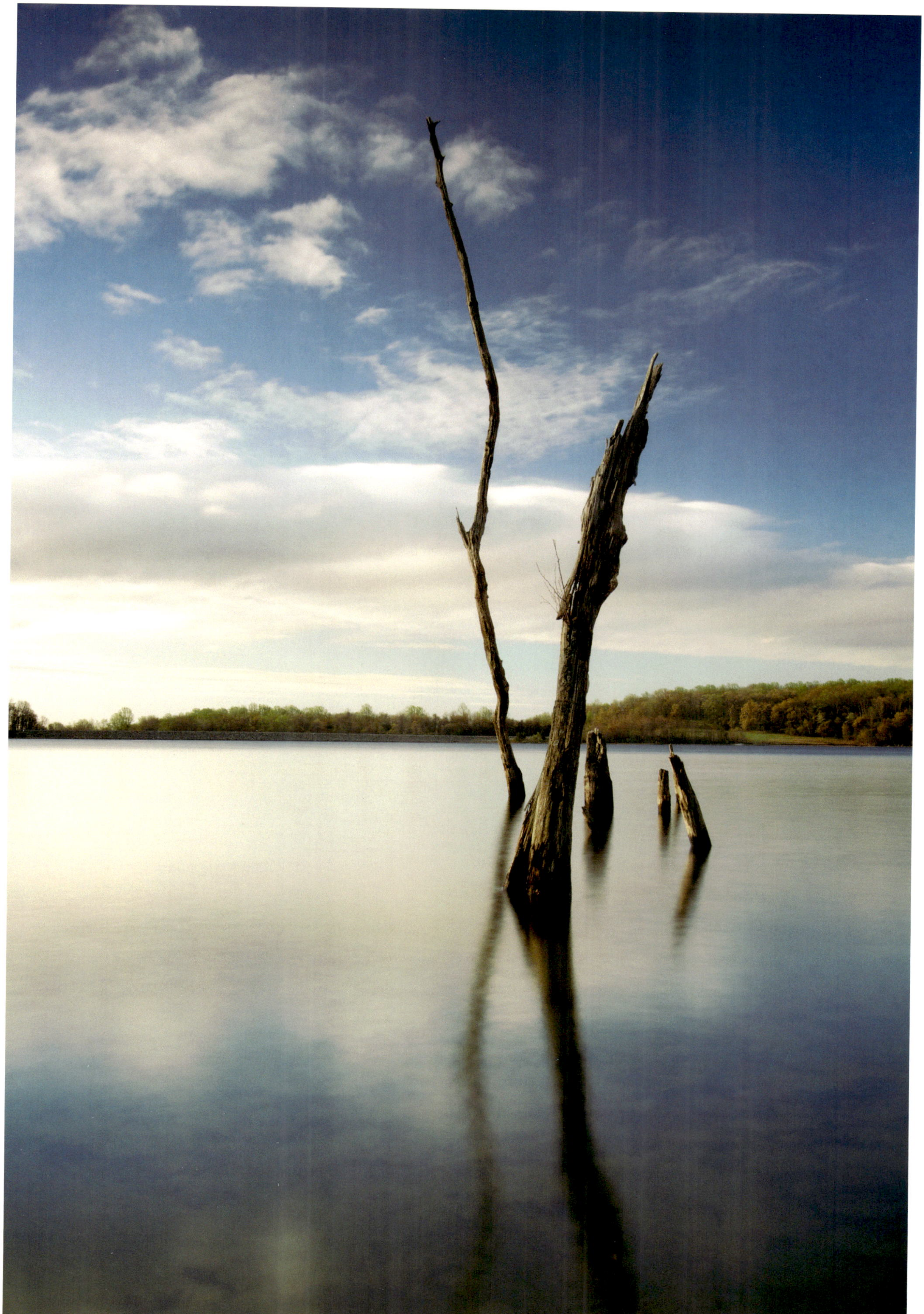

Drowned trees, Merrill Creek Reservoir

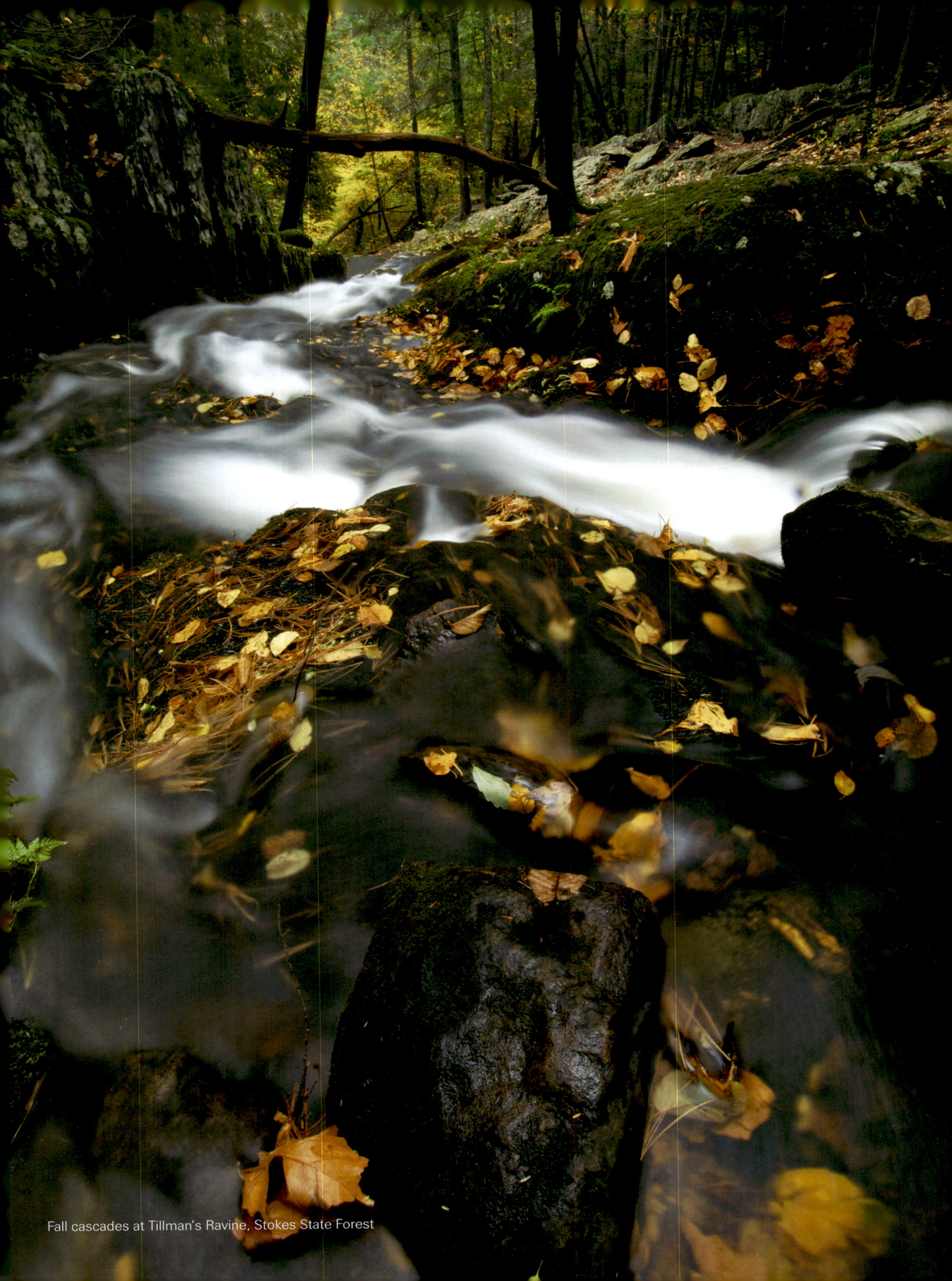

Fall cascades at Tillman's Ravine, Stokes State Forest

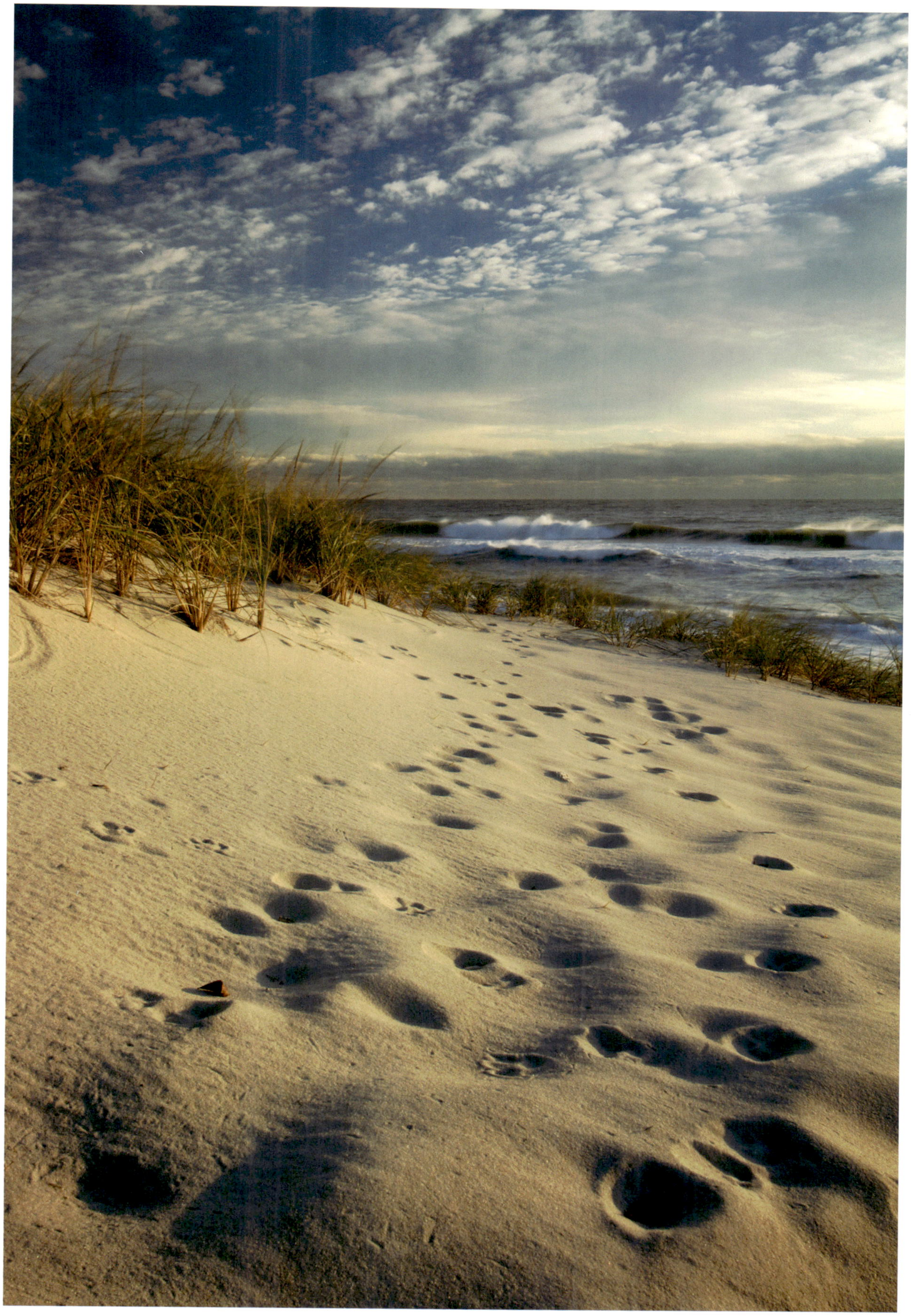

Tracks in the sand, Island Beach State Park

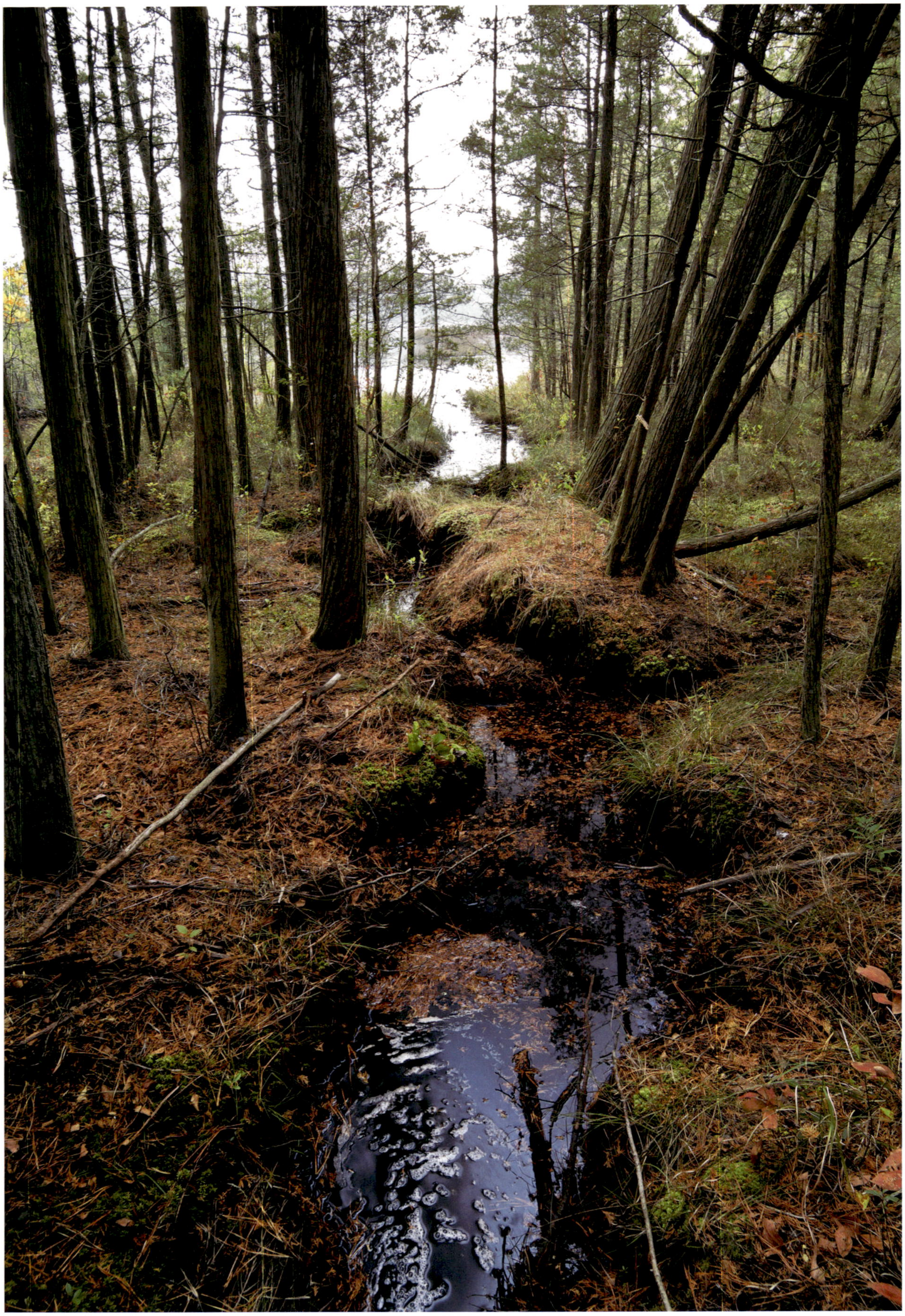

Stream leading to Harrisville Pond, Wharton State Forest

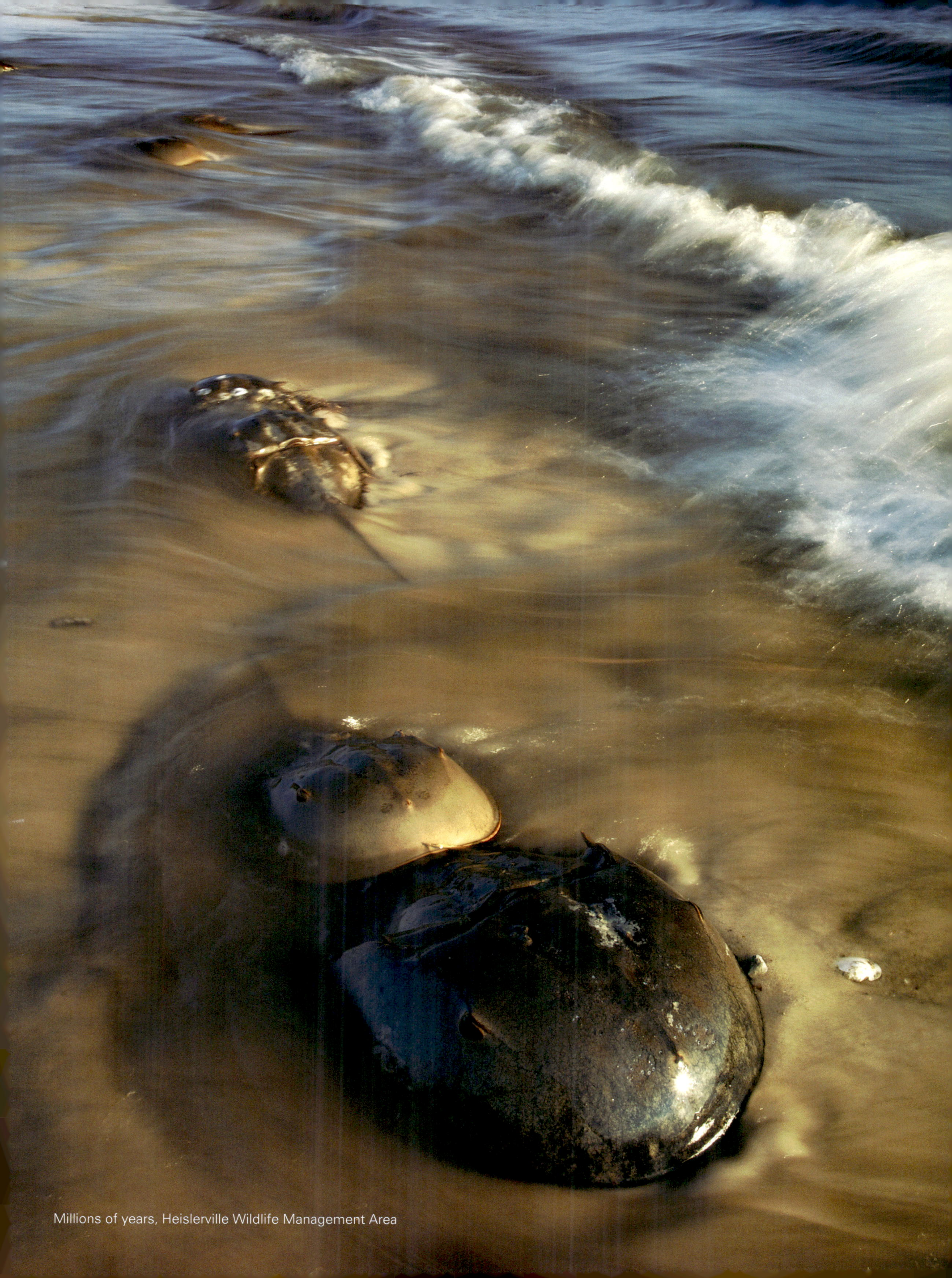

Millions of years, Heislerville Wildlife Management Area

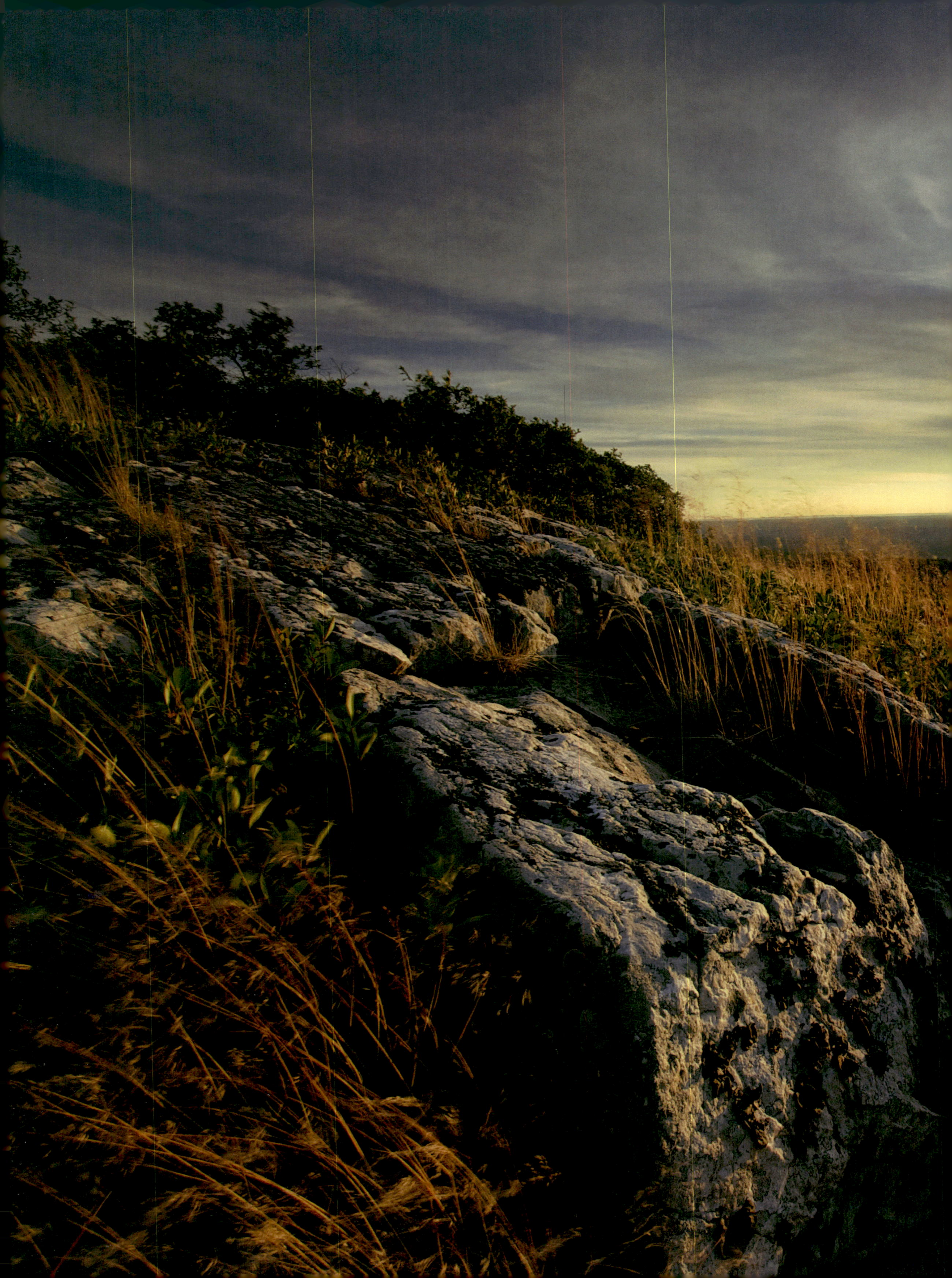

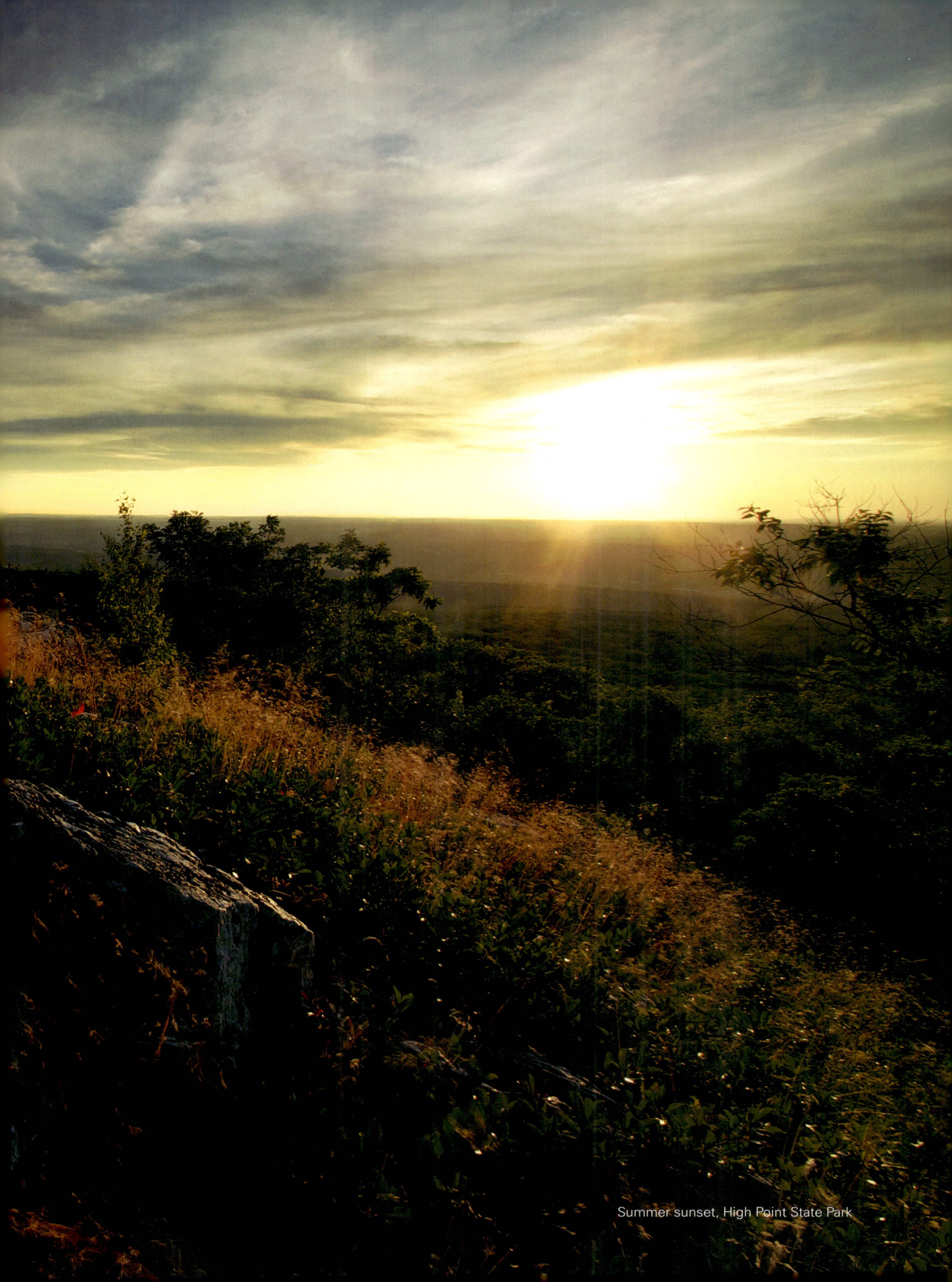

Summer sunset, High Point State Park

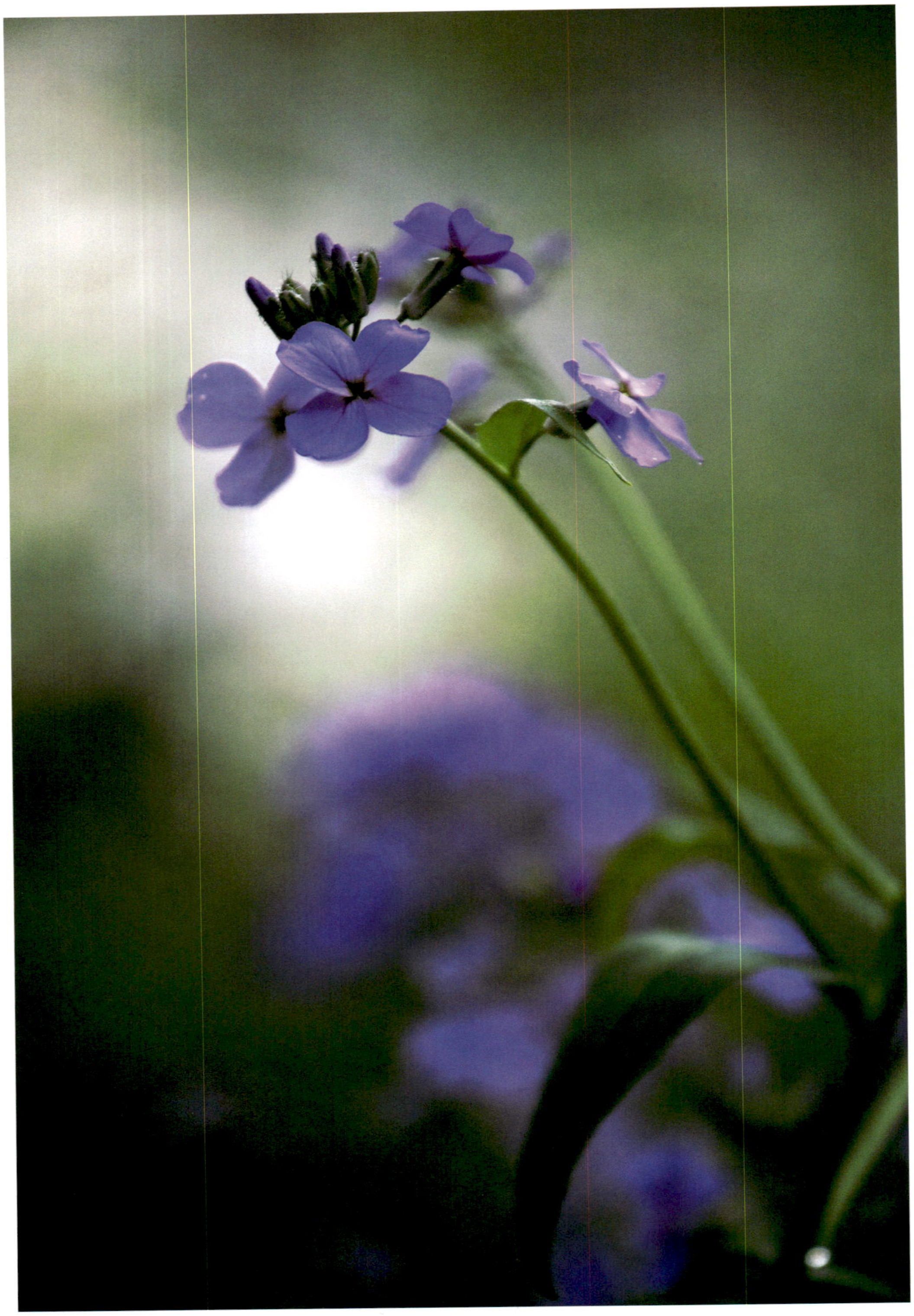

Purple blooms, Point Mountain Reservation

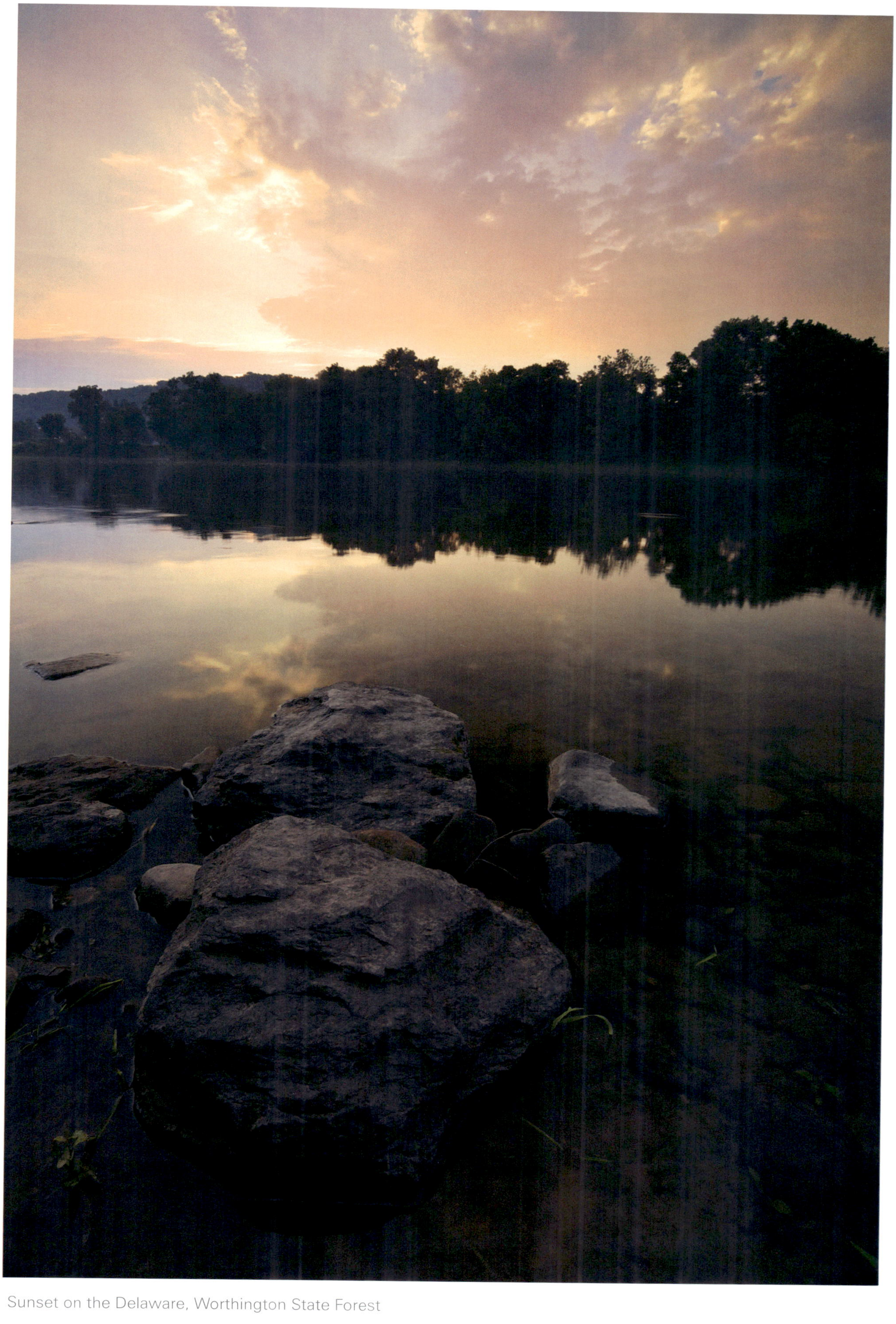

Sunset on the Delaware, Worthington State Forest

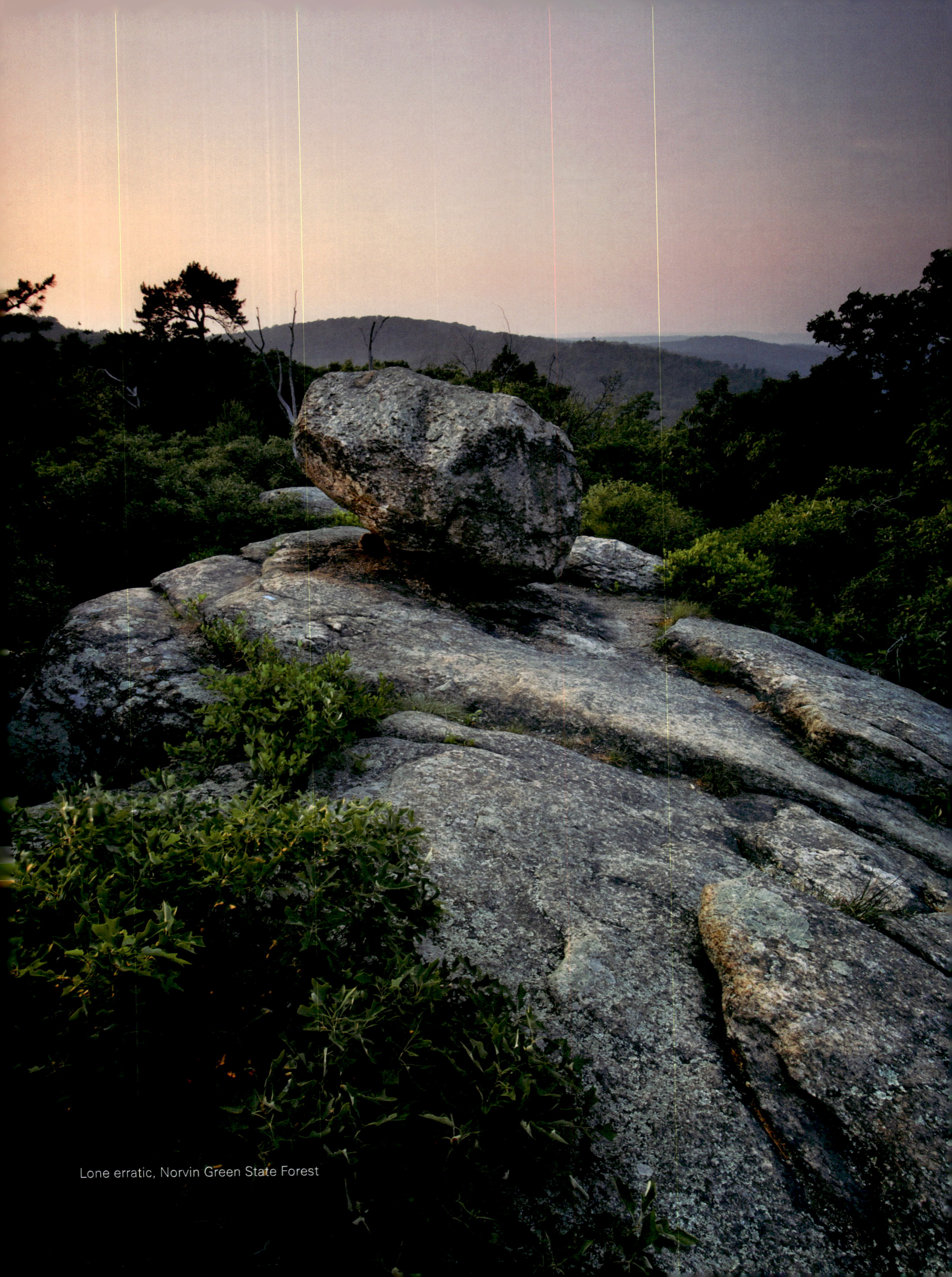

Lone erratic, Norvin Green State Forest

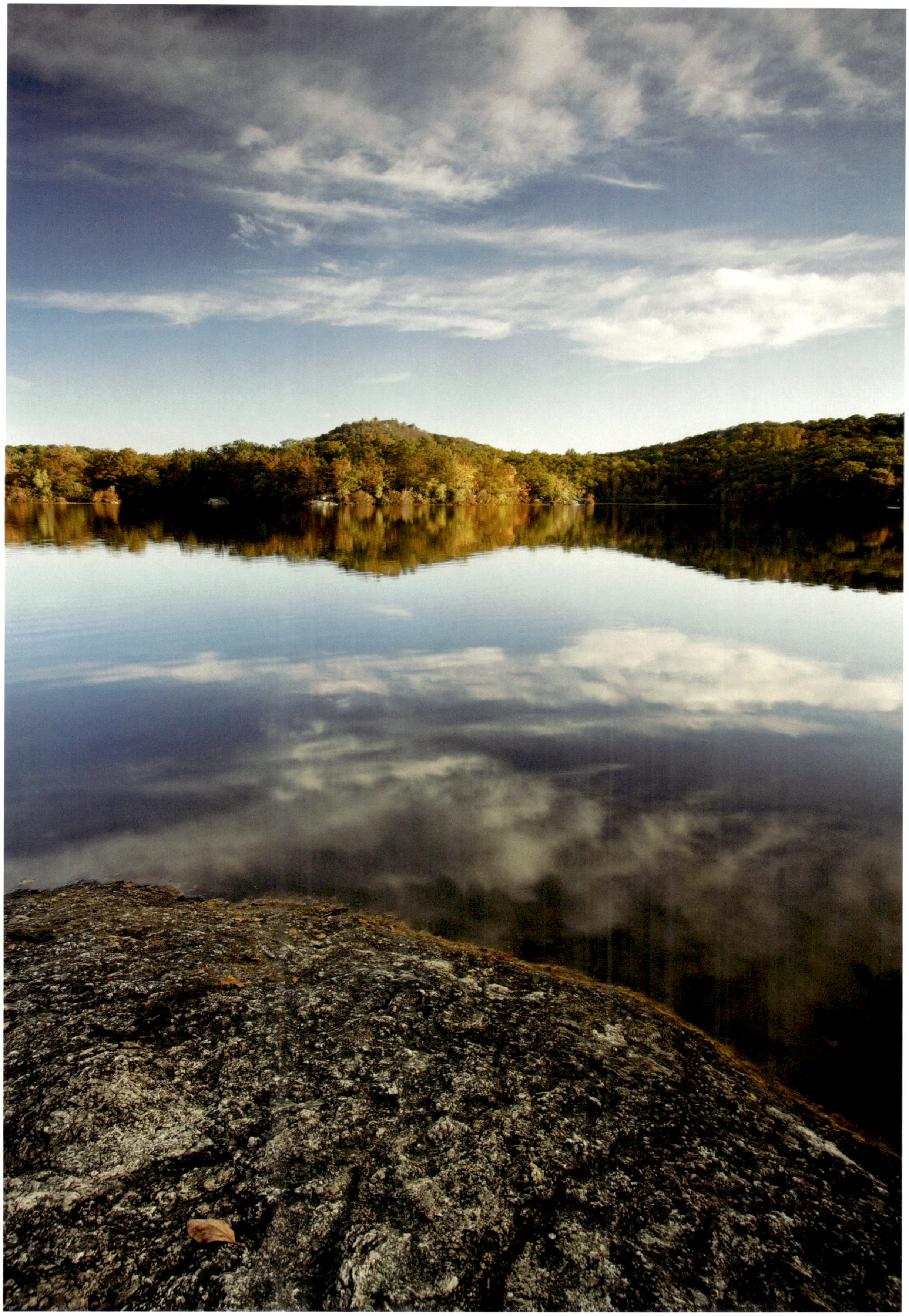

Ramapo Lake, Ramapo Mountain State Forest

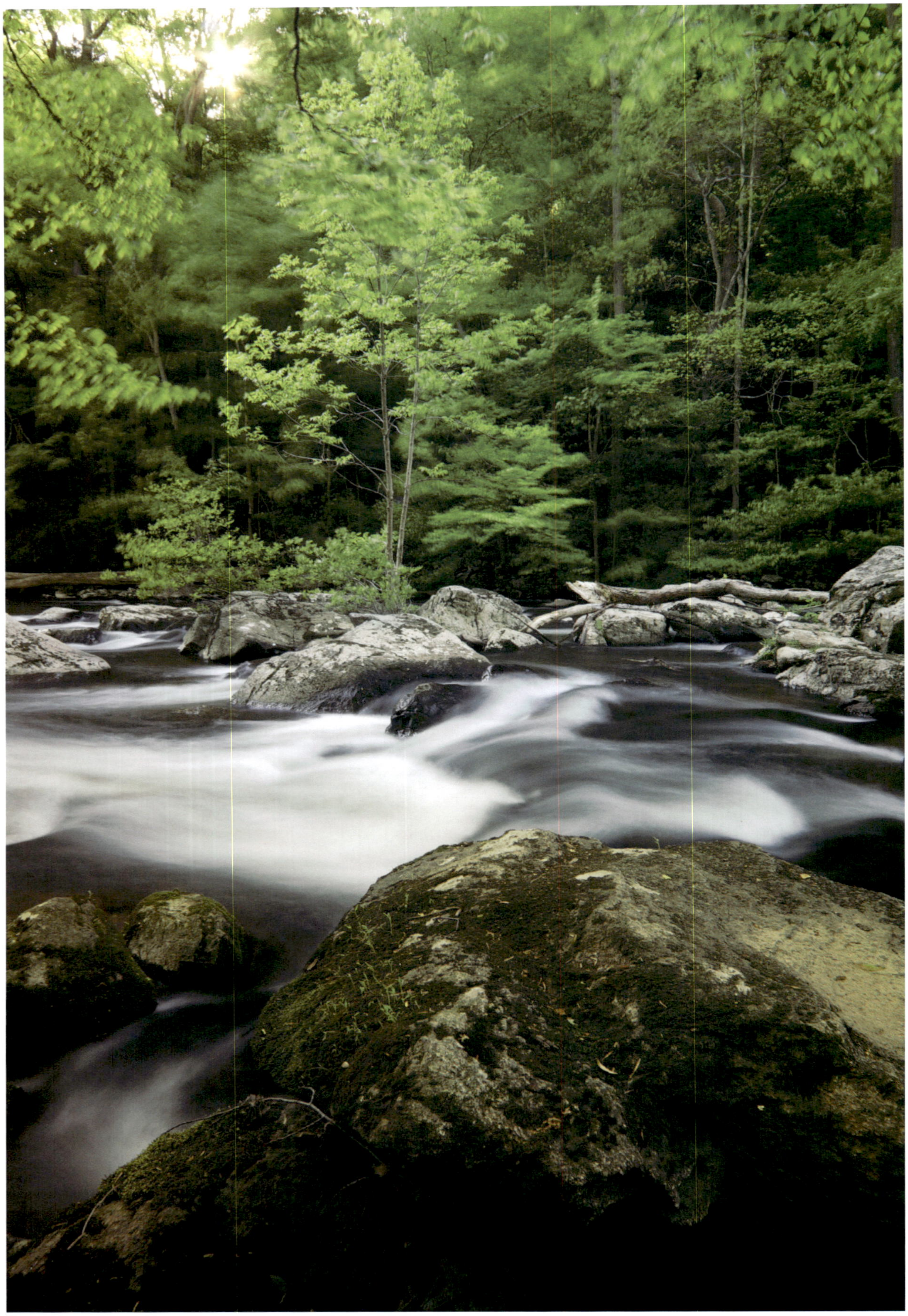

Windy day, Ken Lockwood Gorge Wildlife Management Area

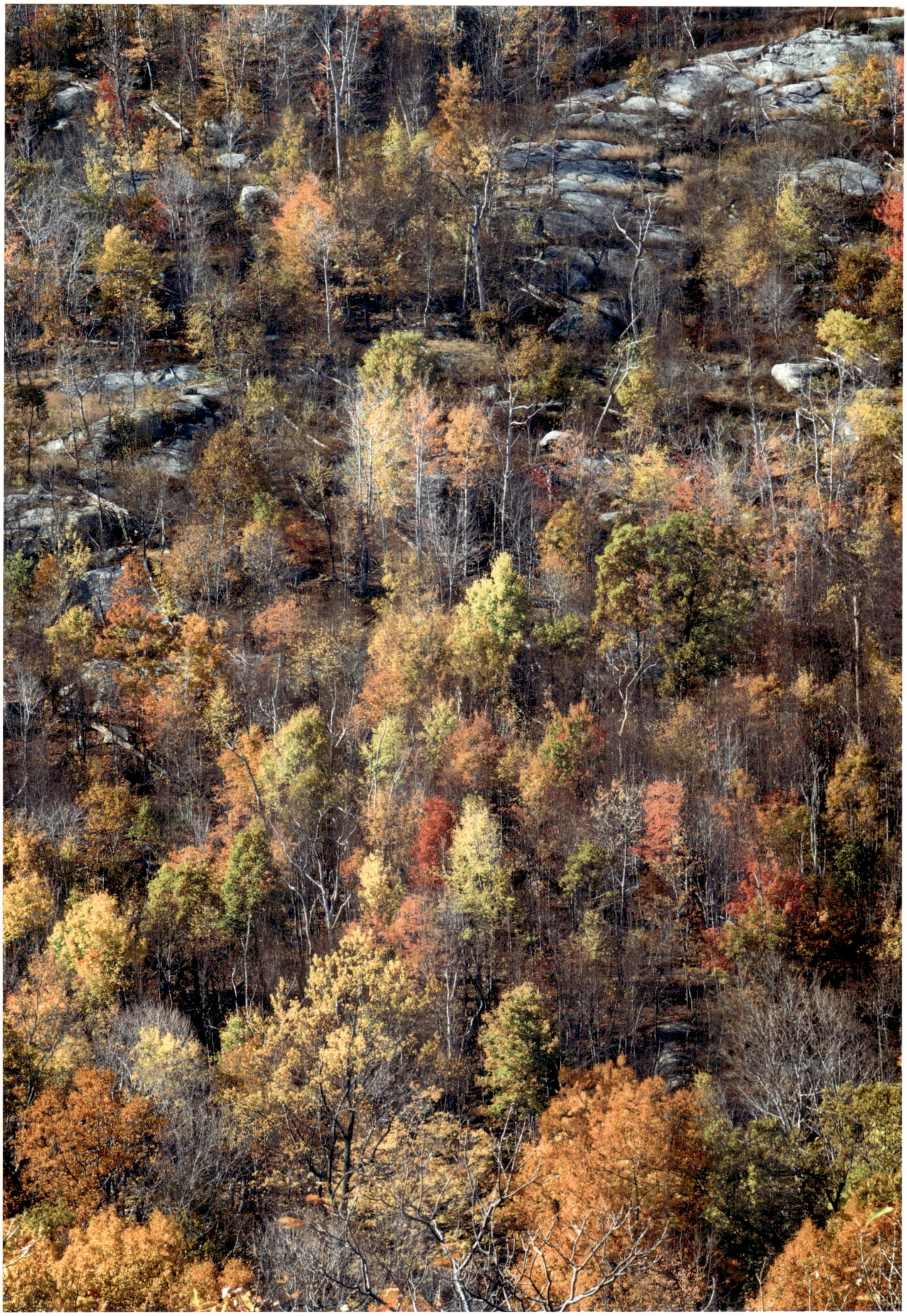
Trees and rocks, Norvin Green State Forest

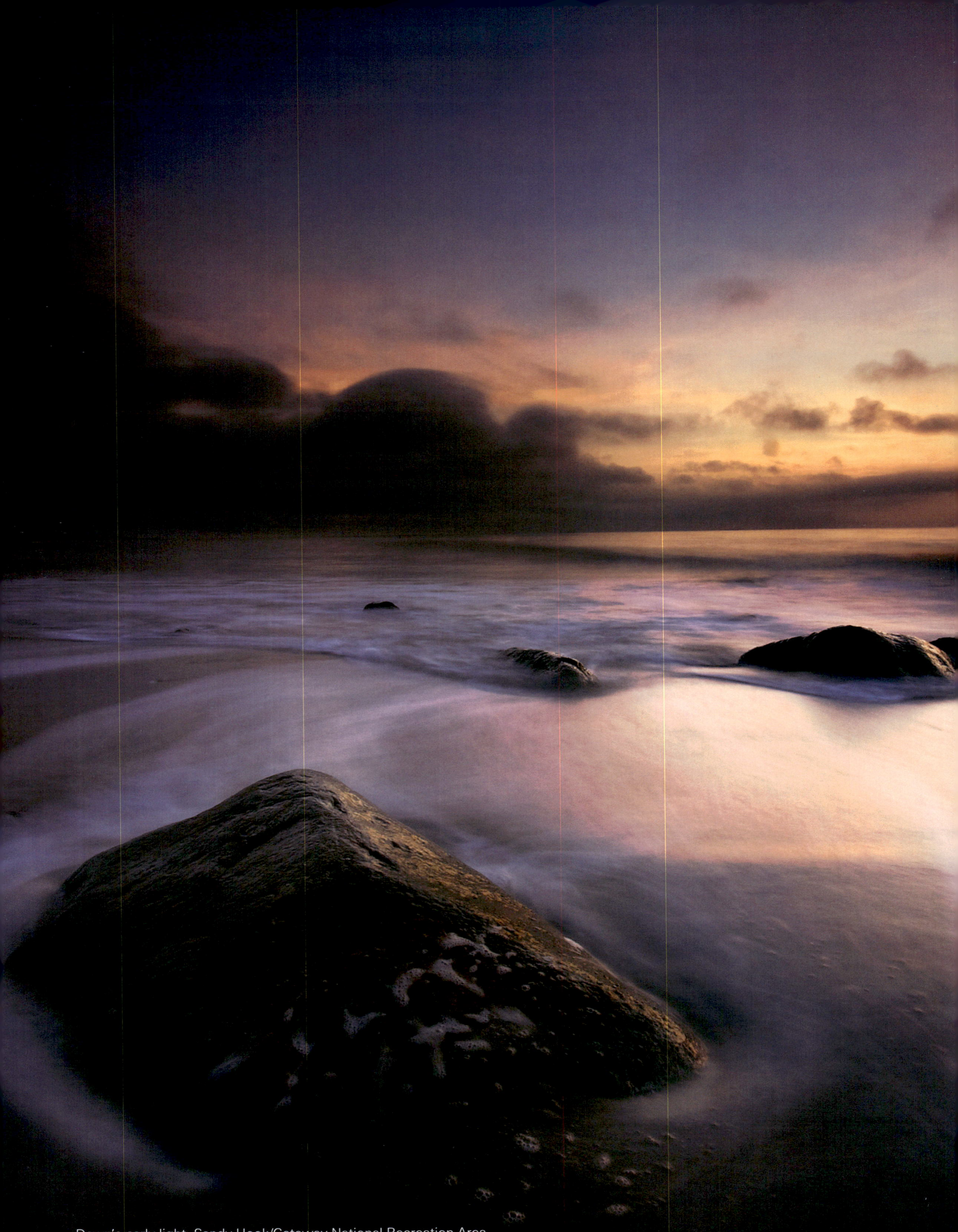

Dawn's early light, Sandy Hook/Gateway National Recreation Area

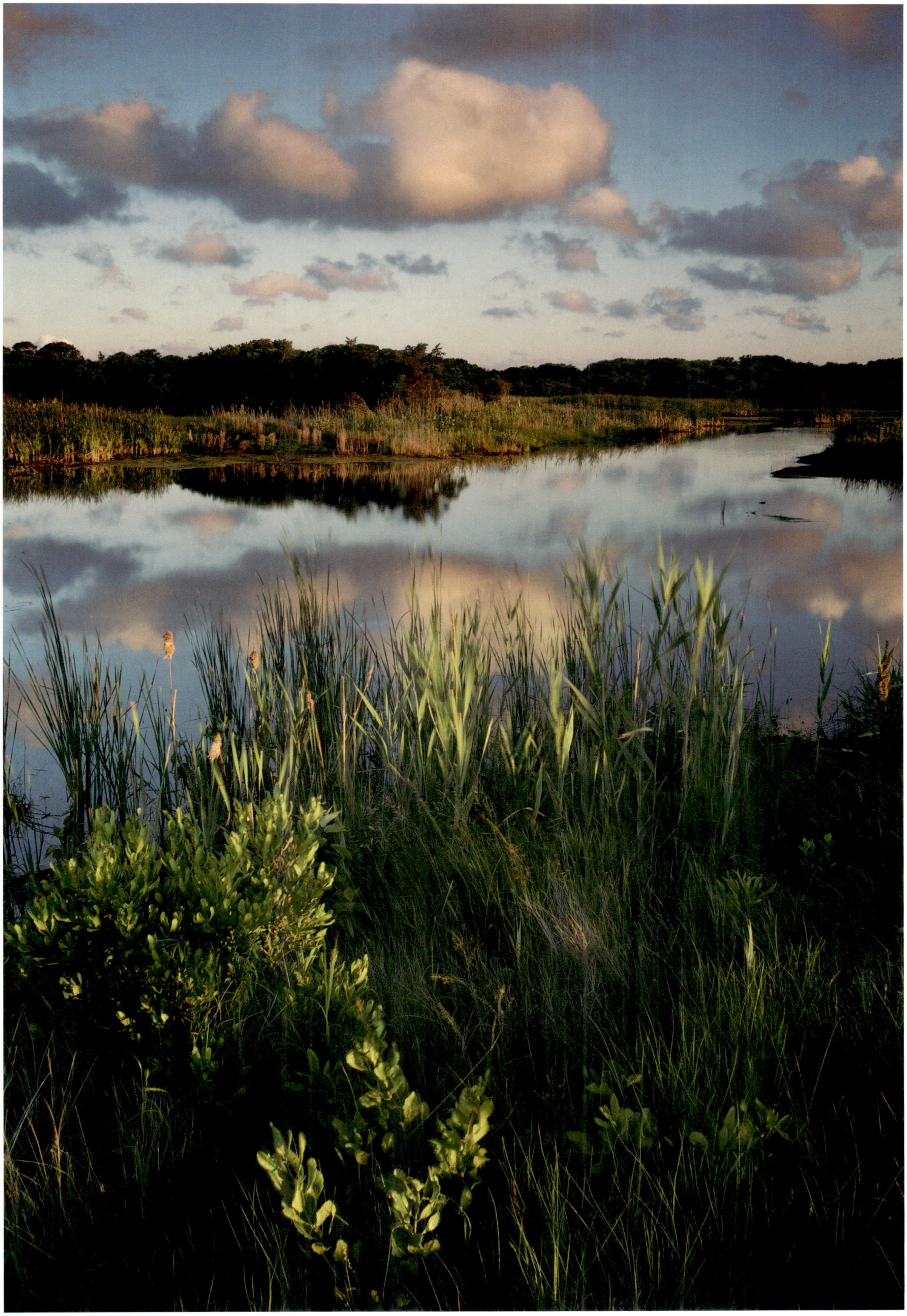

Early morning solitude, South Cape May Meadows

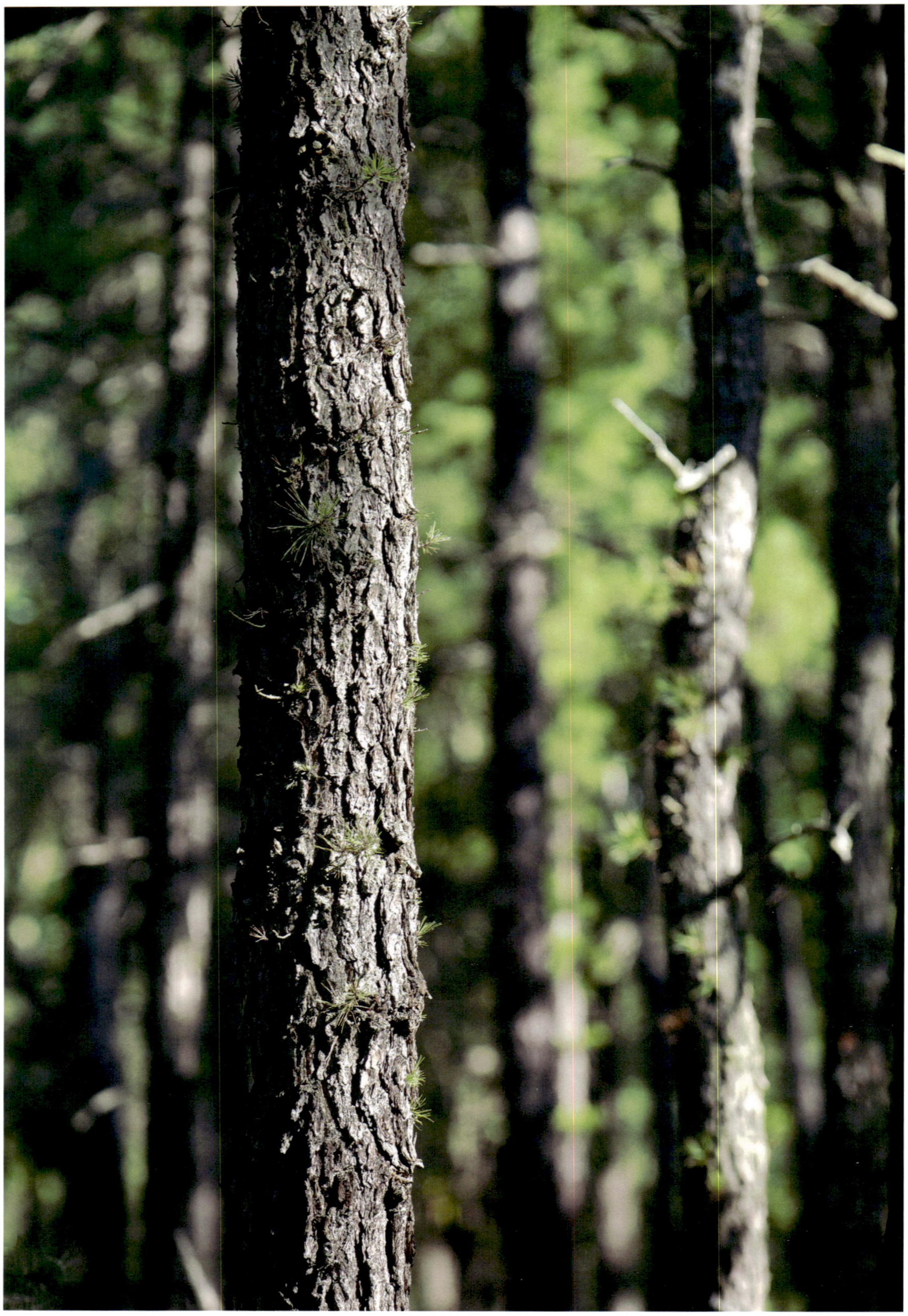

Pines, Brendan T. Byrne State Forest

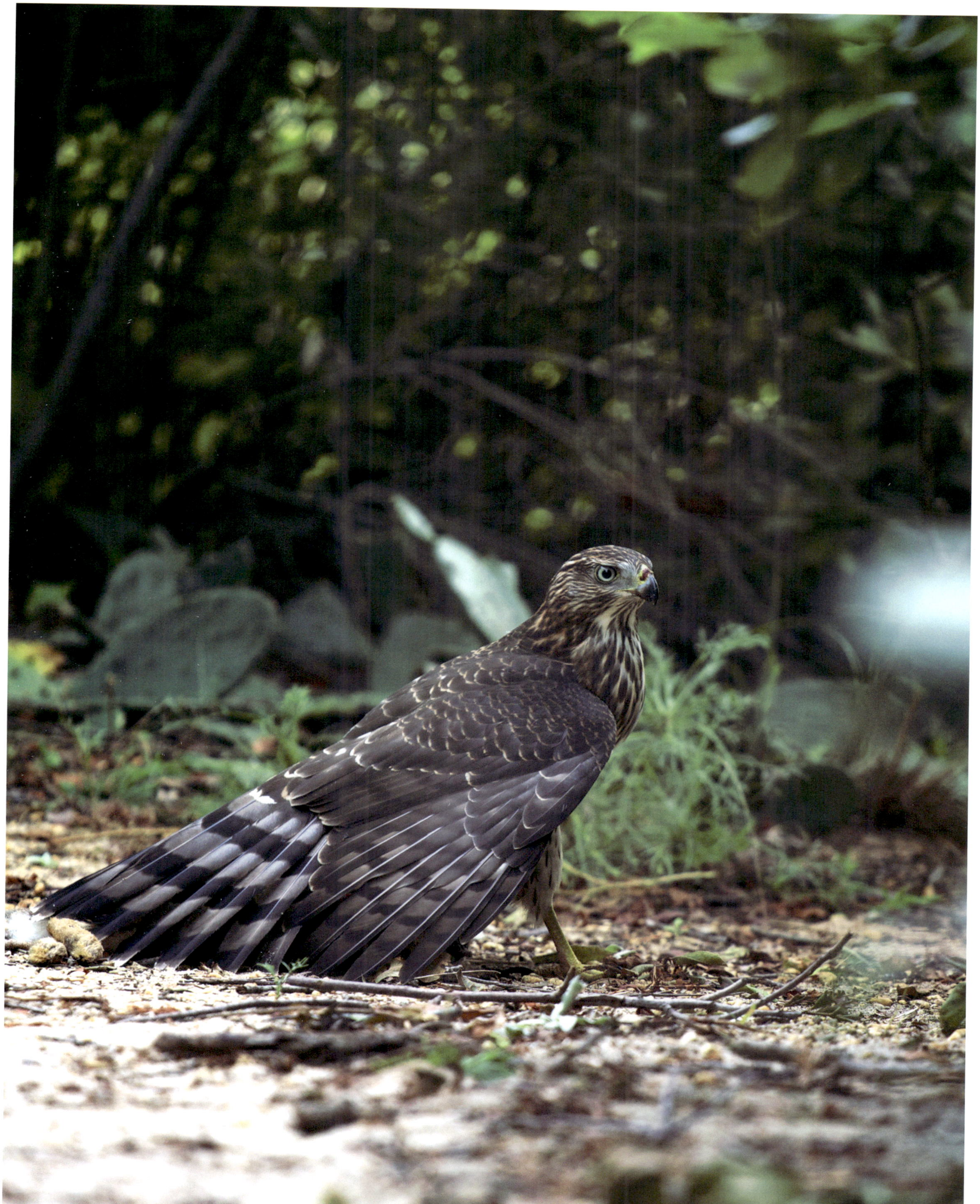

Coopers Hawk, Sandy Hook/Gateway National Recreation Area

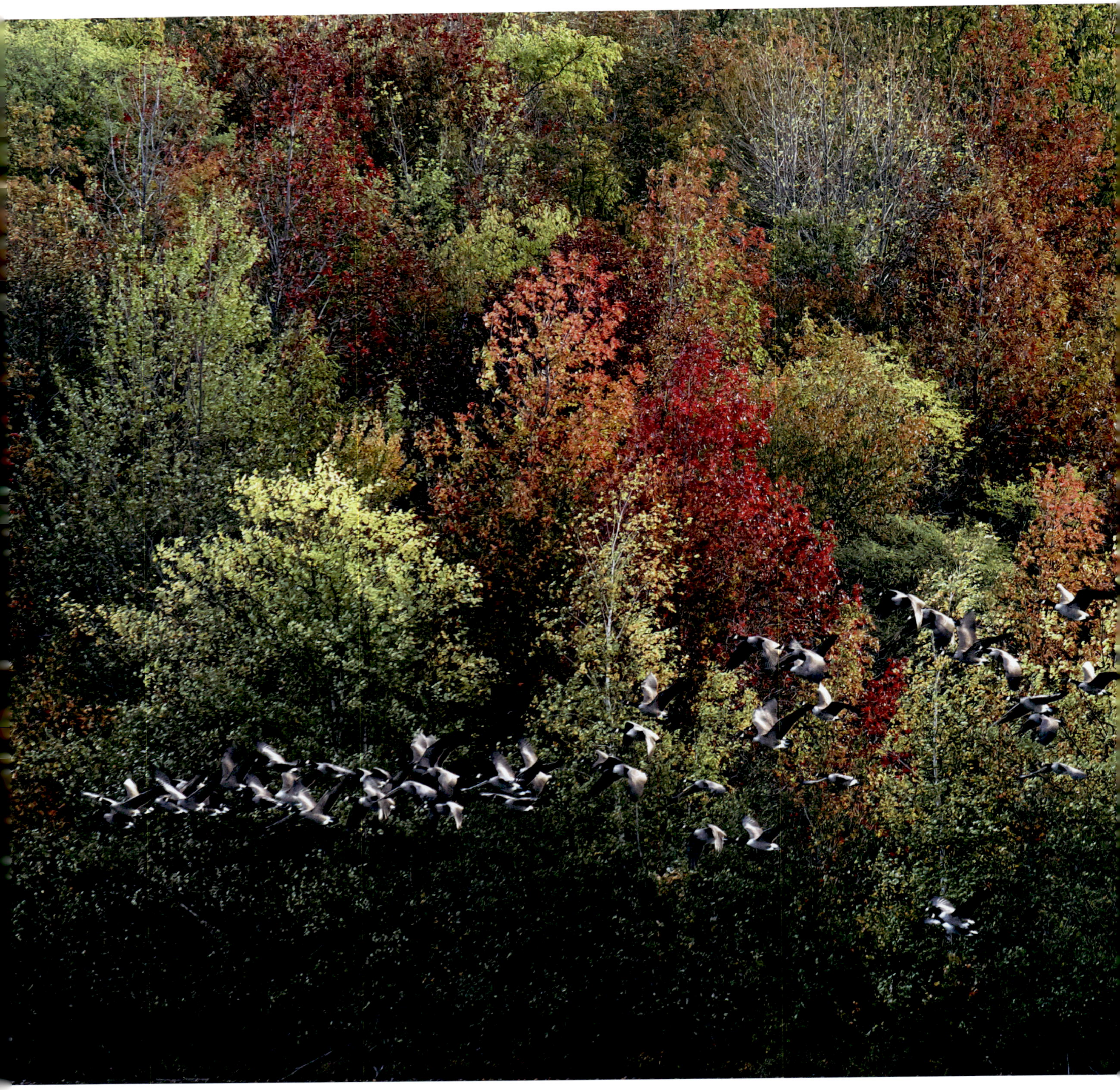

Coming in for a landing, Plainsboro Preserve

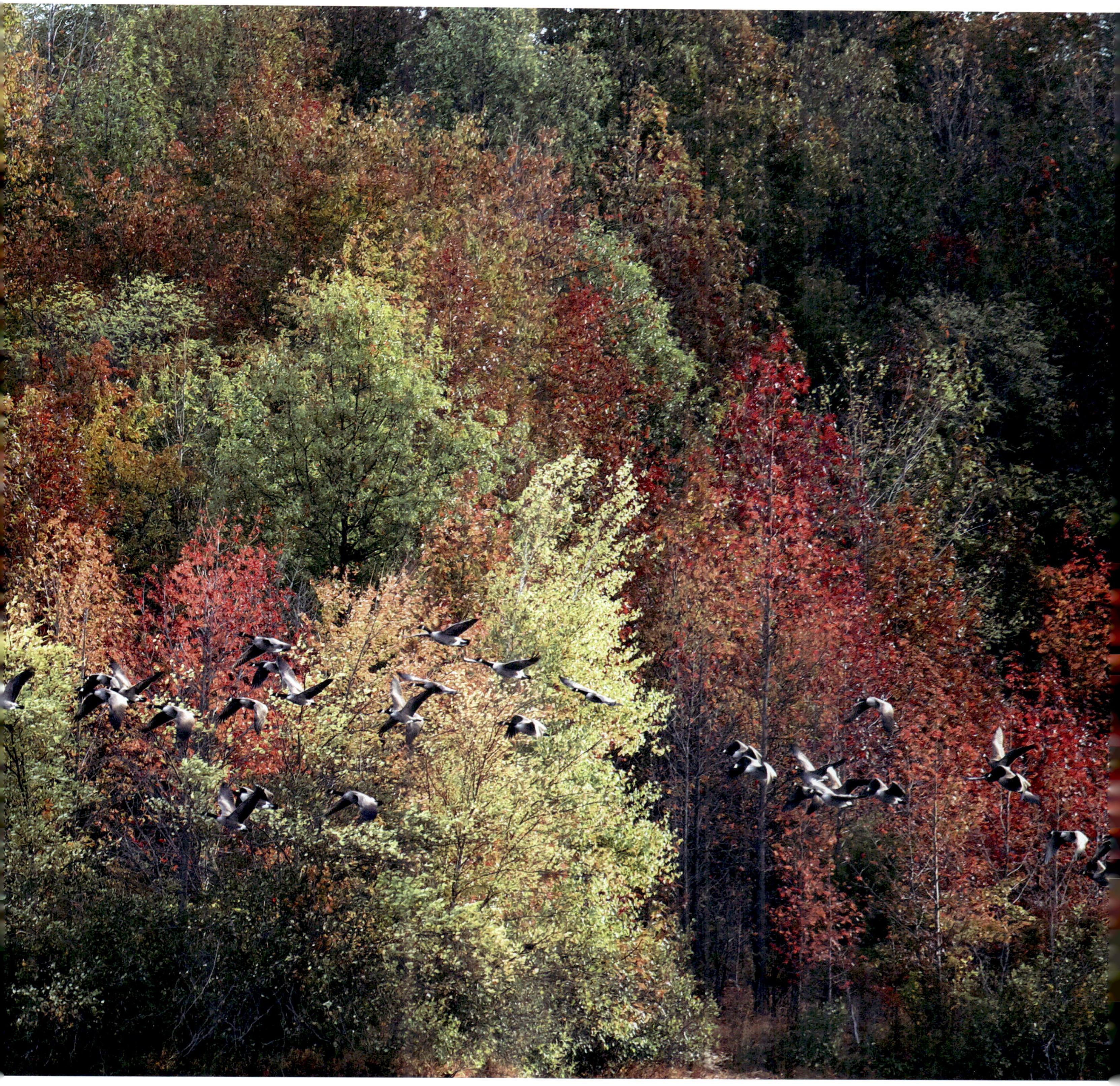

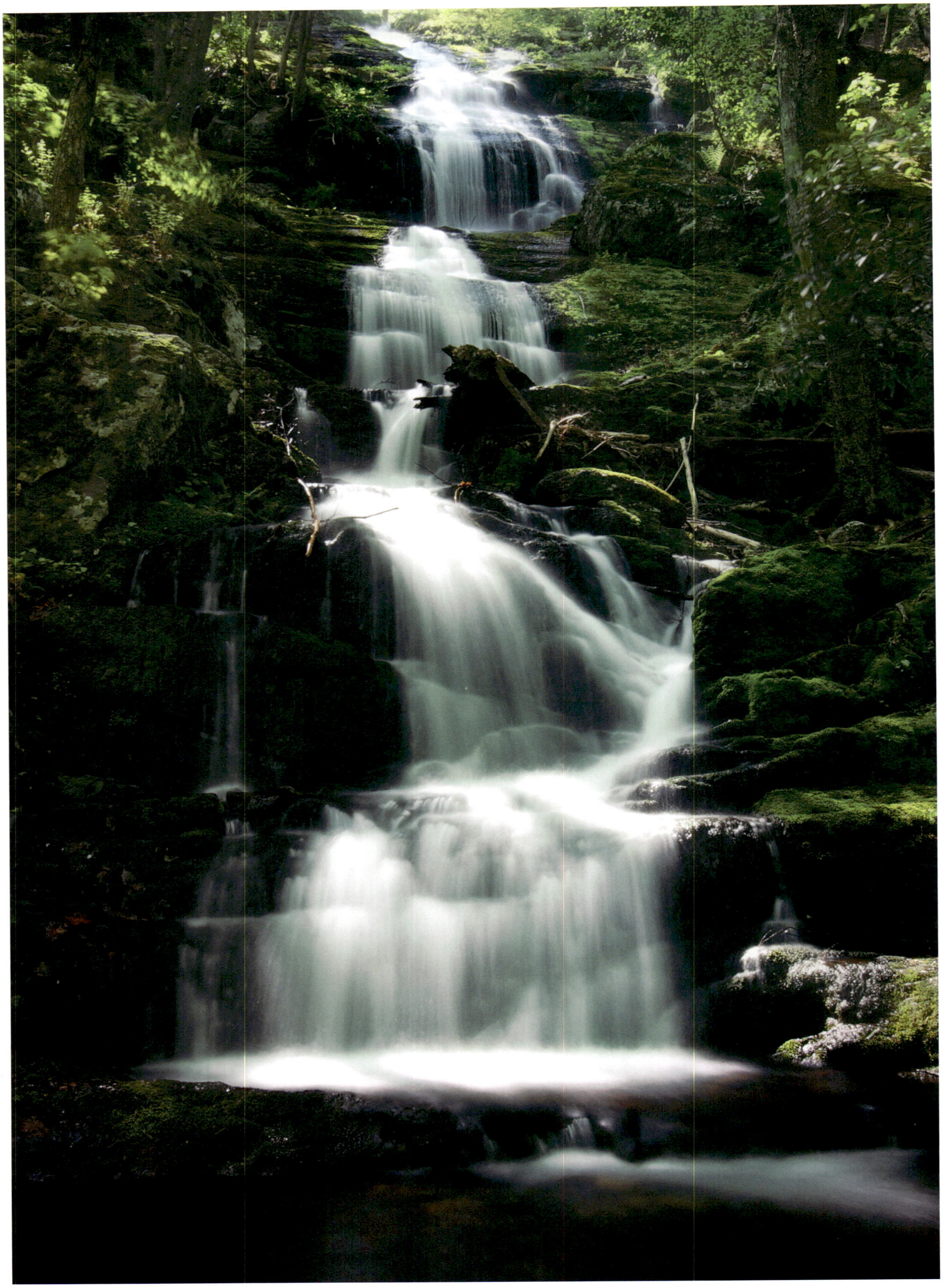

Buttermilk Falls, Delaware Water Gap National Recreation Area

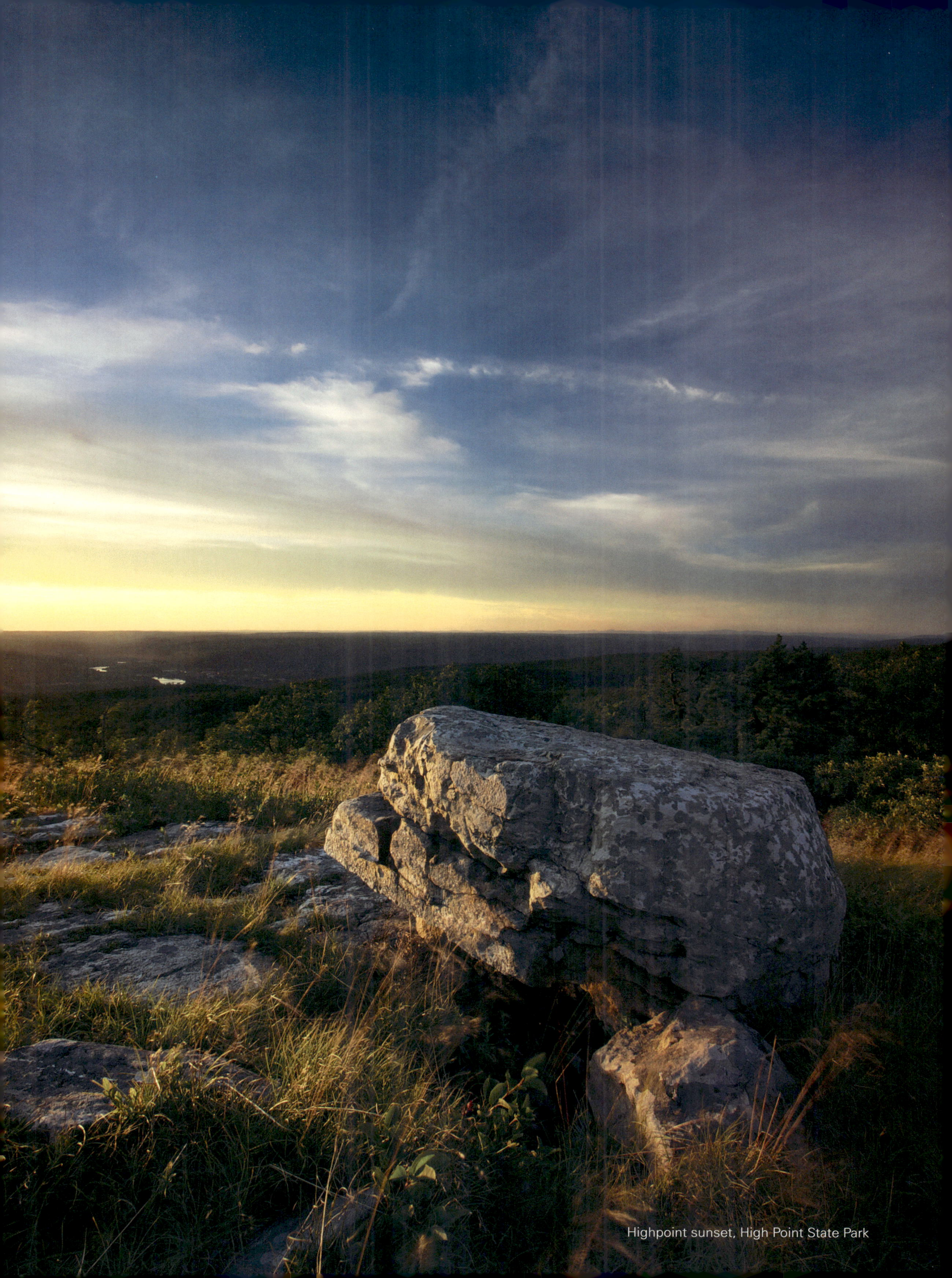

Highpoint sunset, High Point State Park

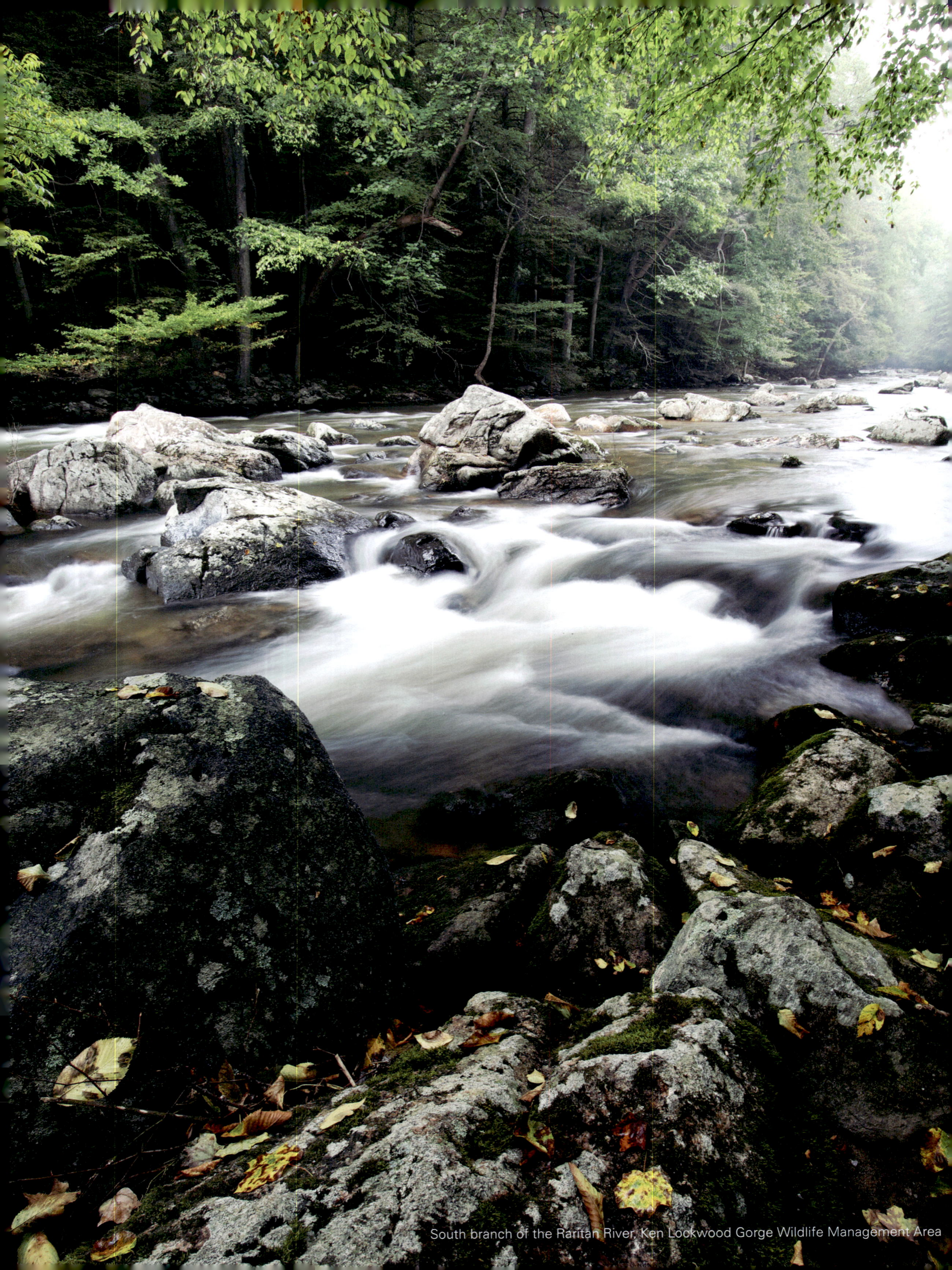

South branch of the Raritan River, Ken Lockwood Gorge Wildlife Management Area

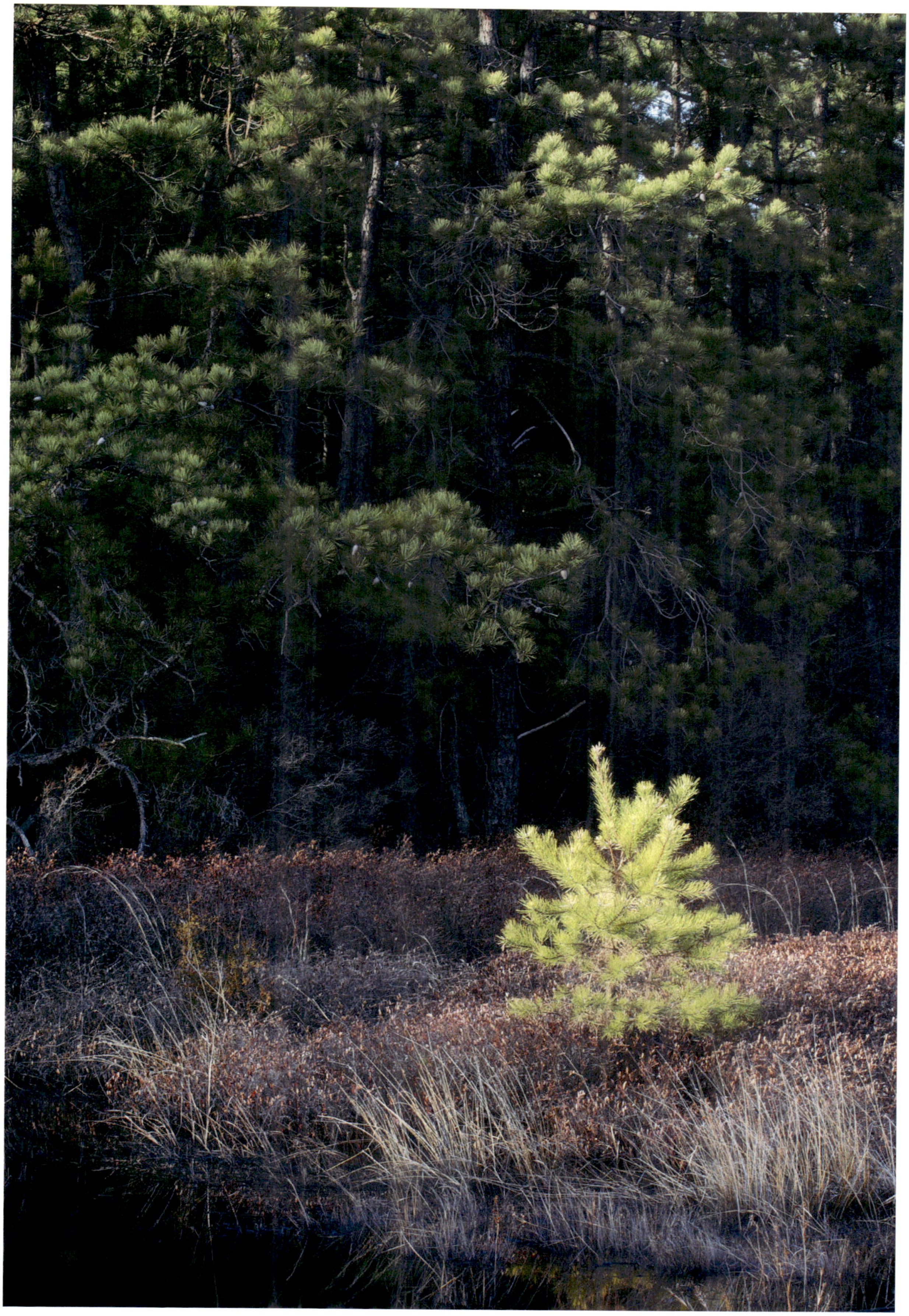

Lone yellow pine, Franklin Parker Preserve

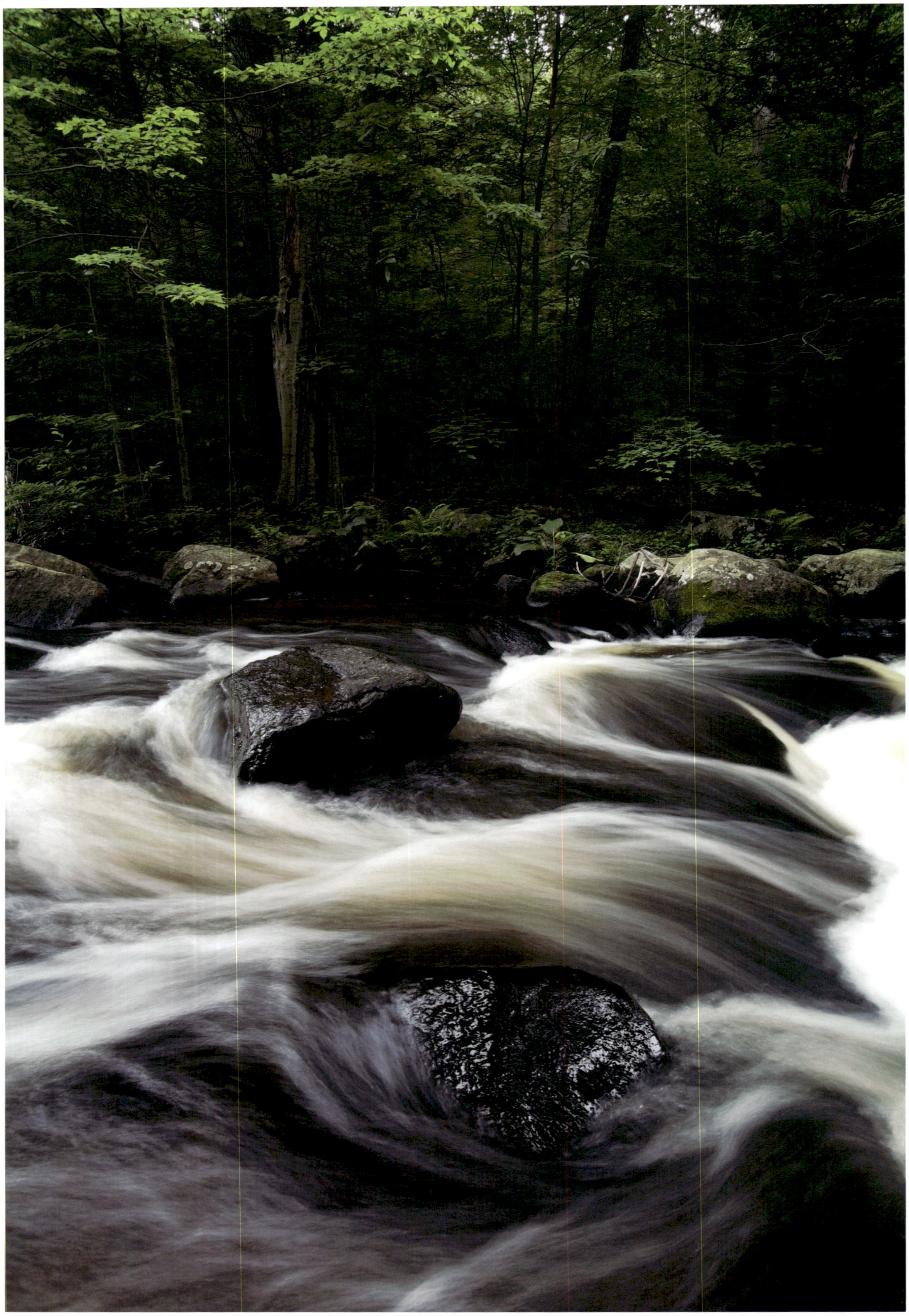

Black River cascades, Hacklebarney State Park

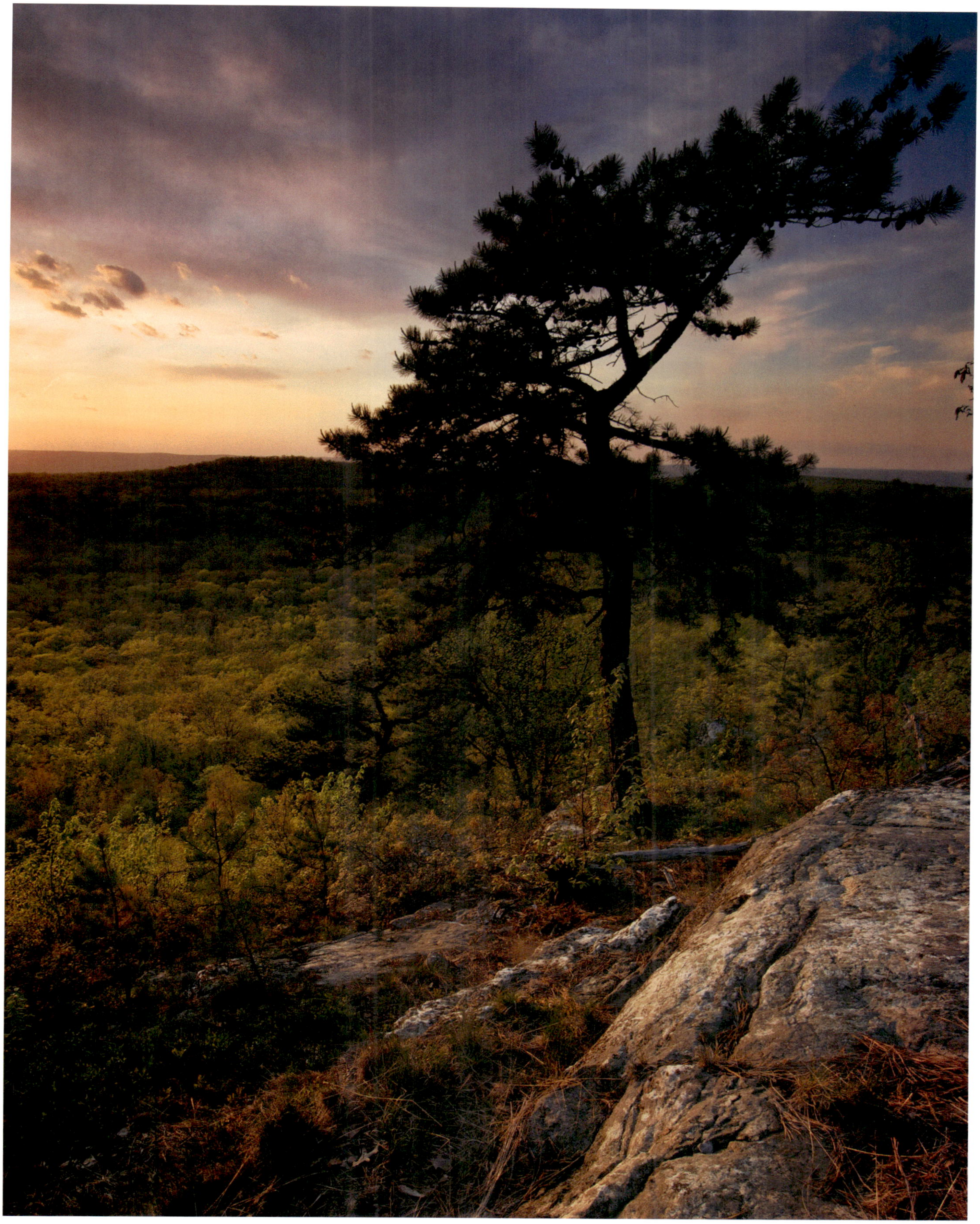

Pine tree sunset, High Point State Park

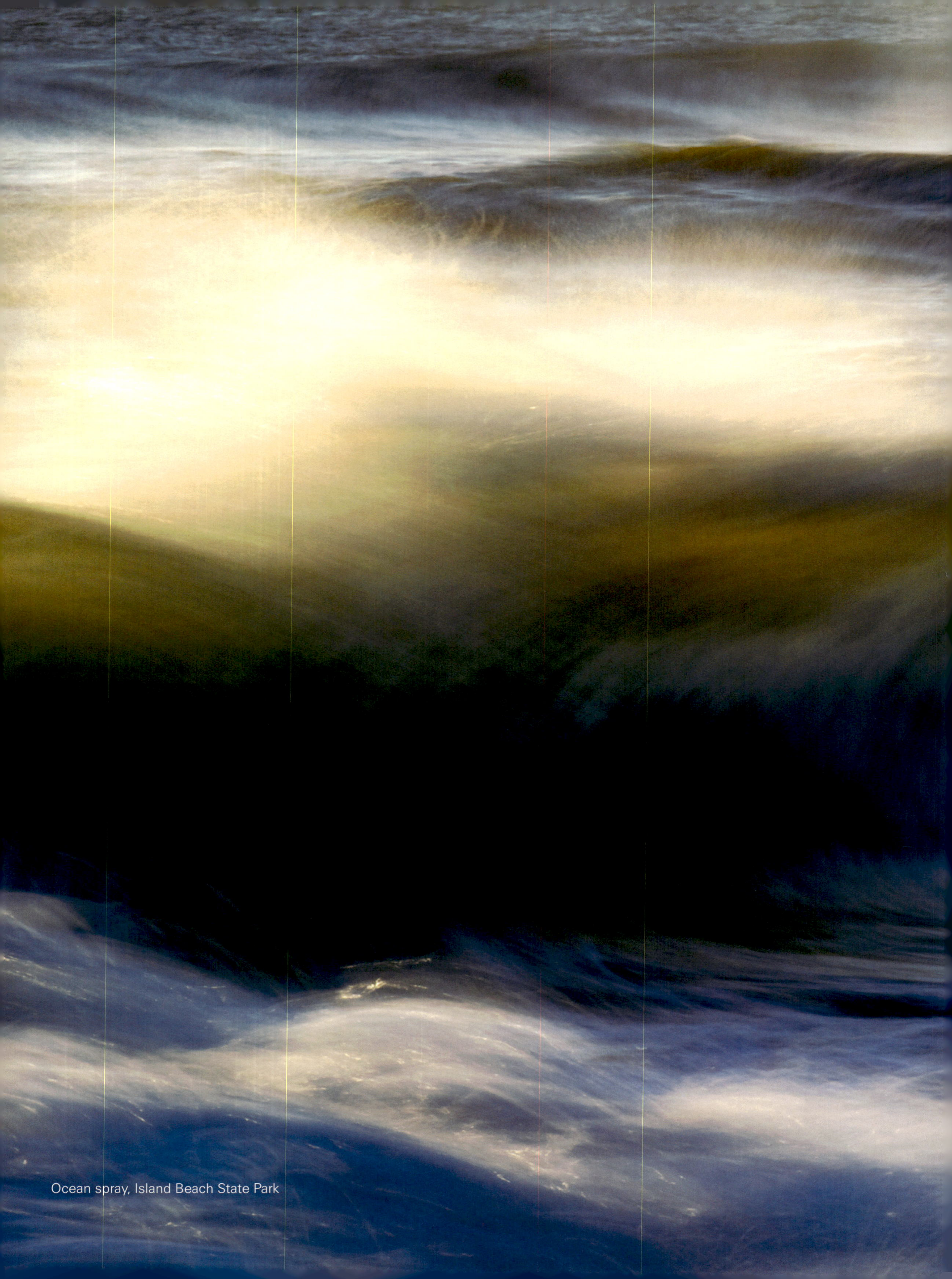

Ocean spray, Island Beach State Park

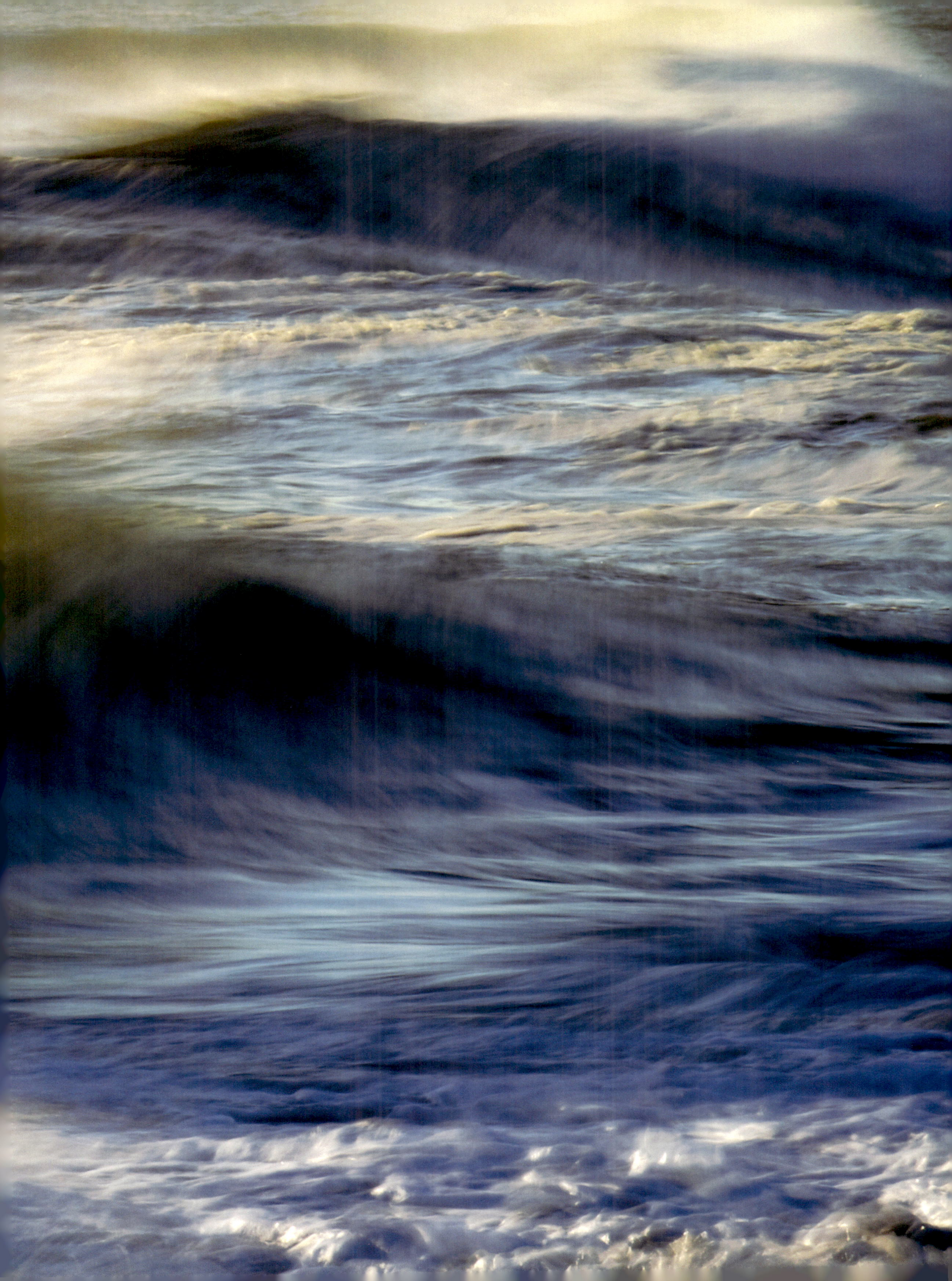

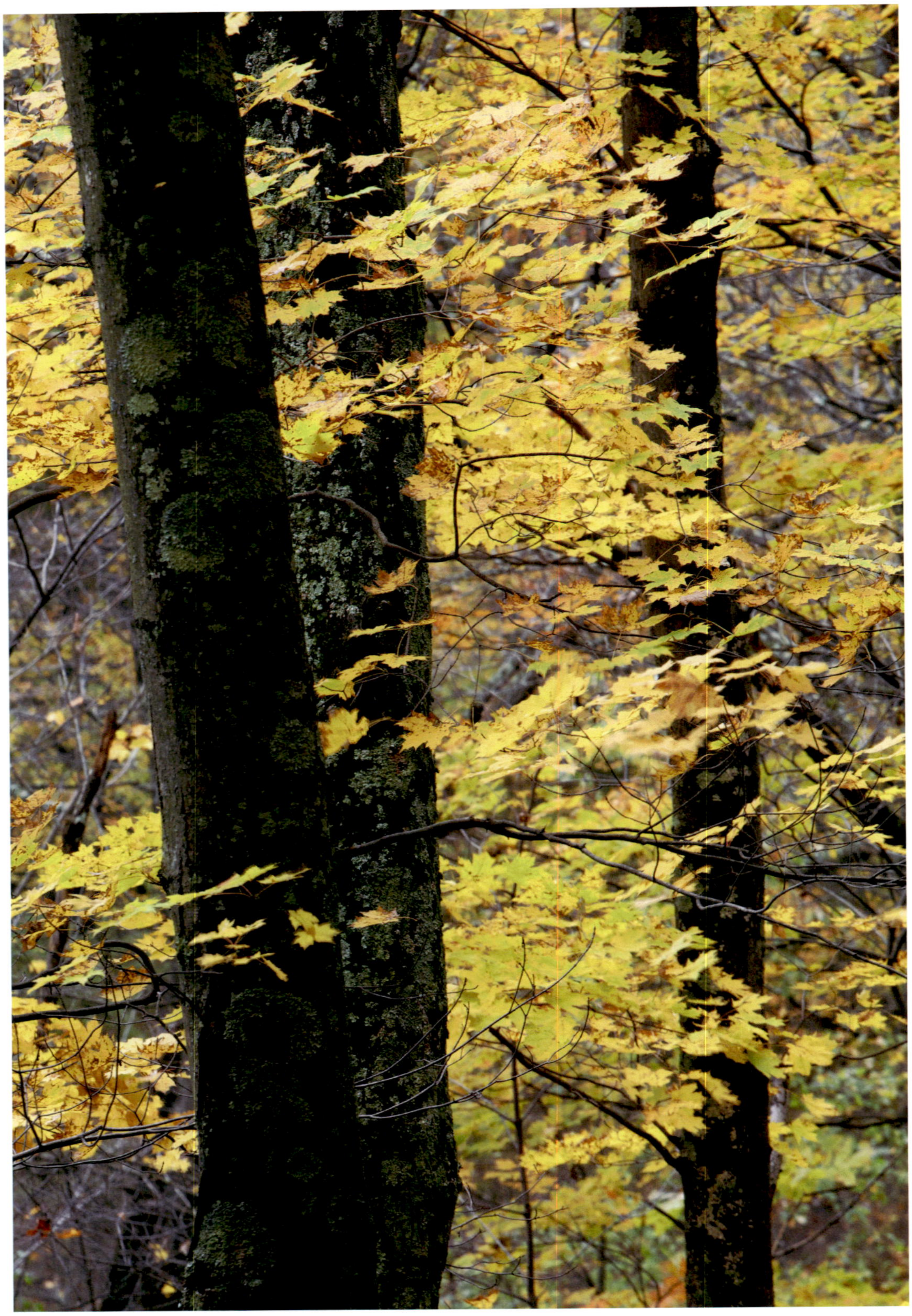

Yellow fall Leaves, Delaware Water Gap National Recreation Area

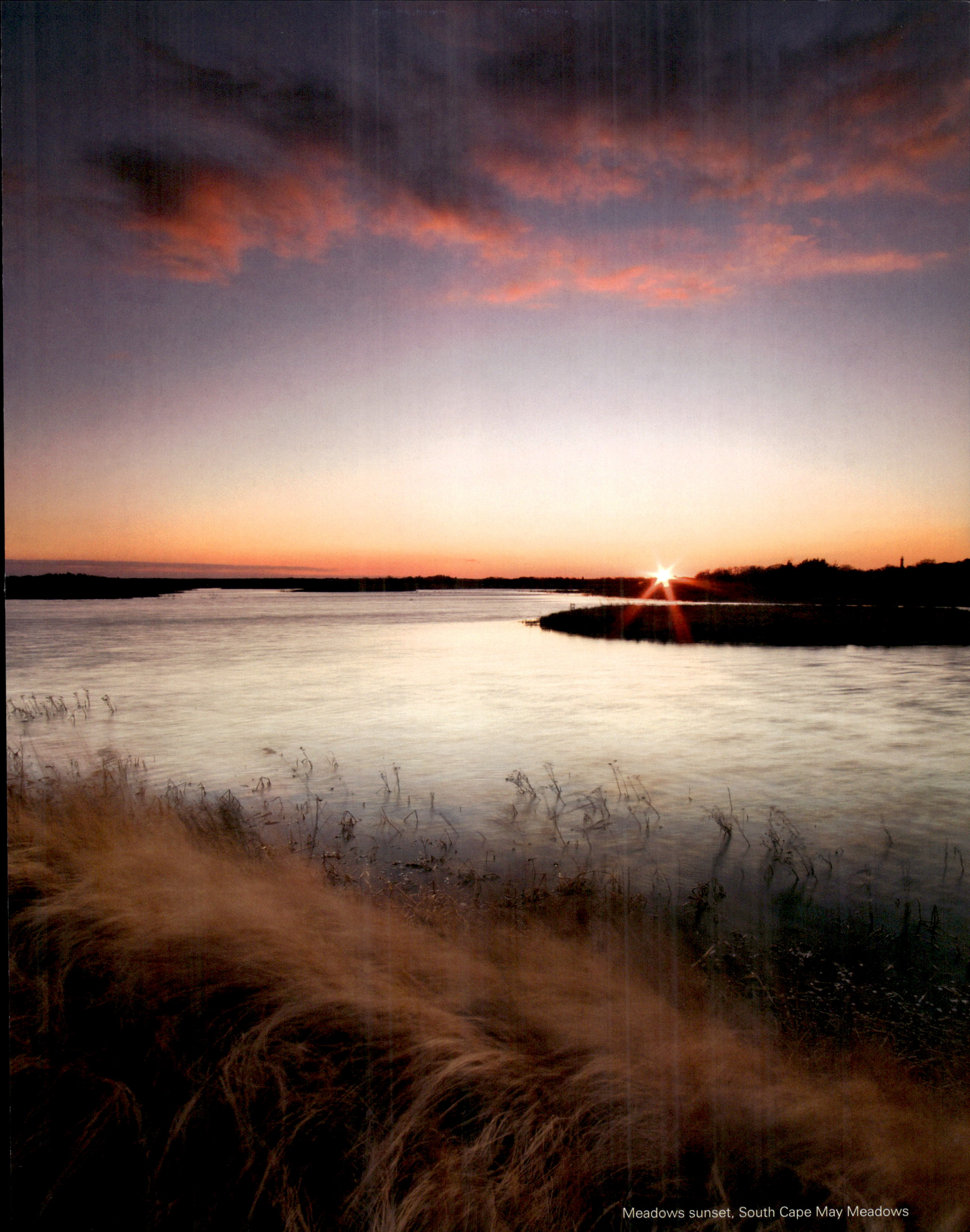

Meadows sunset, South Cape May Meadows

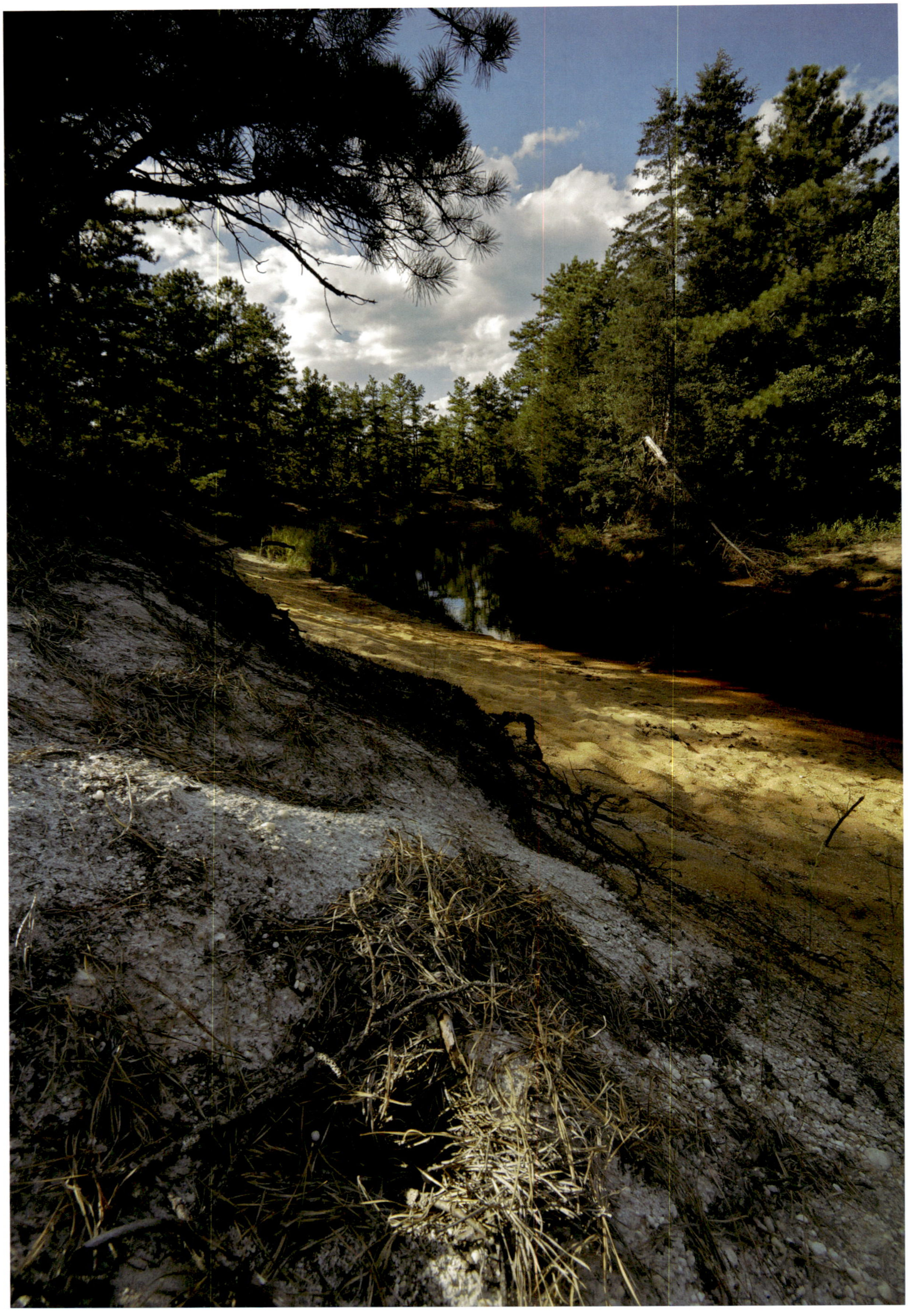

Mullica River, Wharton State Forest

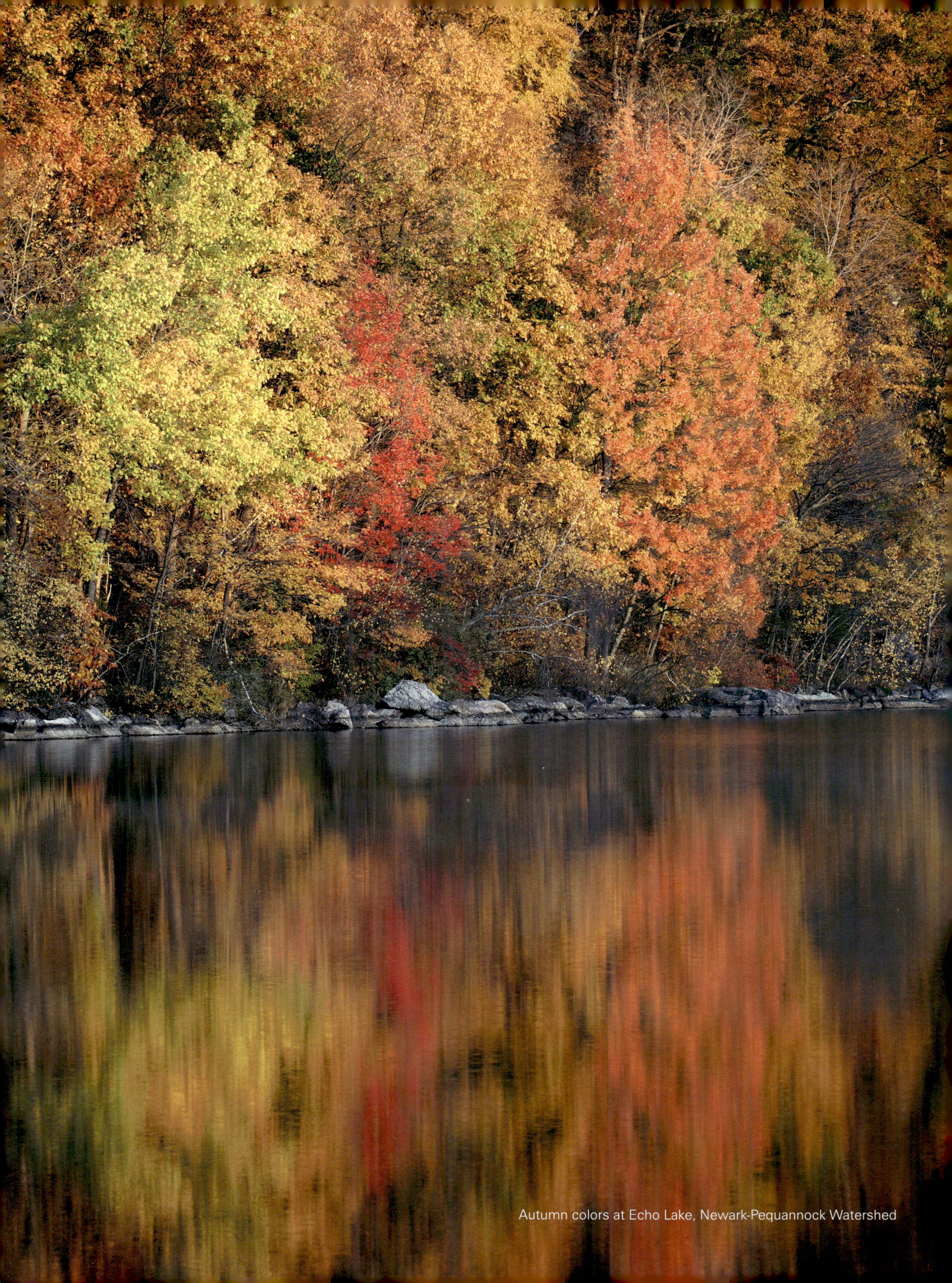

Autumn colors at Echo Lake, Newark-Pequannock Watershed

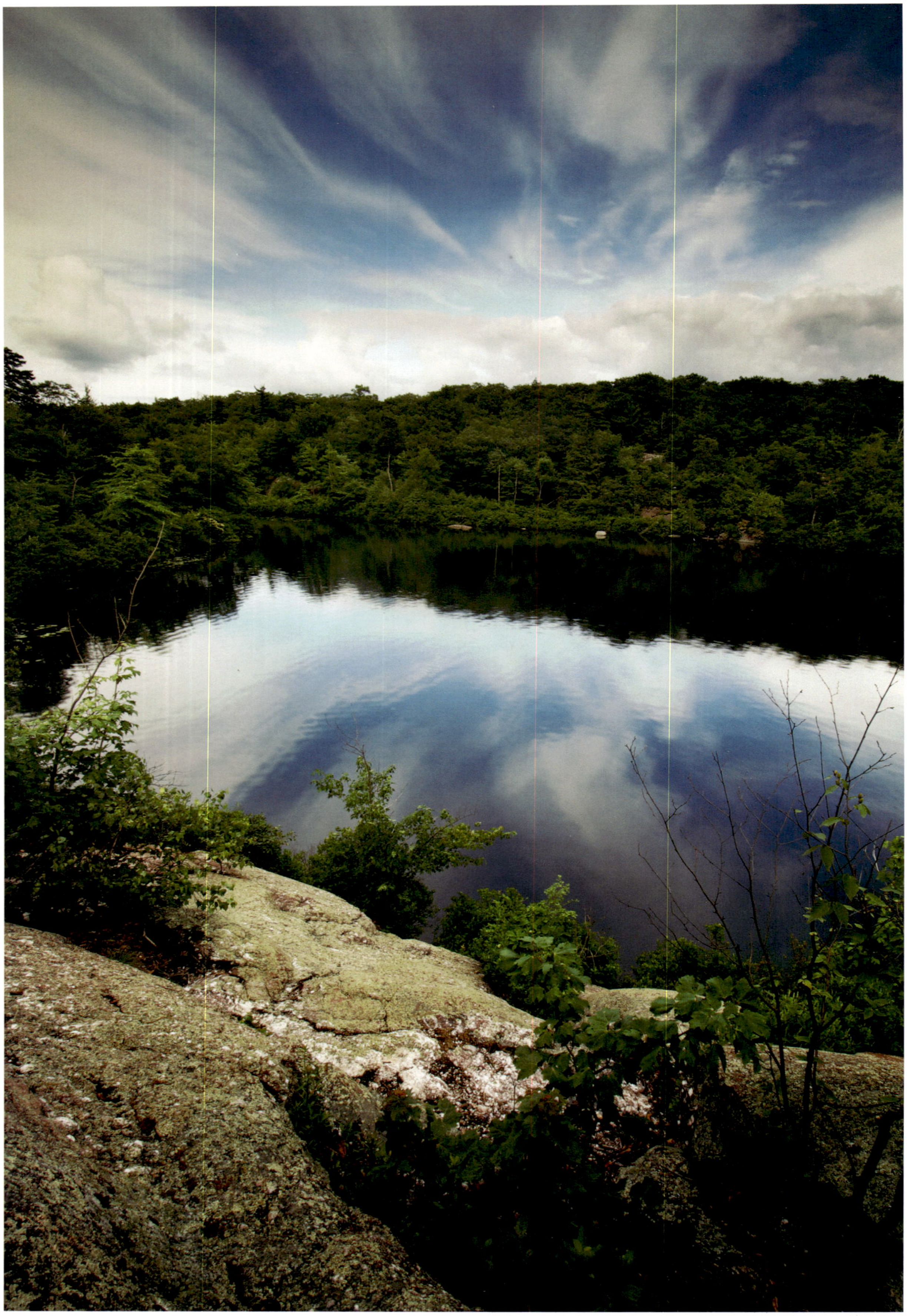

Terrace Pond reflections, Wawayanda State Park

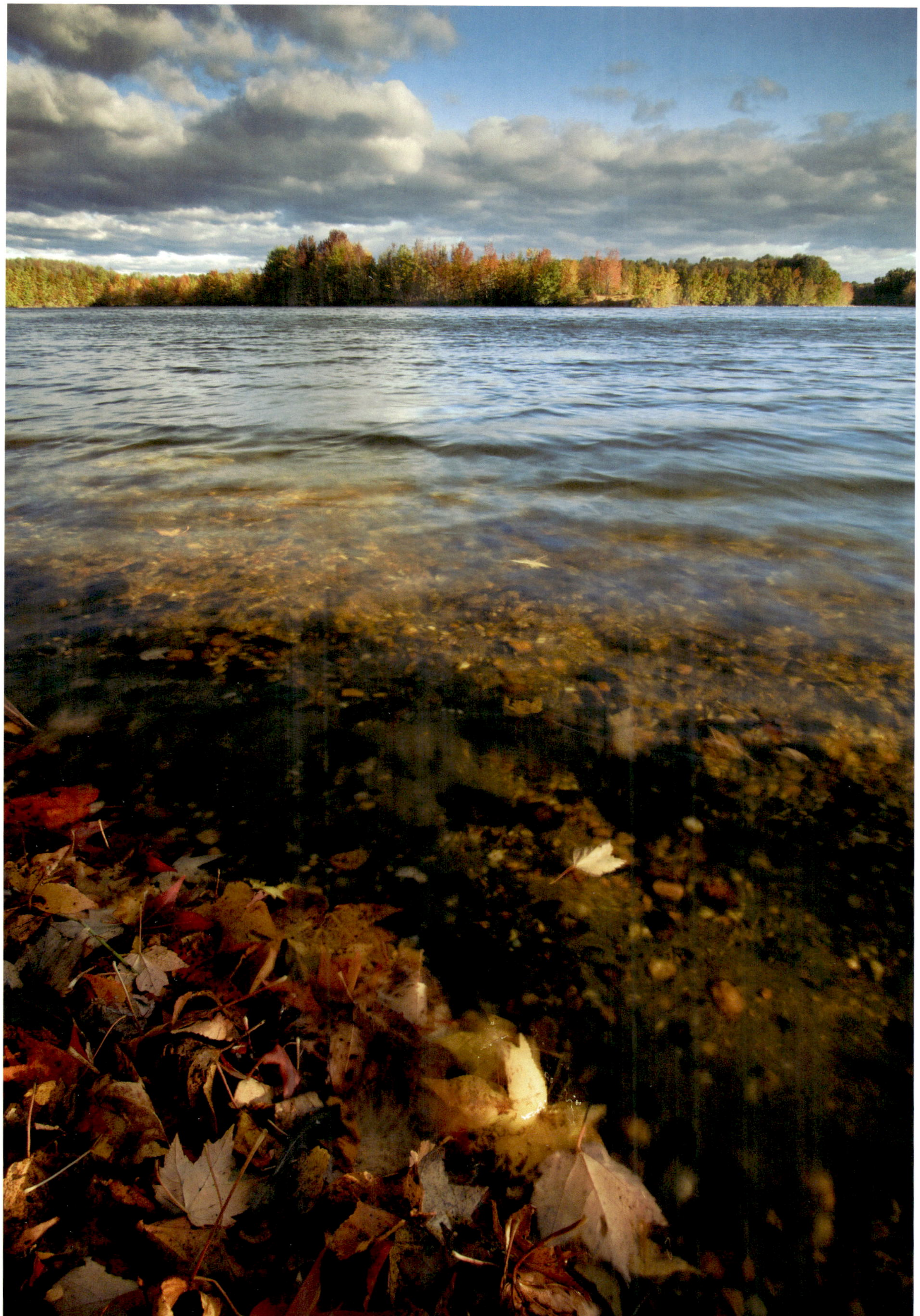

McCormack Lake, Plainsboro Preserve

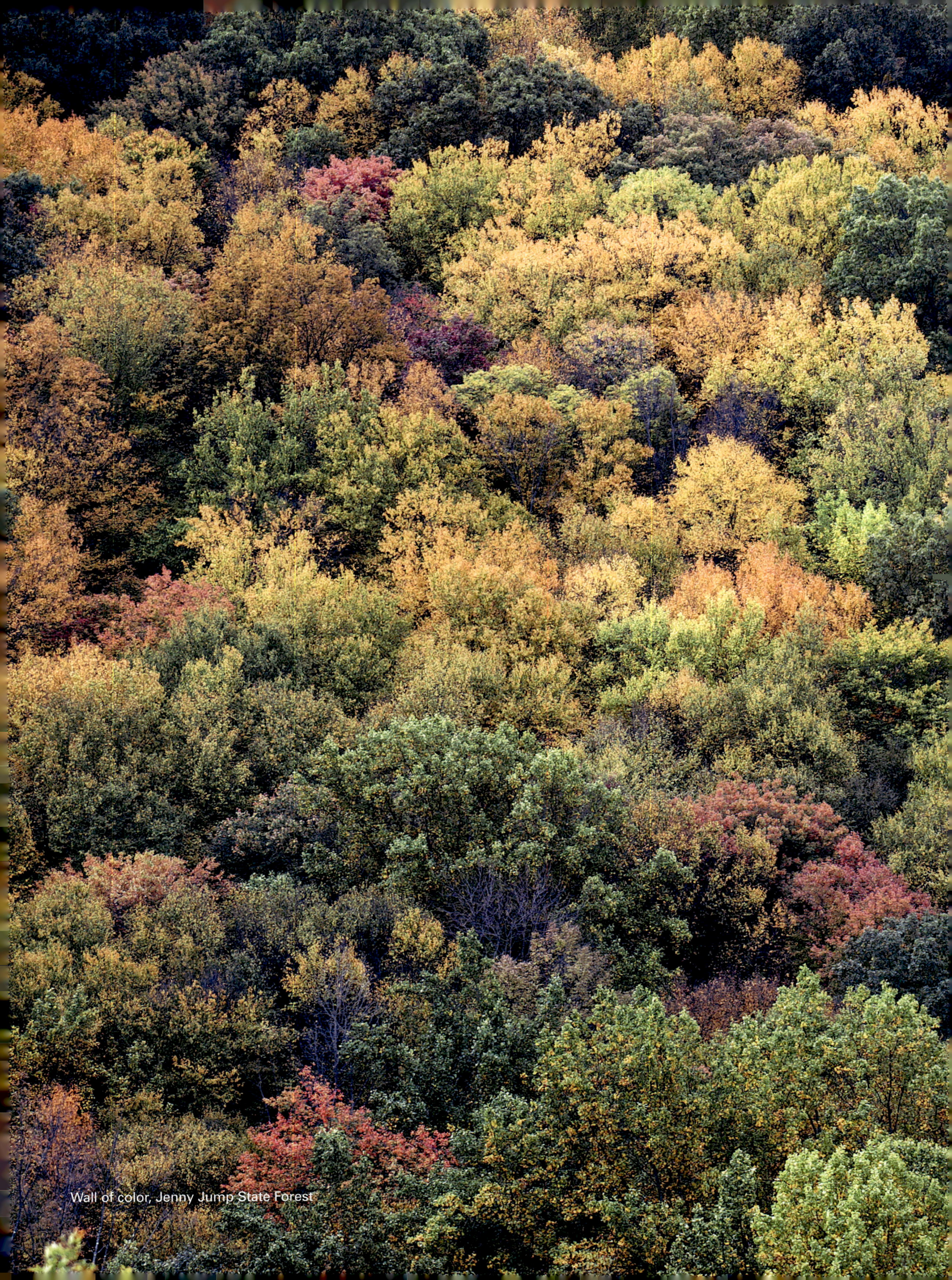

Wall of color, Jenny Jump State Forest

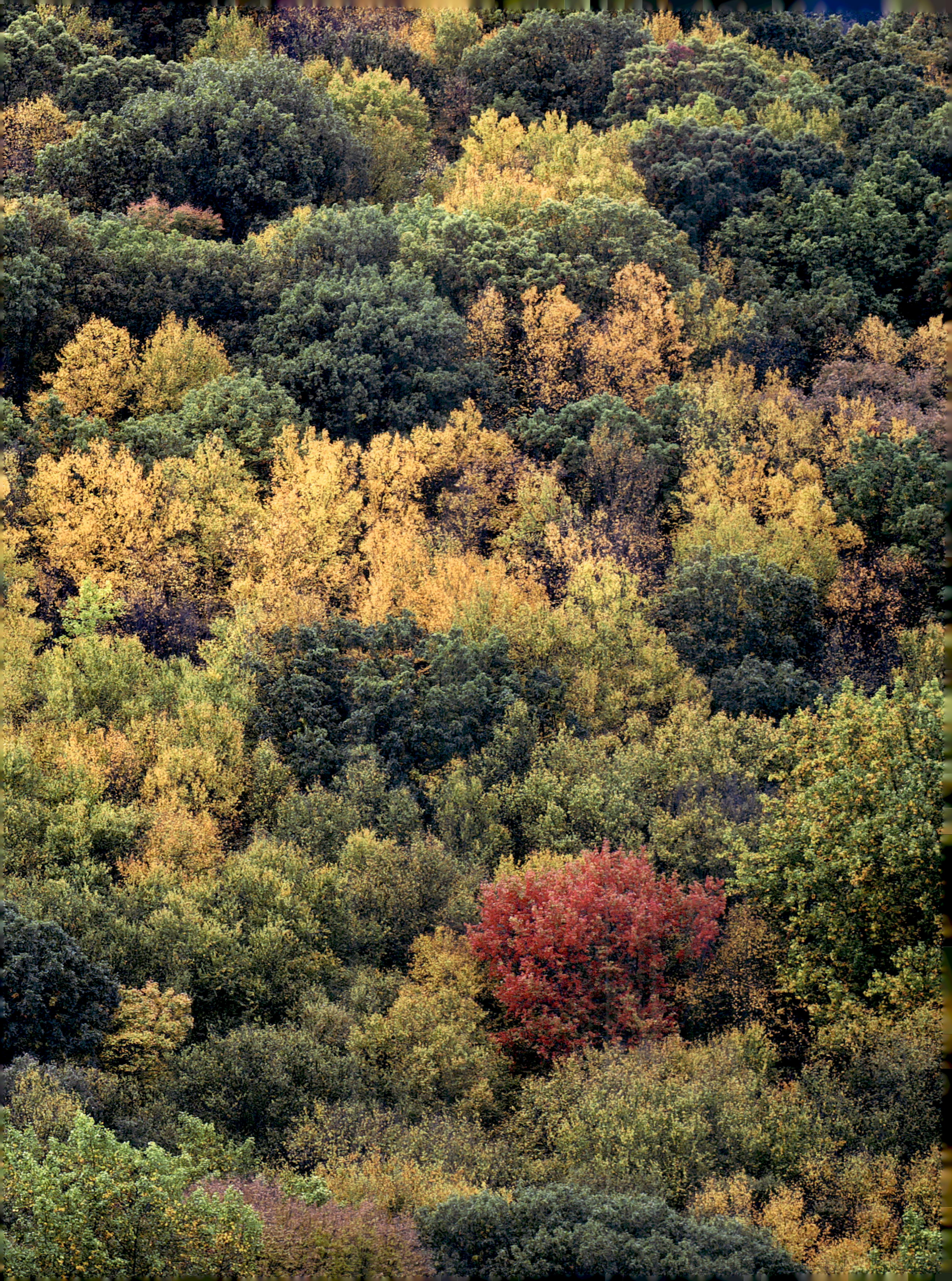

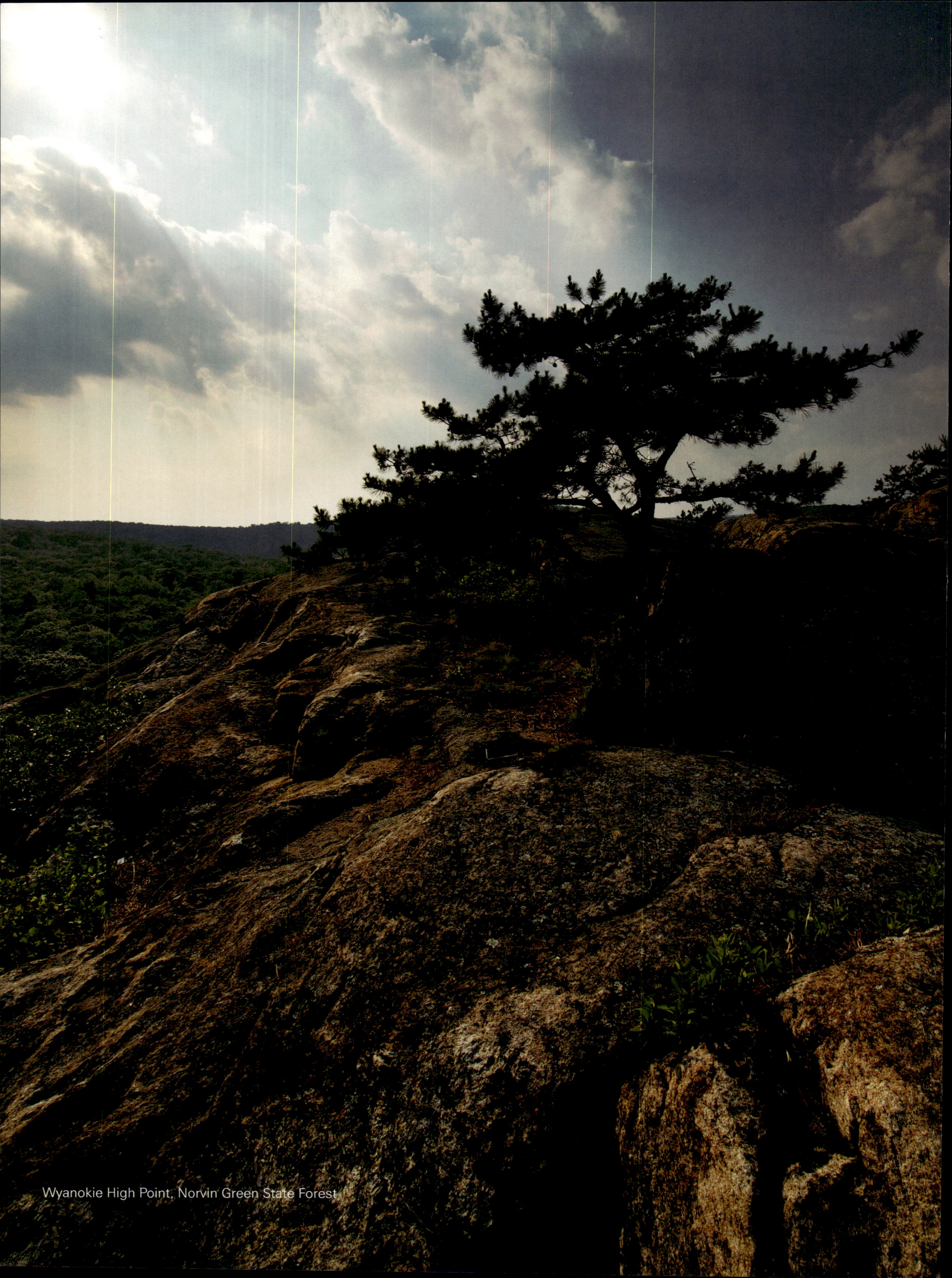

Wyanokie High Point, Norvin Green State Forest

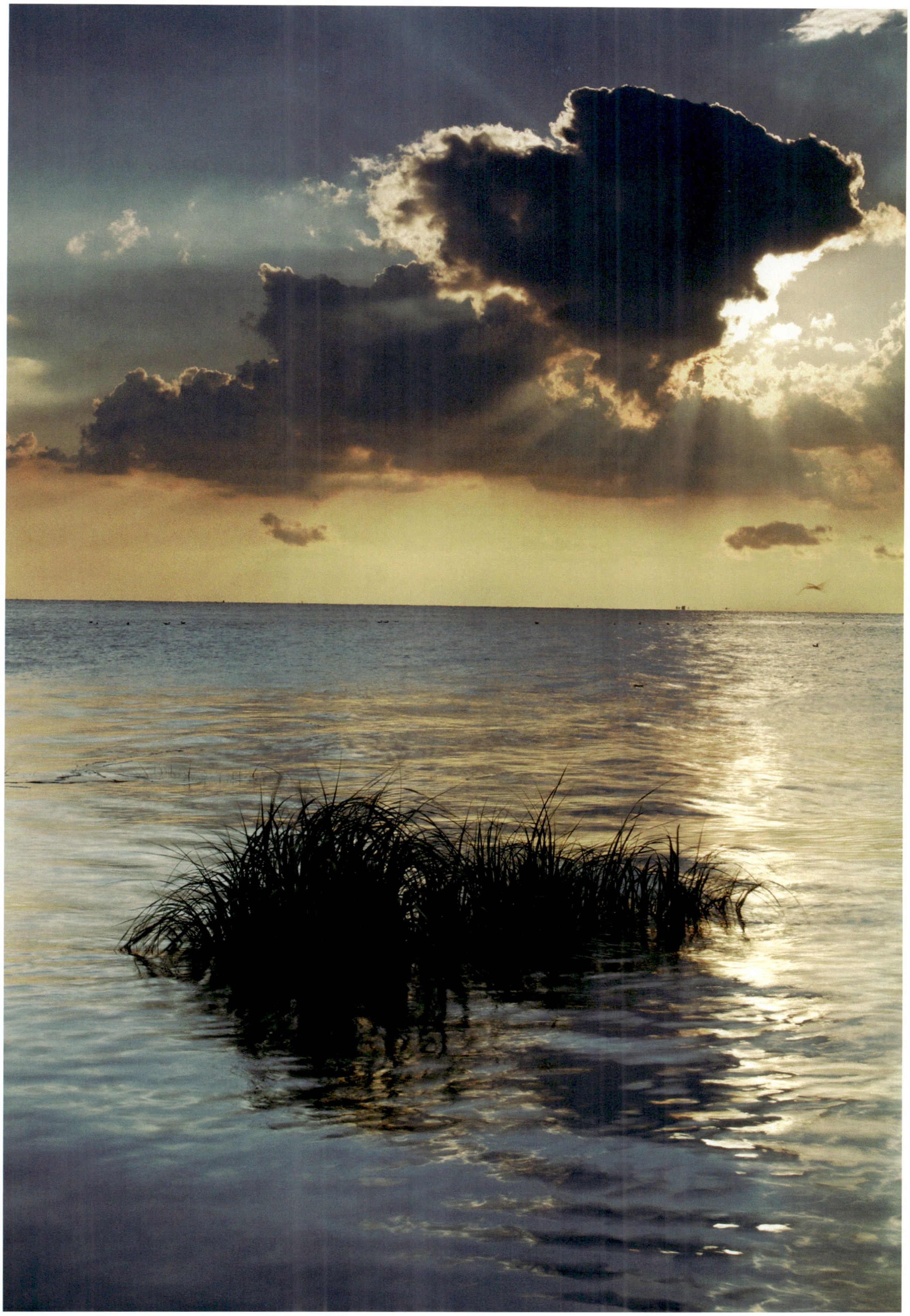

Delaware Bay sunset, Heislerville Wildlife Management Area

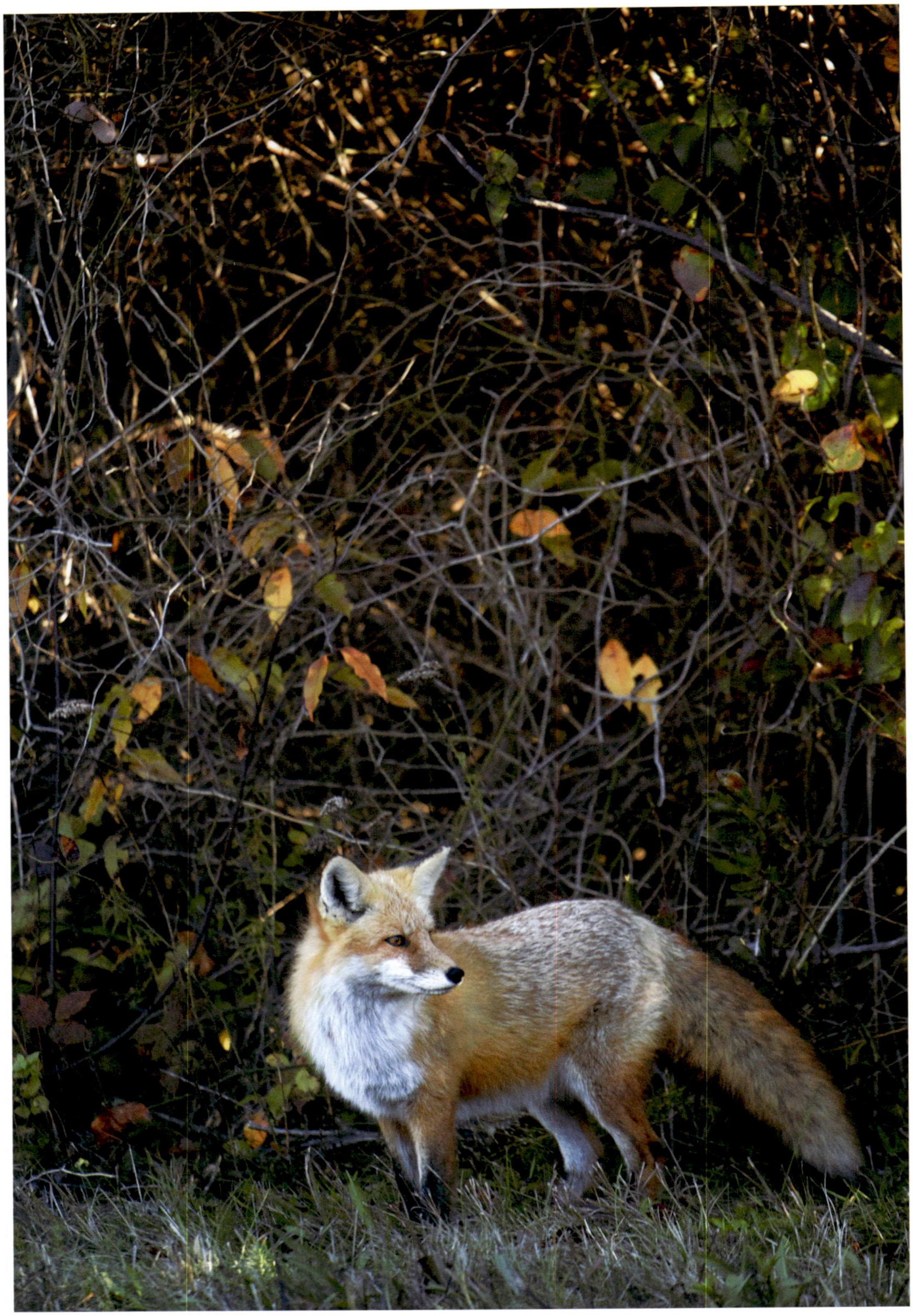

Beautiful Red Fox, Island Beach State Park

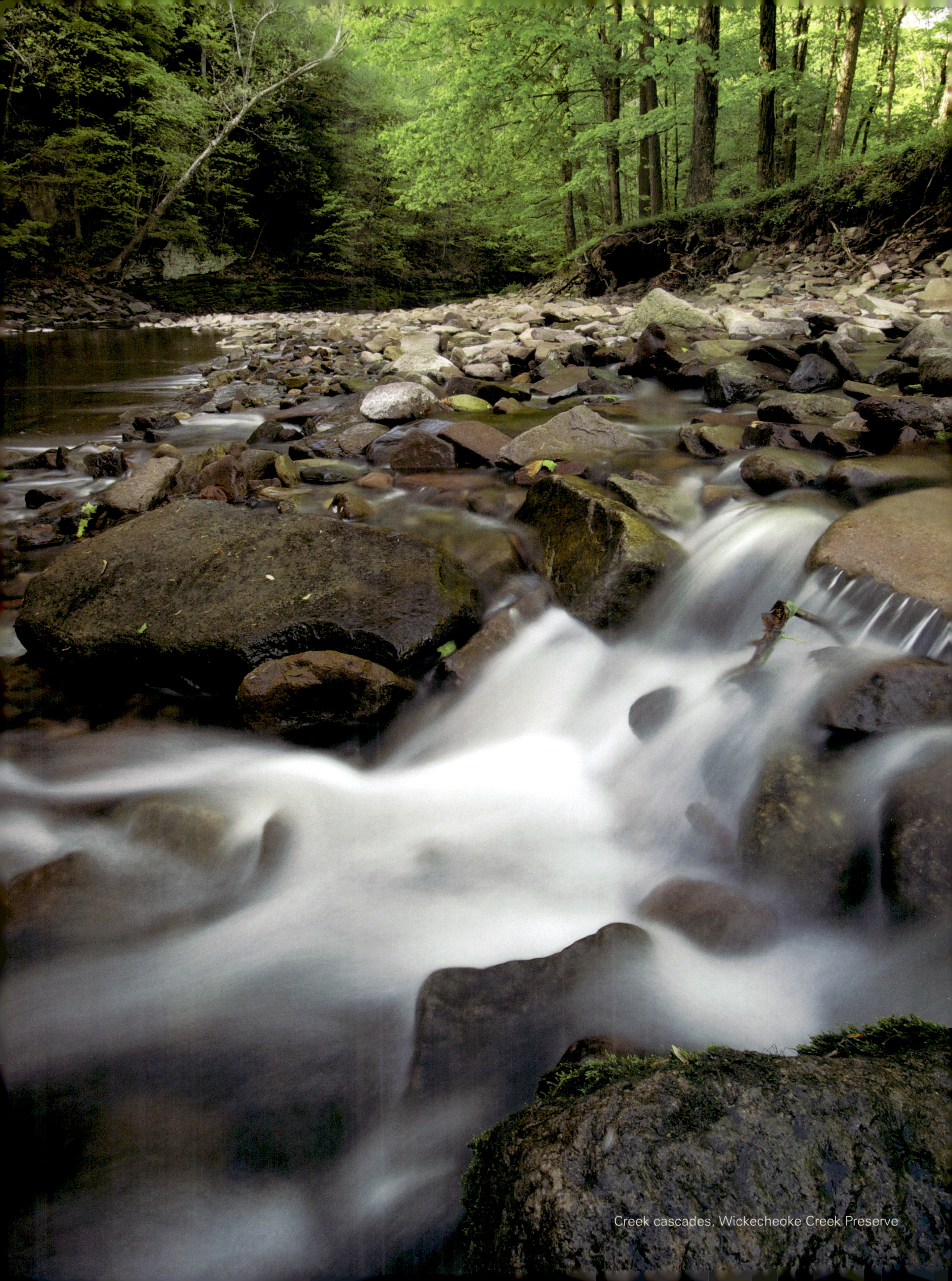

Creek cascades, Wickecheoke Creek Preserve

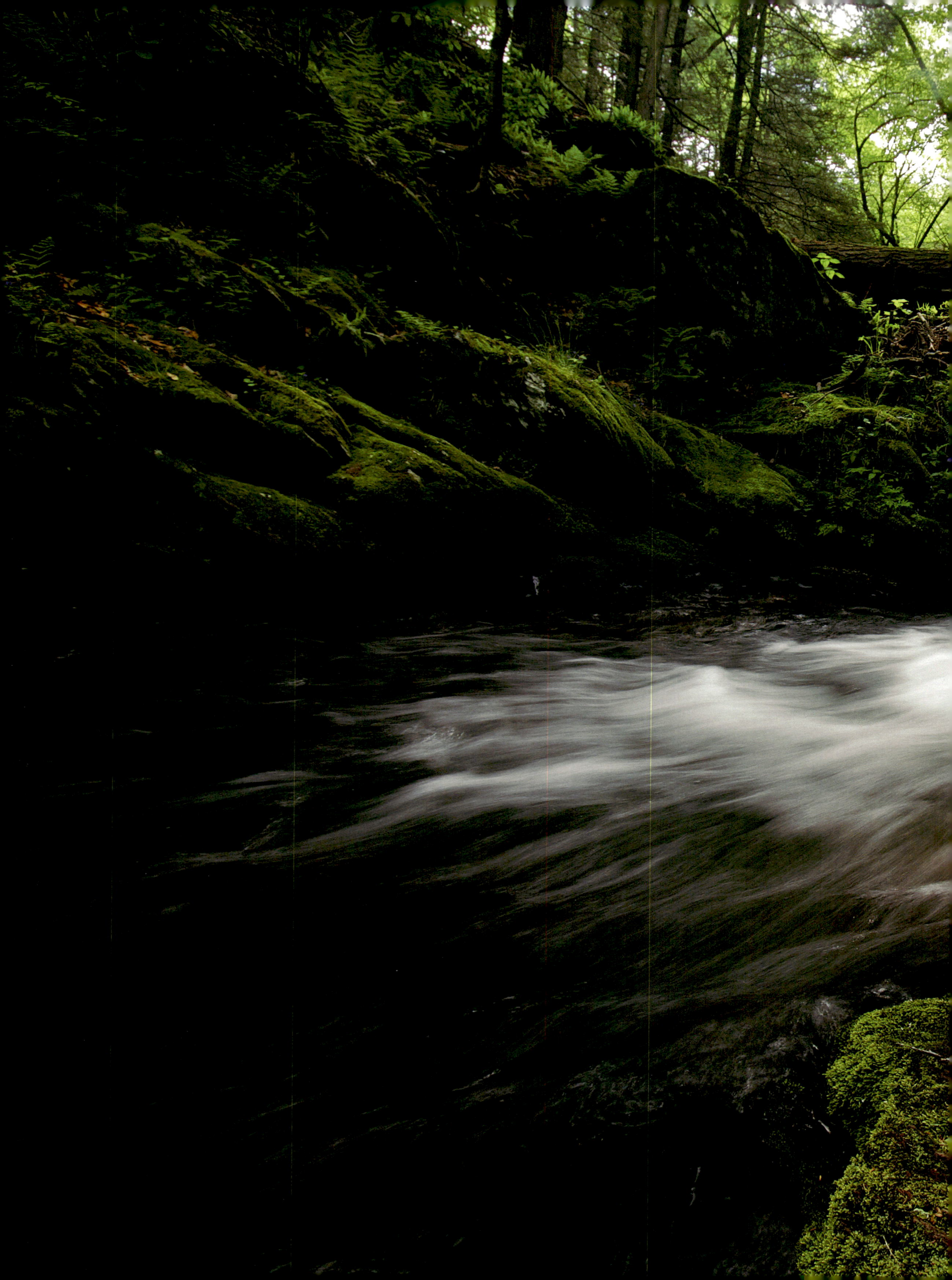

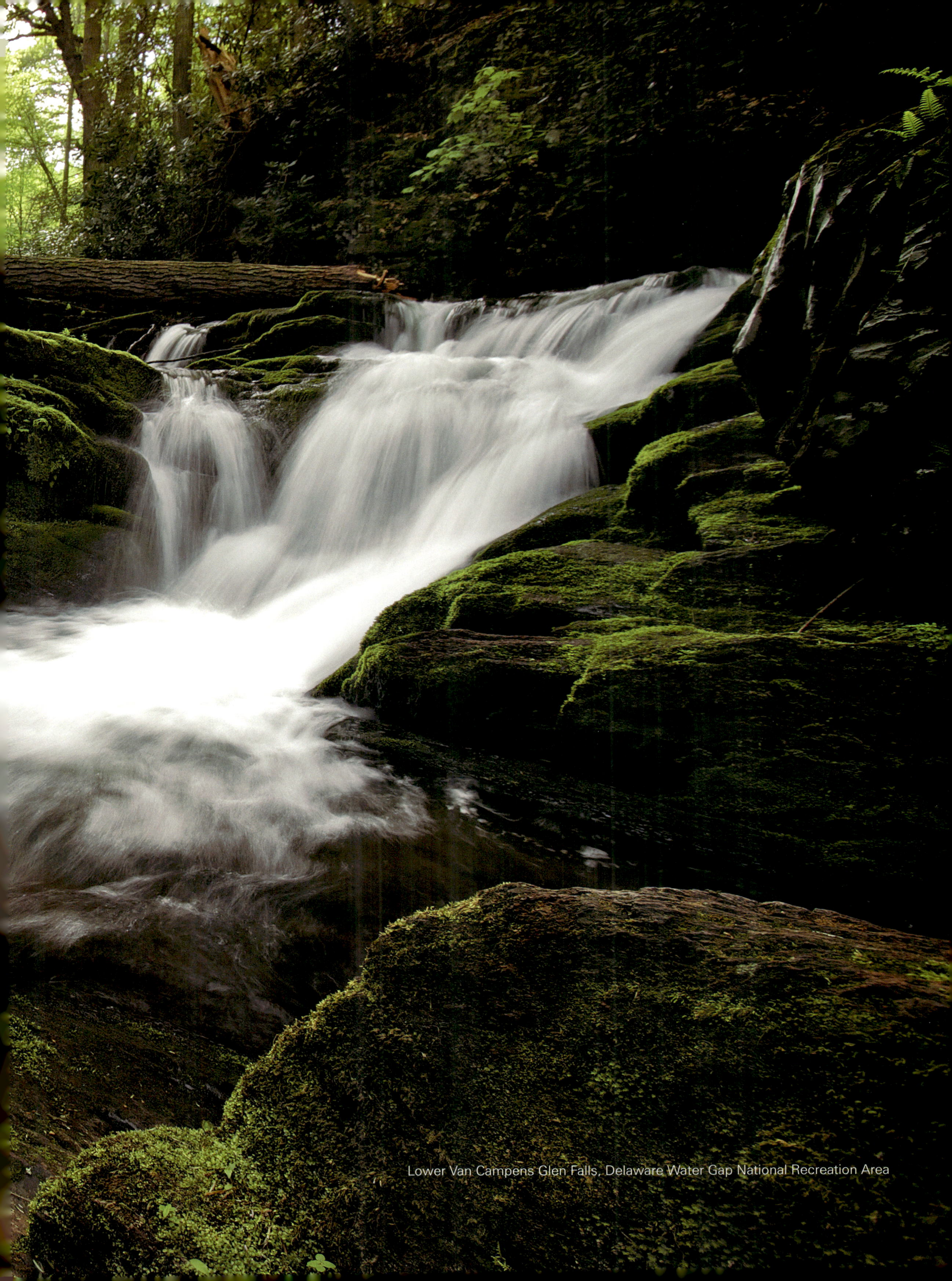

Lower Van Campens Glen Falls, Delaware Water Gap National Recreation Area

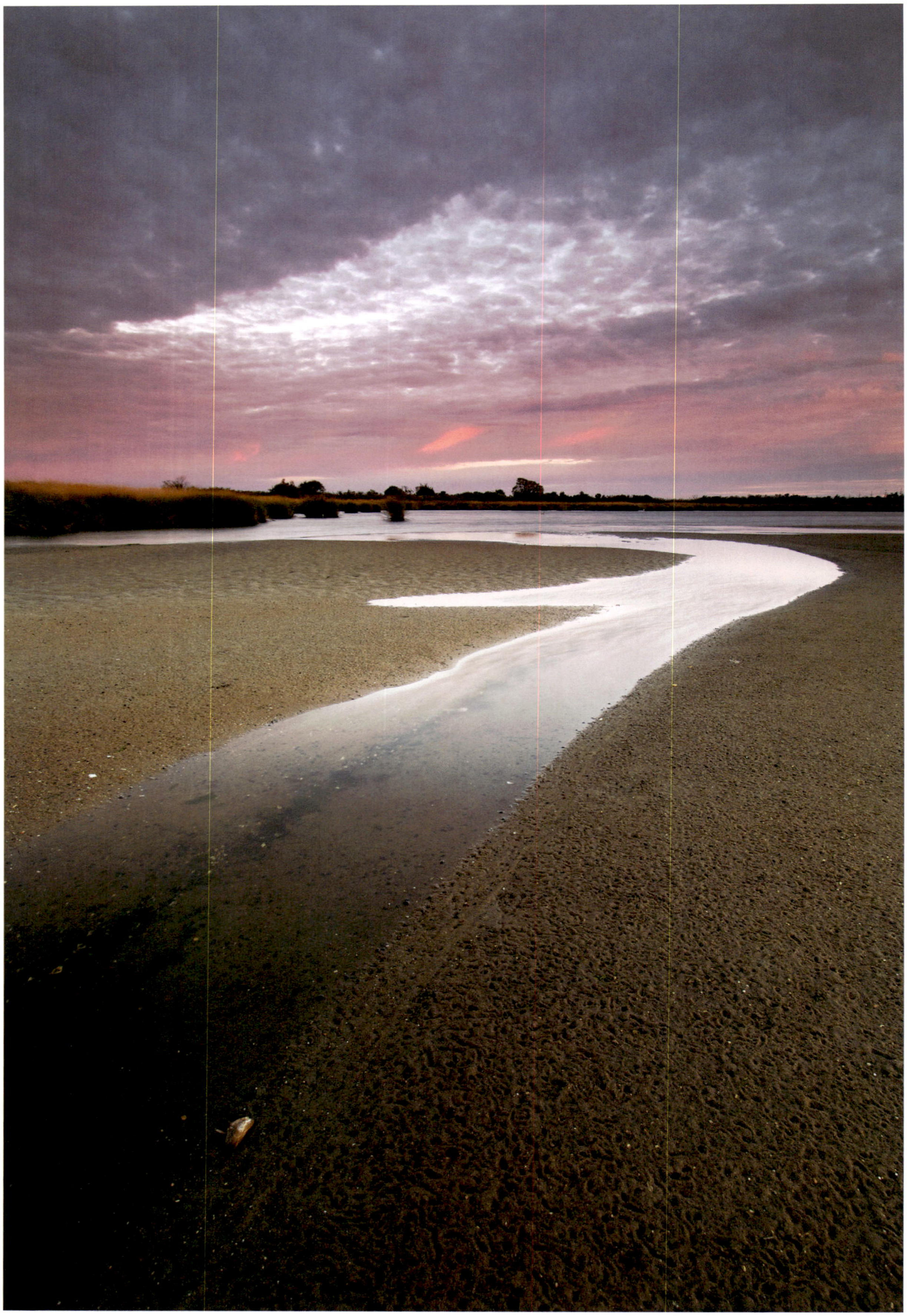

Tidal pools, Sandy Hook/Gateway National Recreation Area

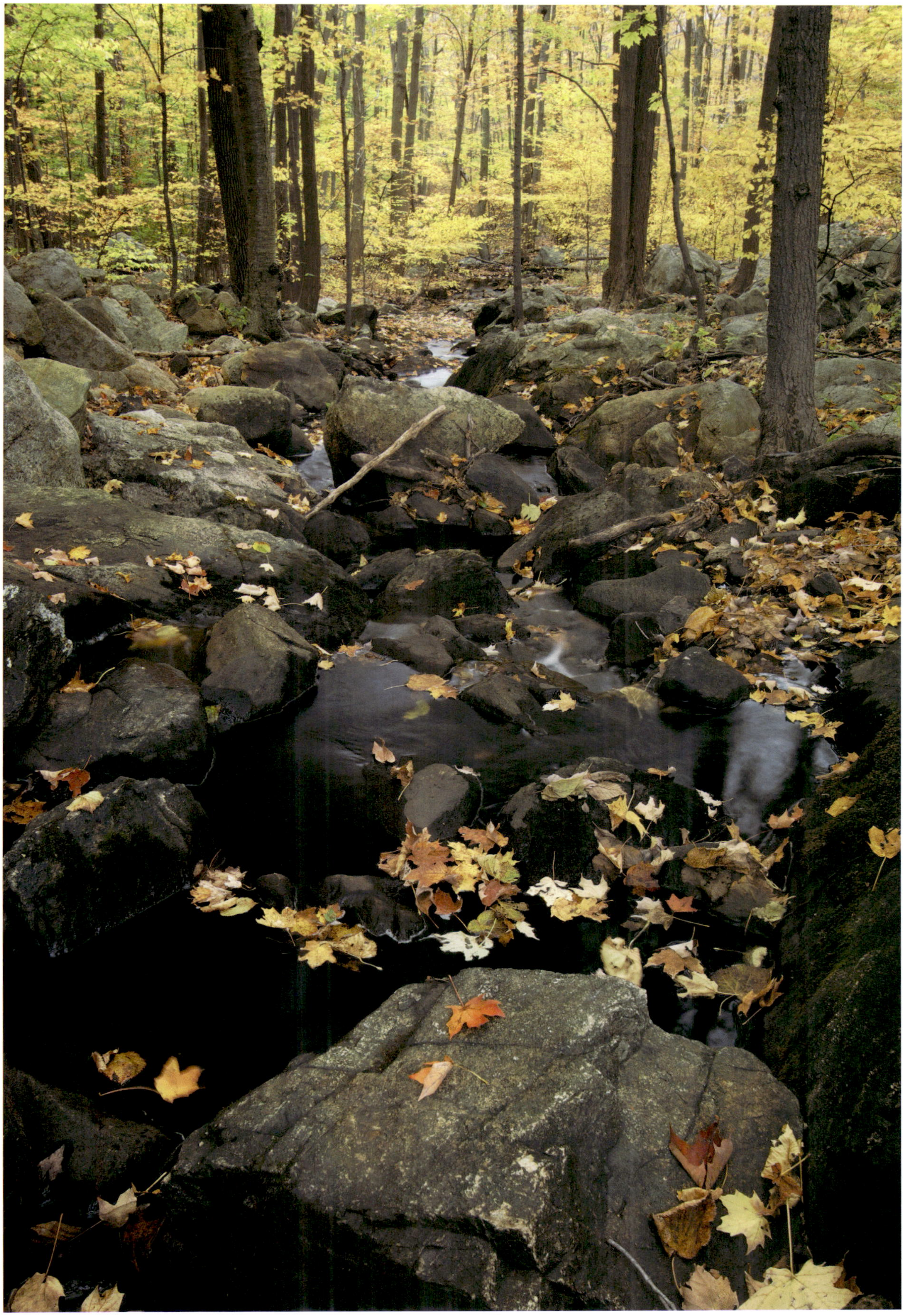

Fall stream, Mahlon Dickerson Reservation

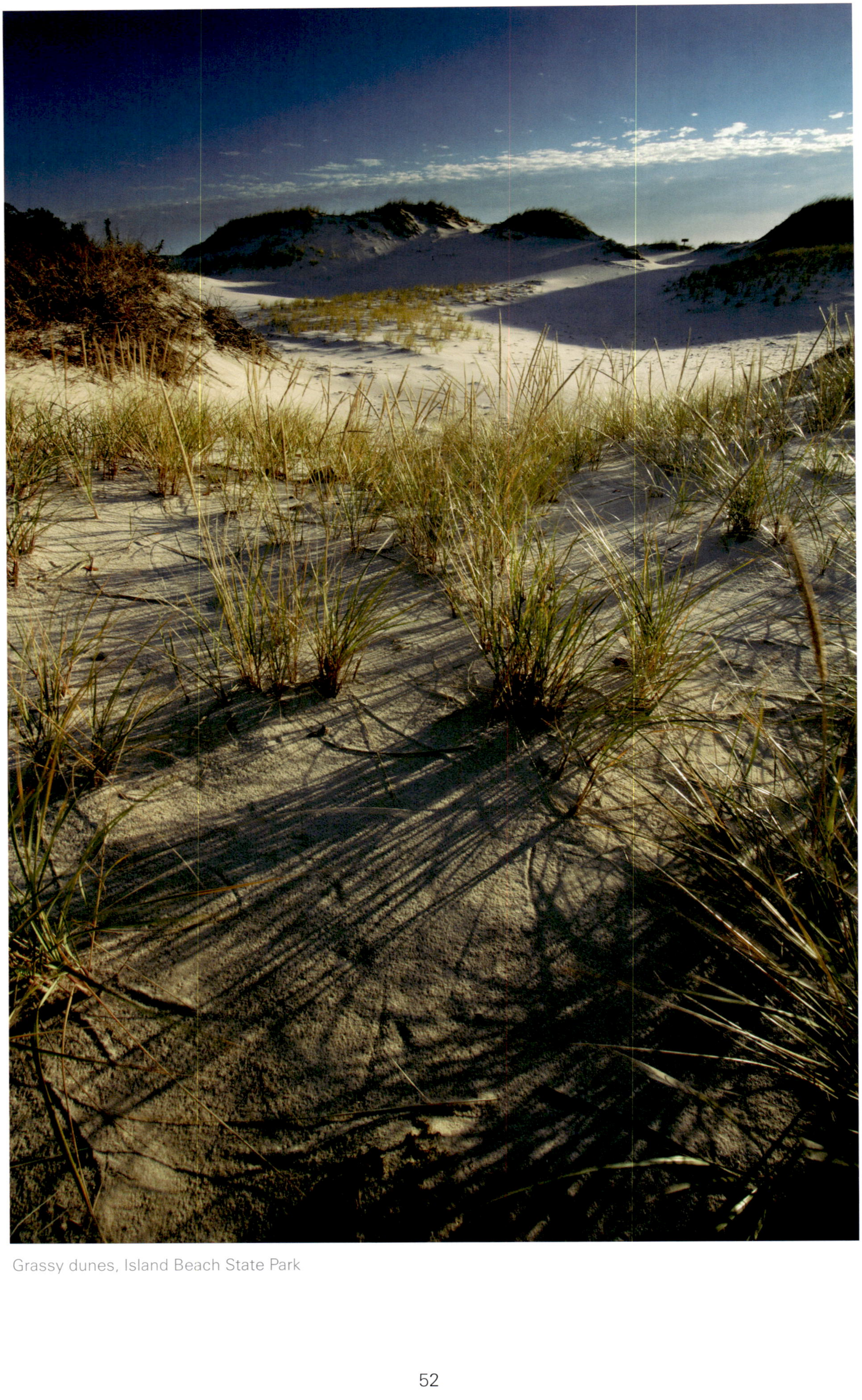

Grassy dunes, Island Beach State Park

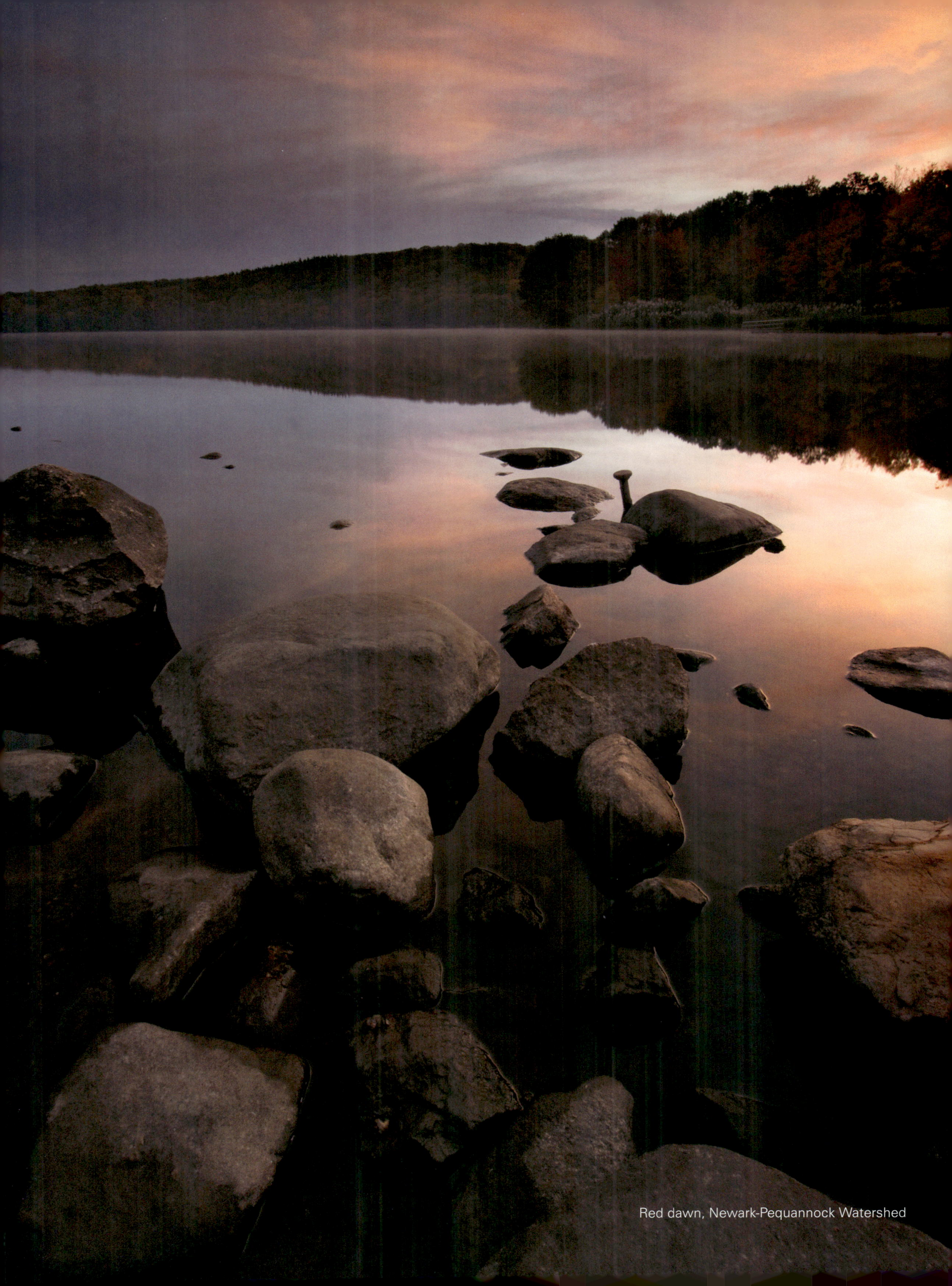

Red dawn, Newark-Pequannock Watershed

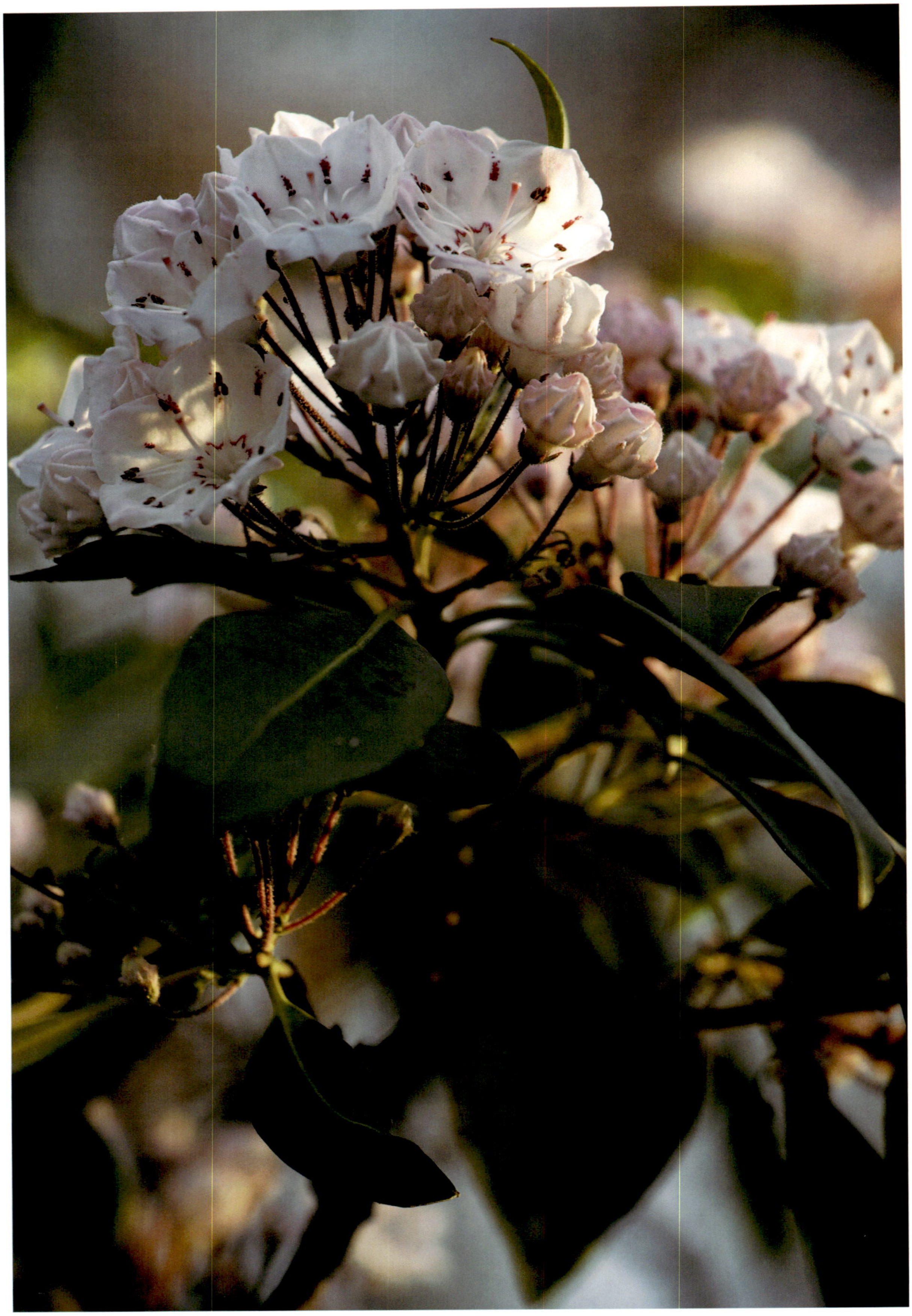

Mountain laurel blooms, Penn State Forest

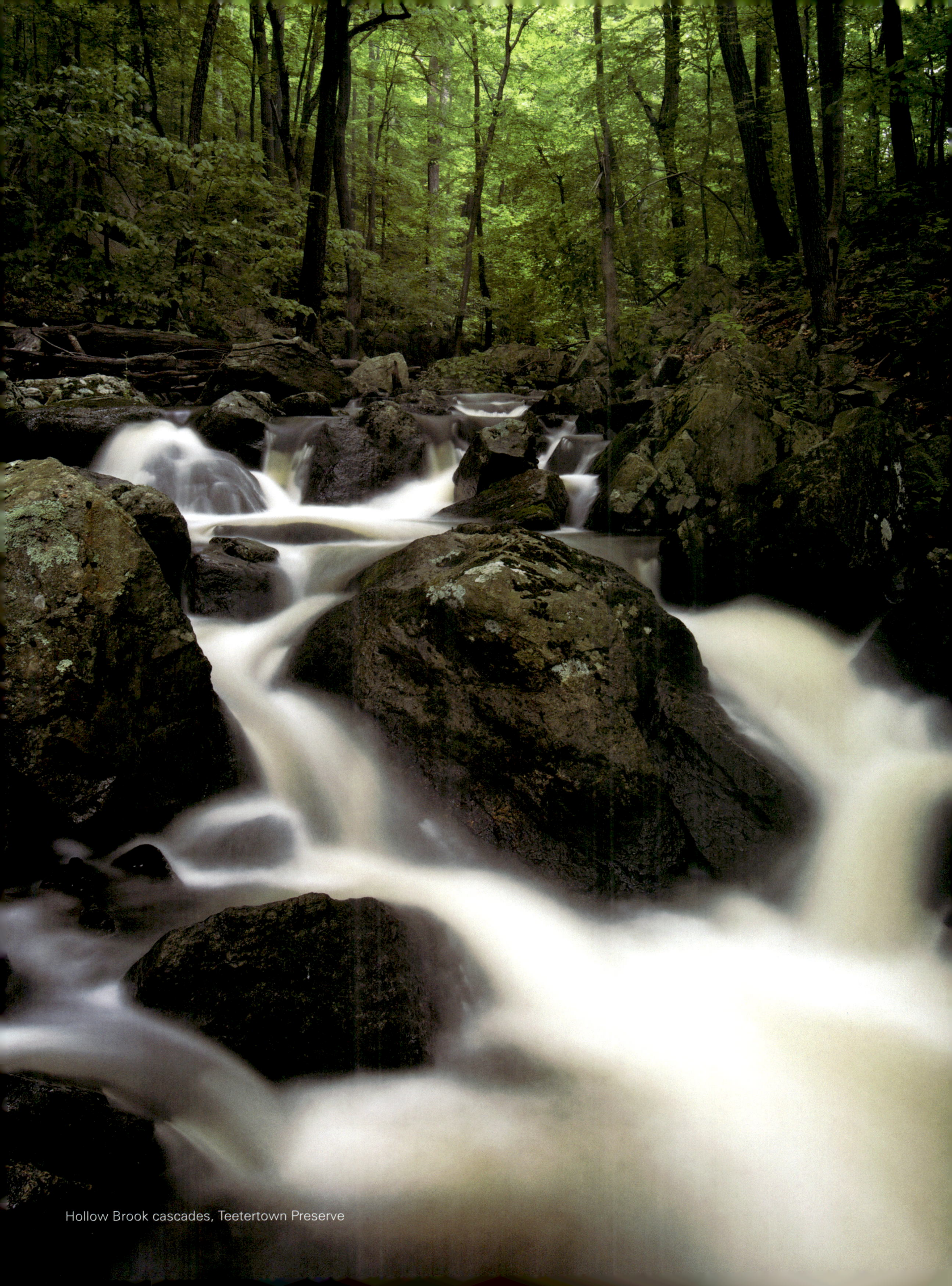

Hollow Brook cascades, Teetertown Preserve

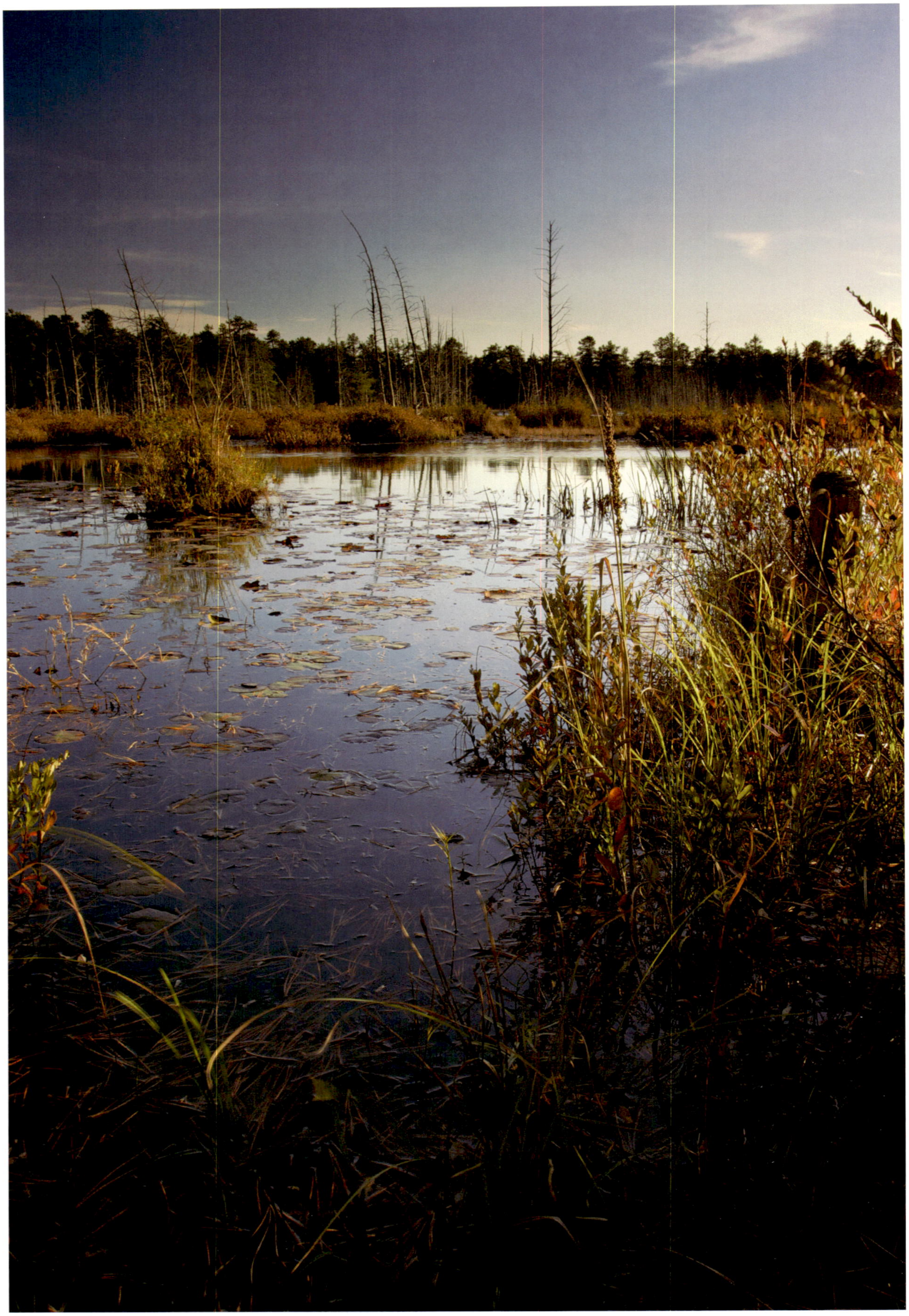

Goshen Pond, Wharton State Forest

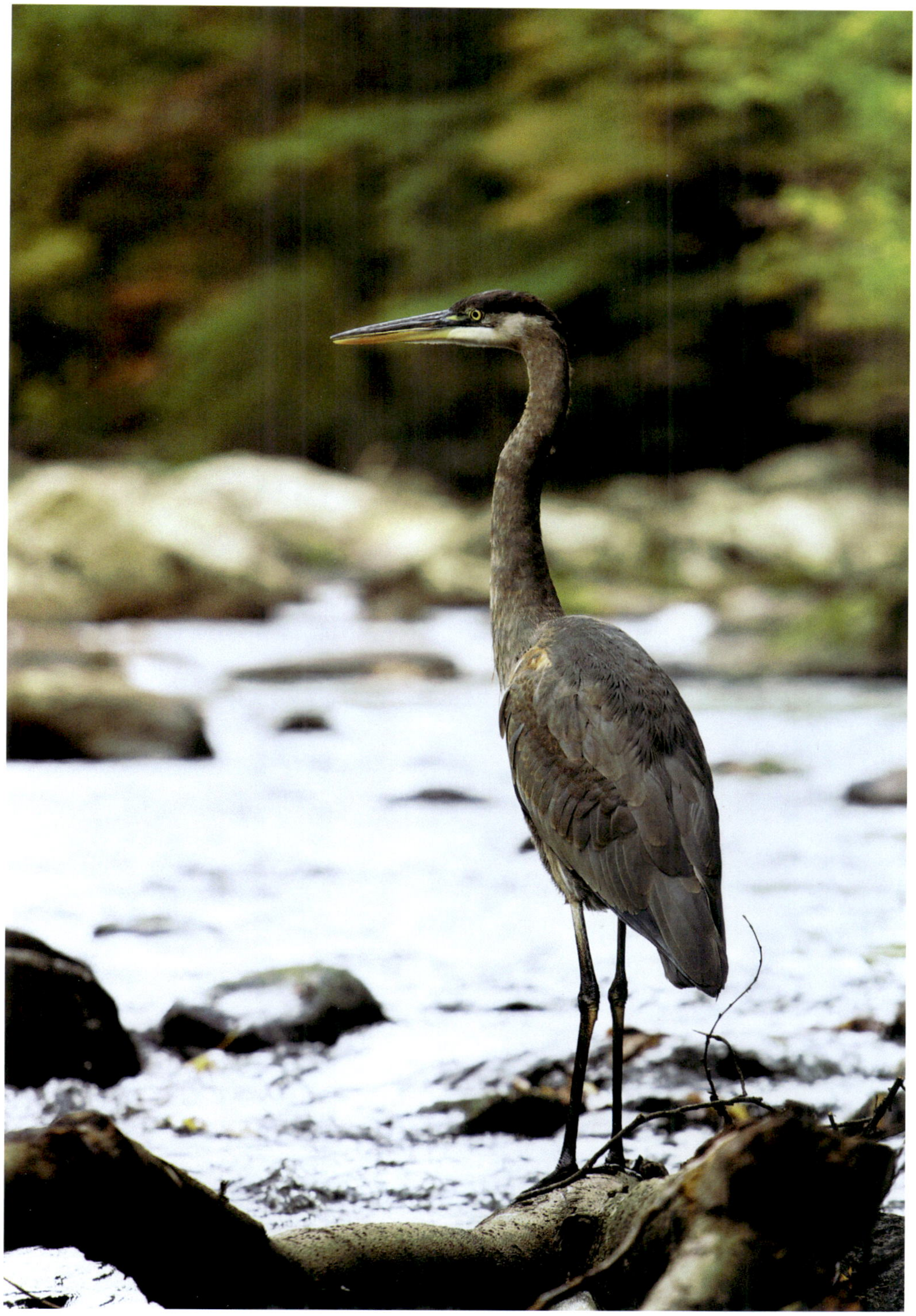

Blue Heron, Ken Lockwood Gorge Wildlife Management Area

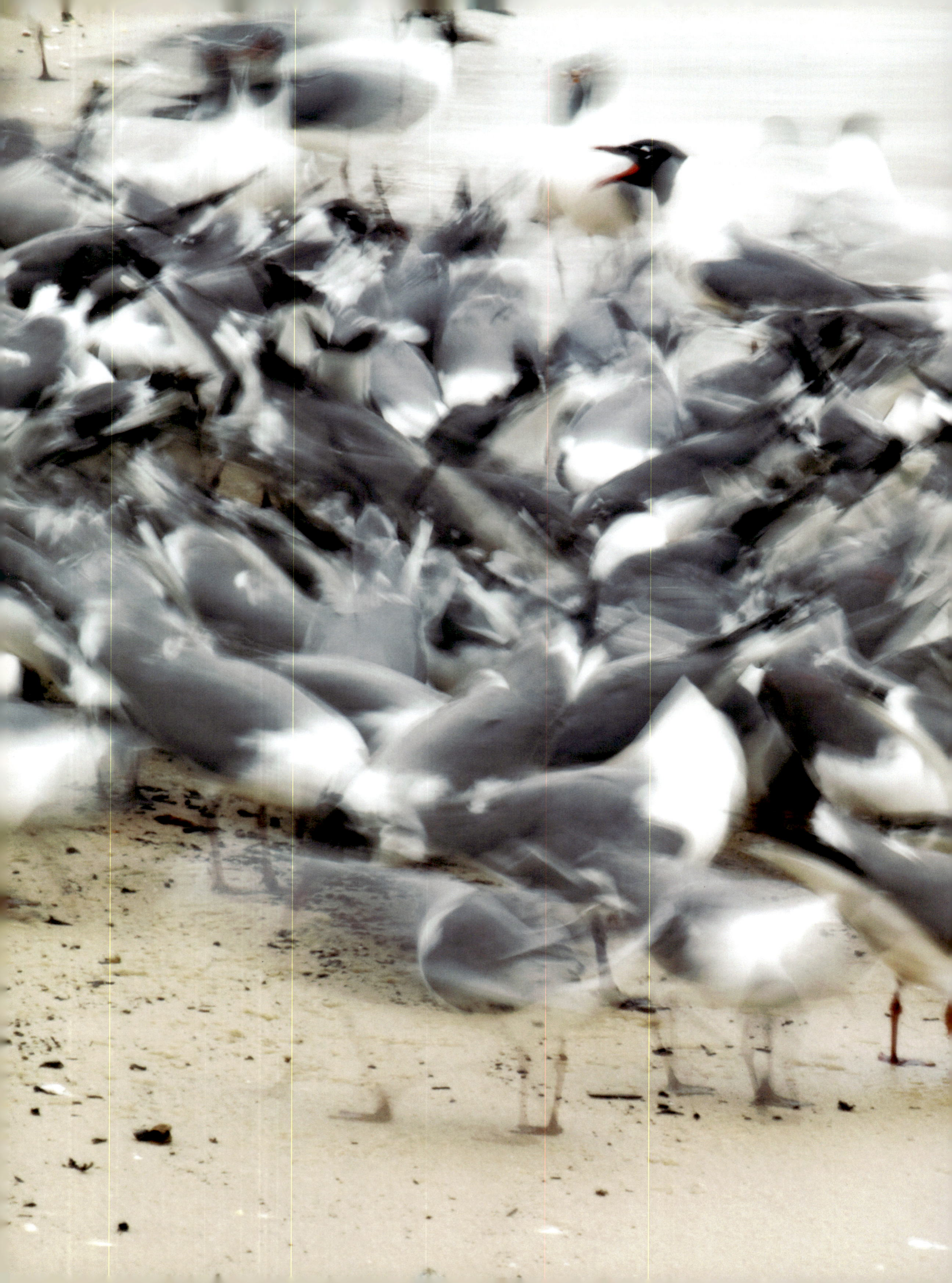

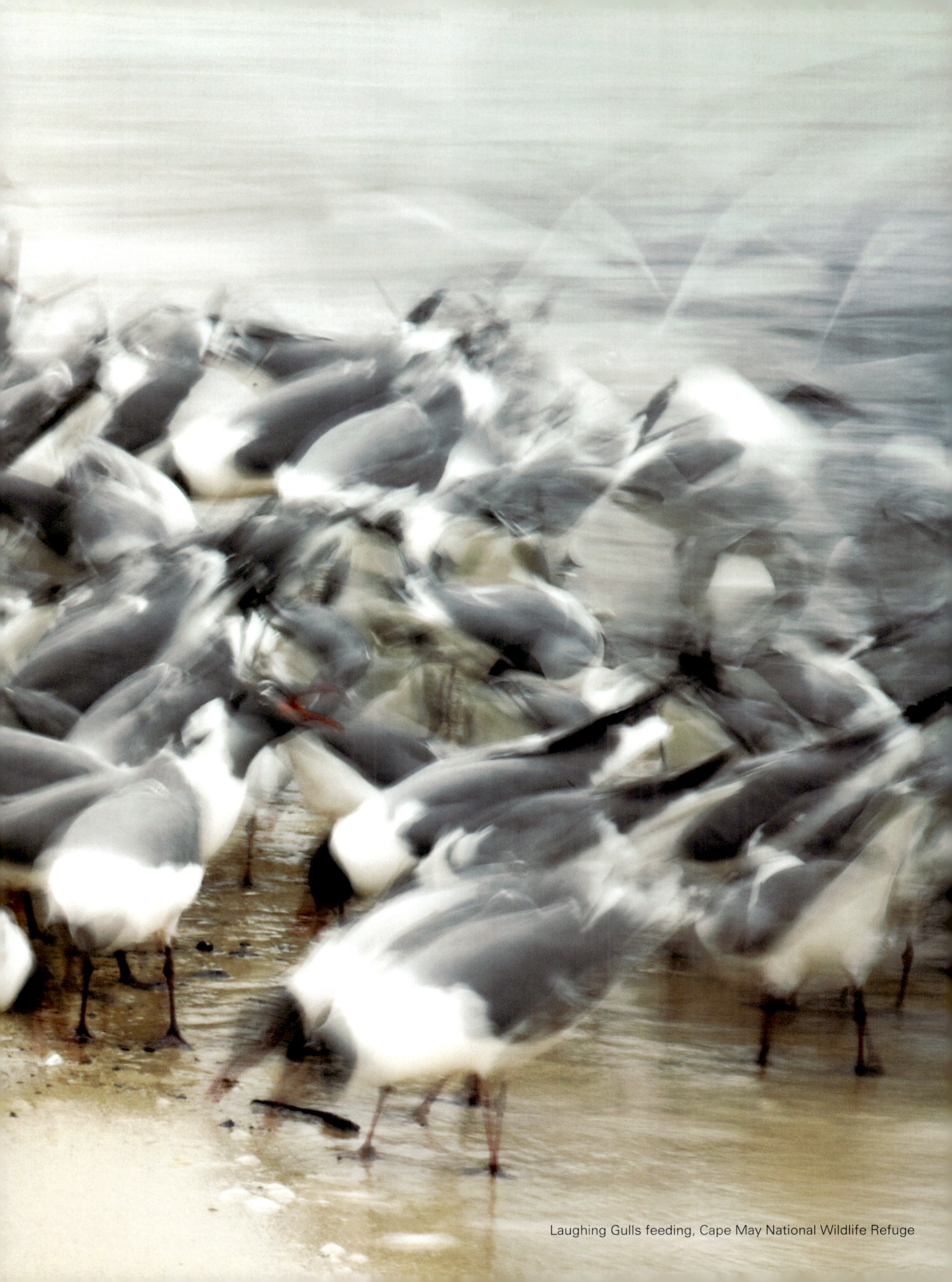

Laughing Gulls feeding, Cape May National Wildlife Refuge

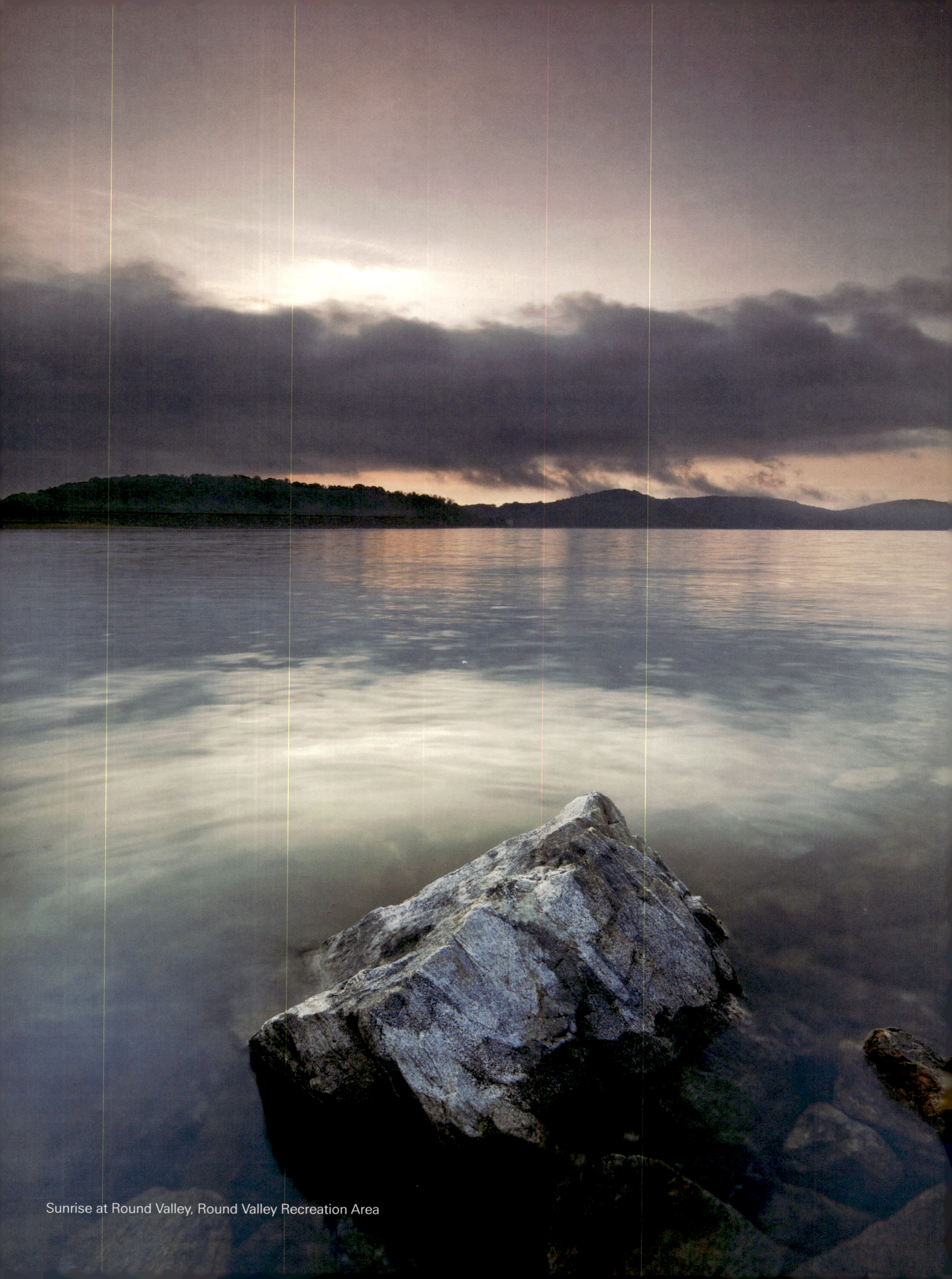
Sunrise at Round Valley, Round Valley Recreation Area

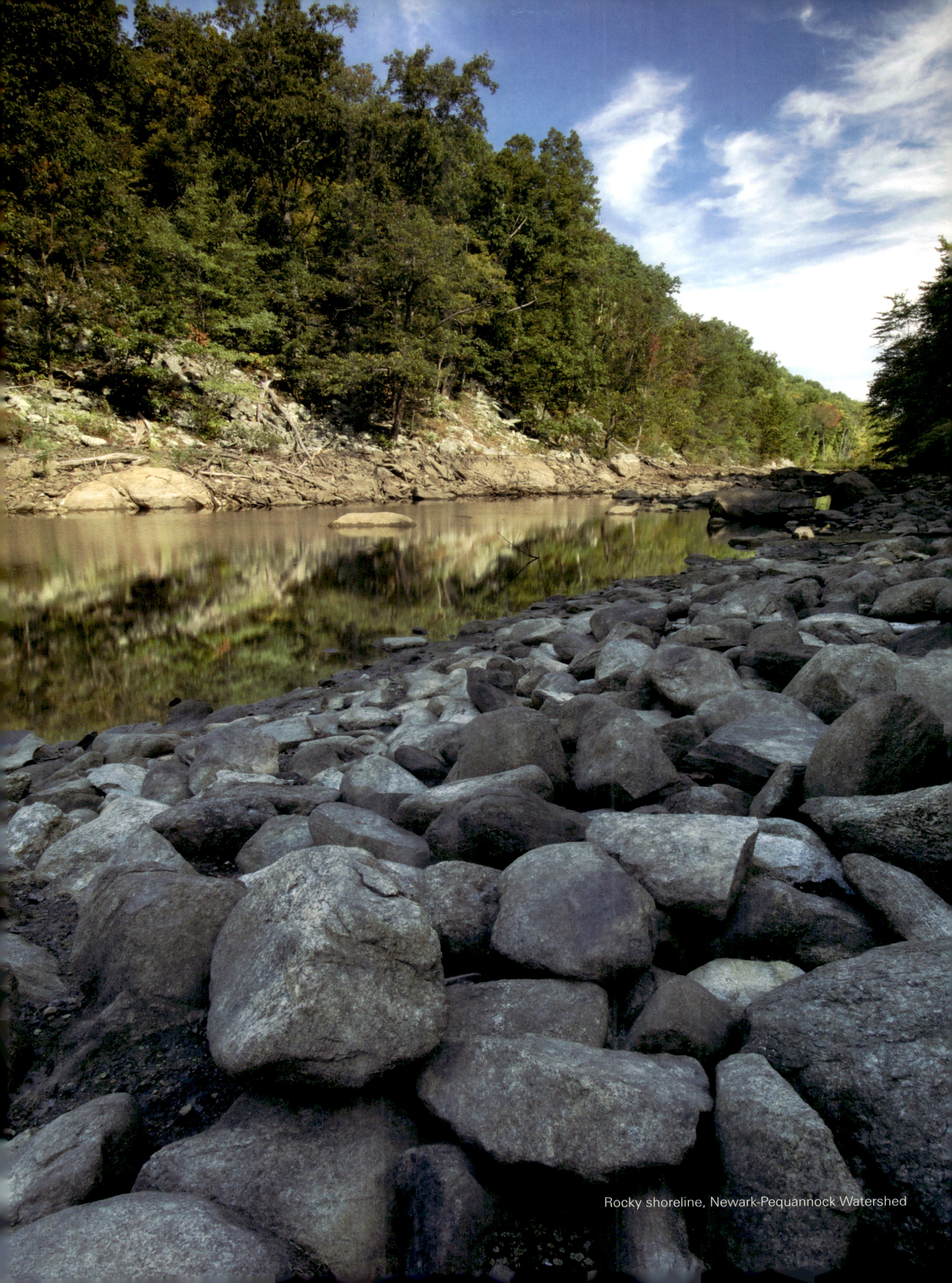

Rocky shoreline, Newark-Pequannock Watershed

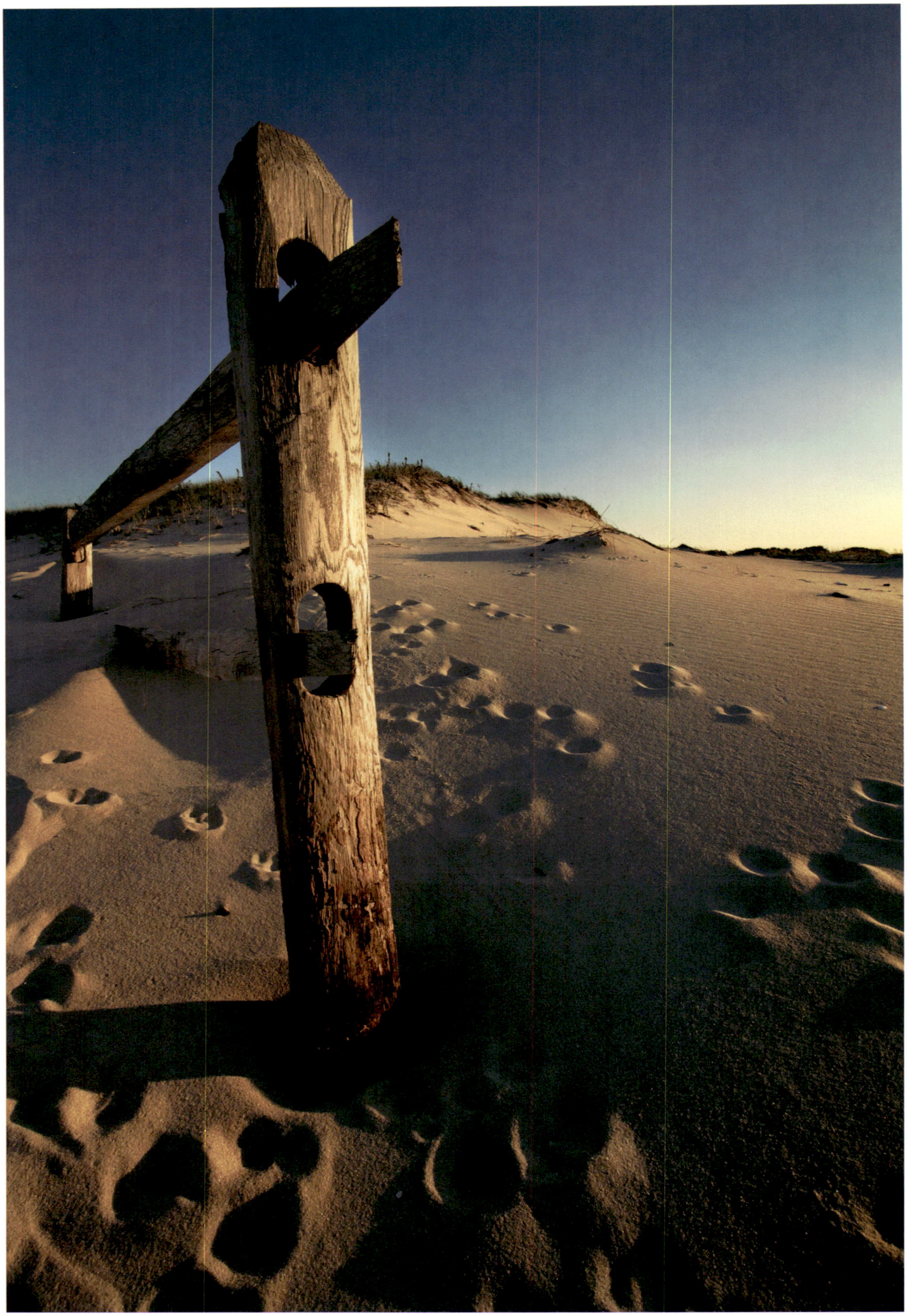

Weathered fence post, Island Beach State Park

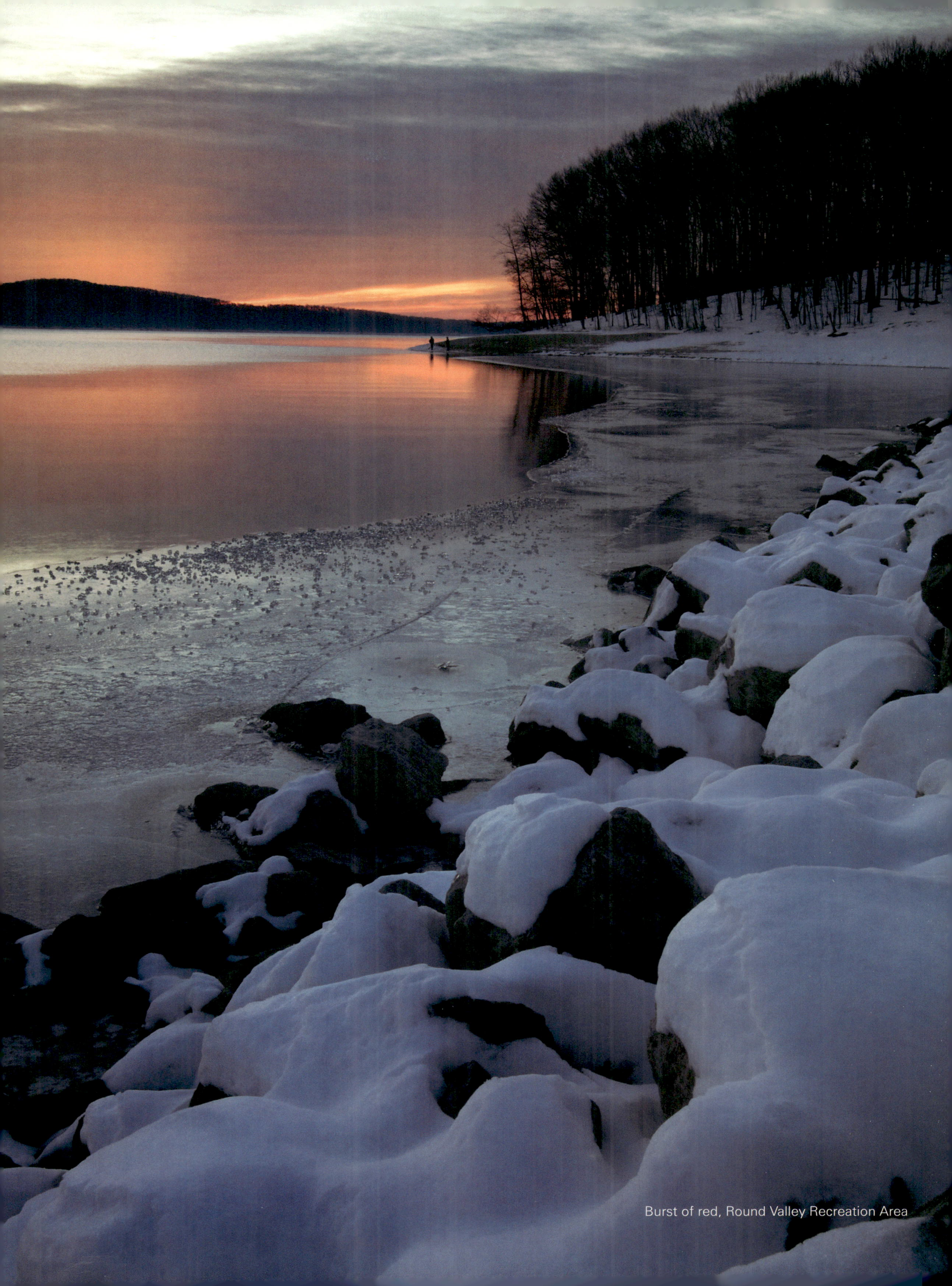

Burst of red, Round Valley Recreation Area

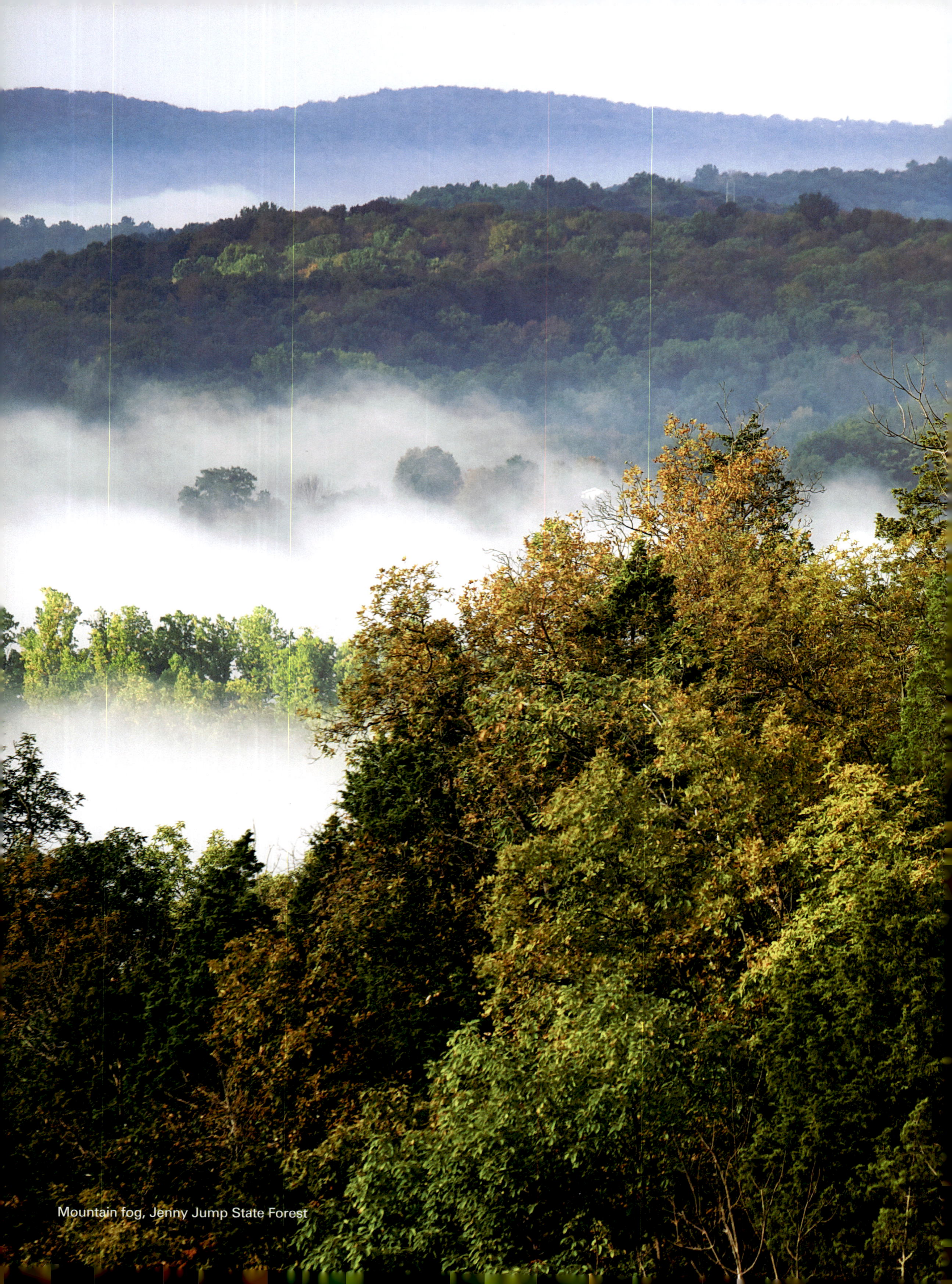

Mountain fog, Jenny Jump State Forest

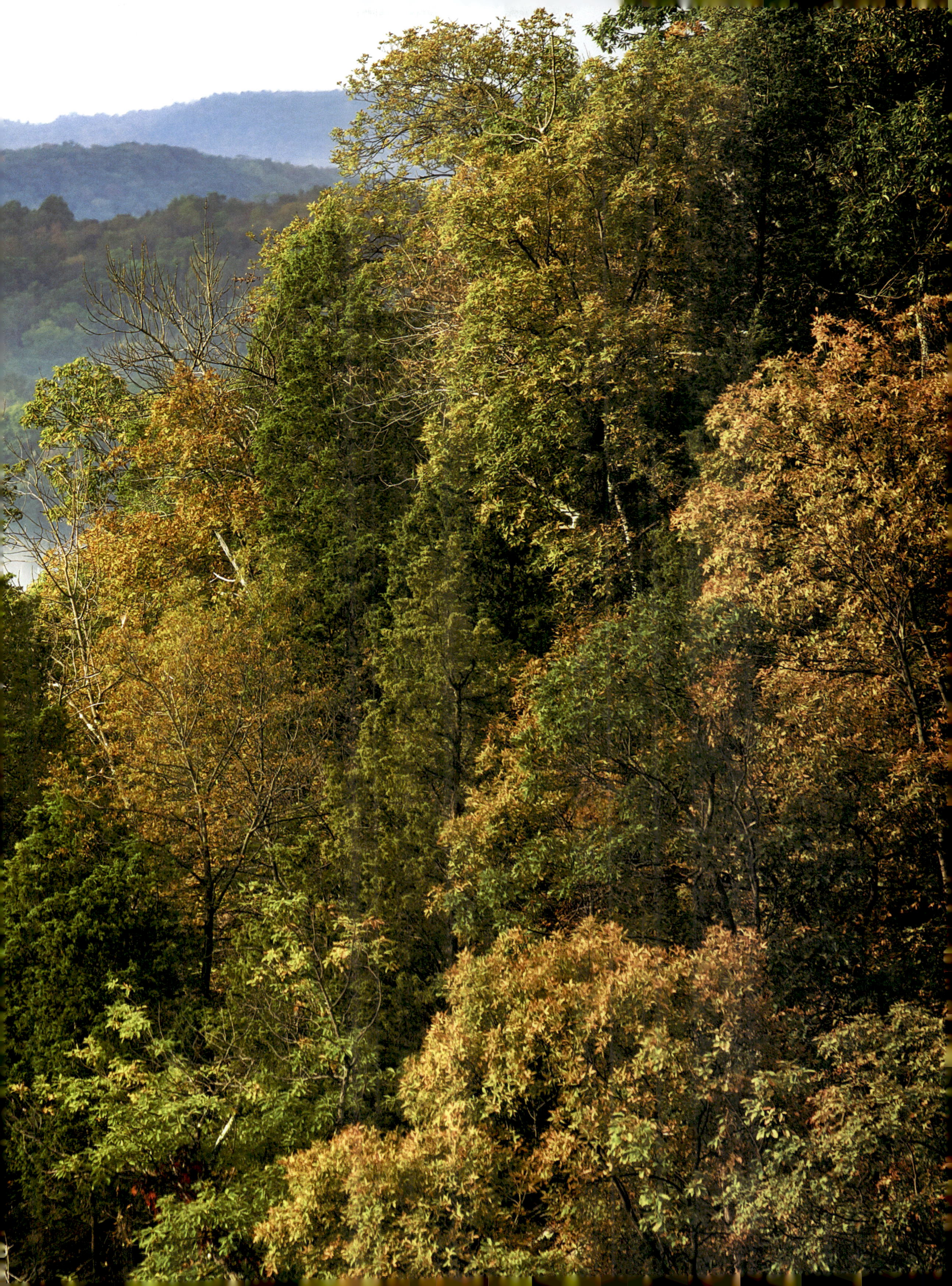

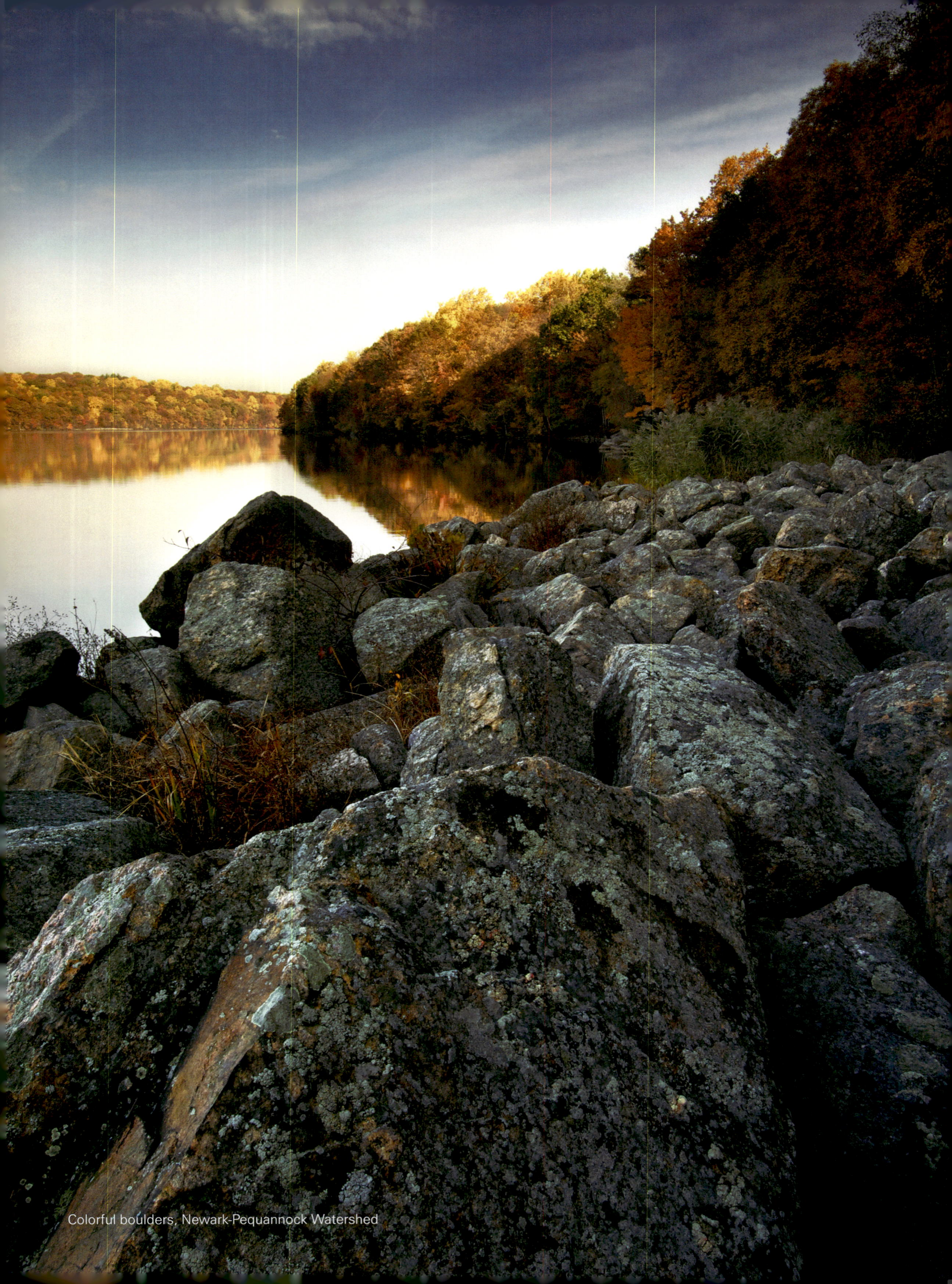

Colorful boulders, Newark-Pequannock Watershed

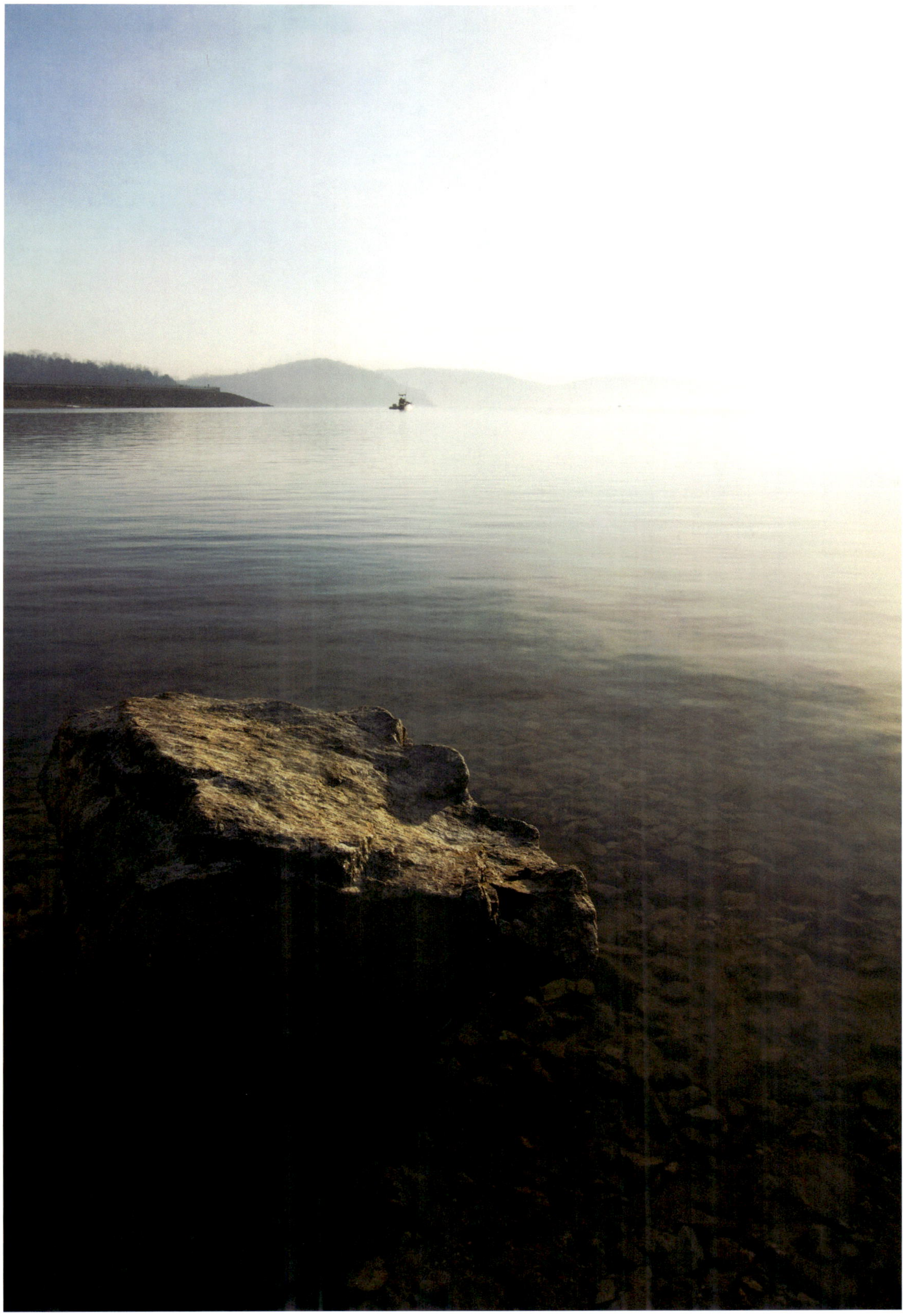

Lake fog, Round Valley Recreation Area

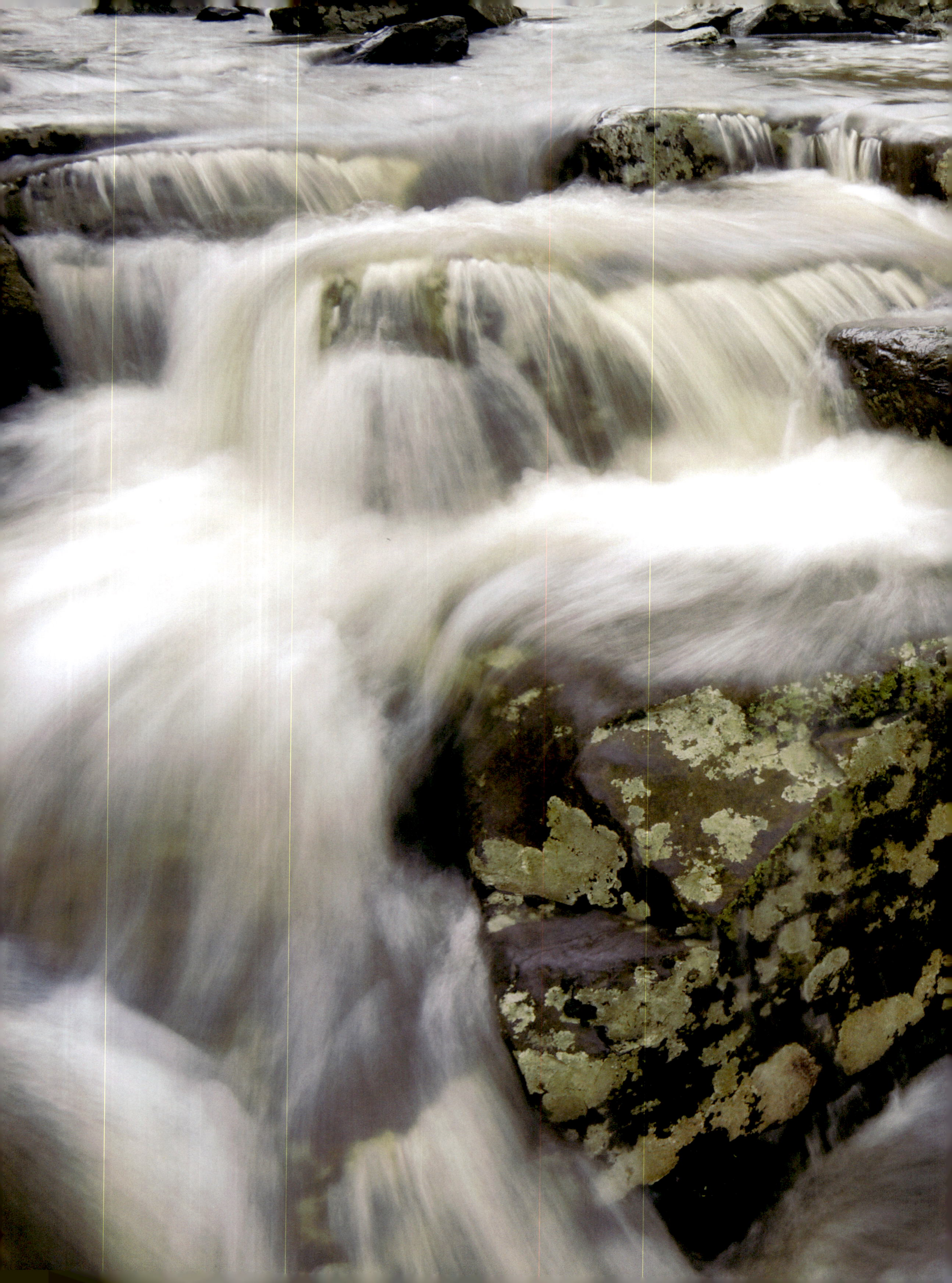

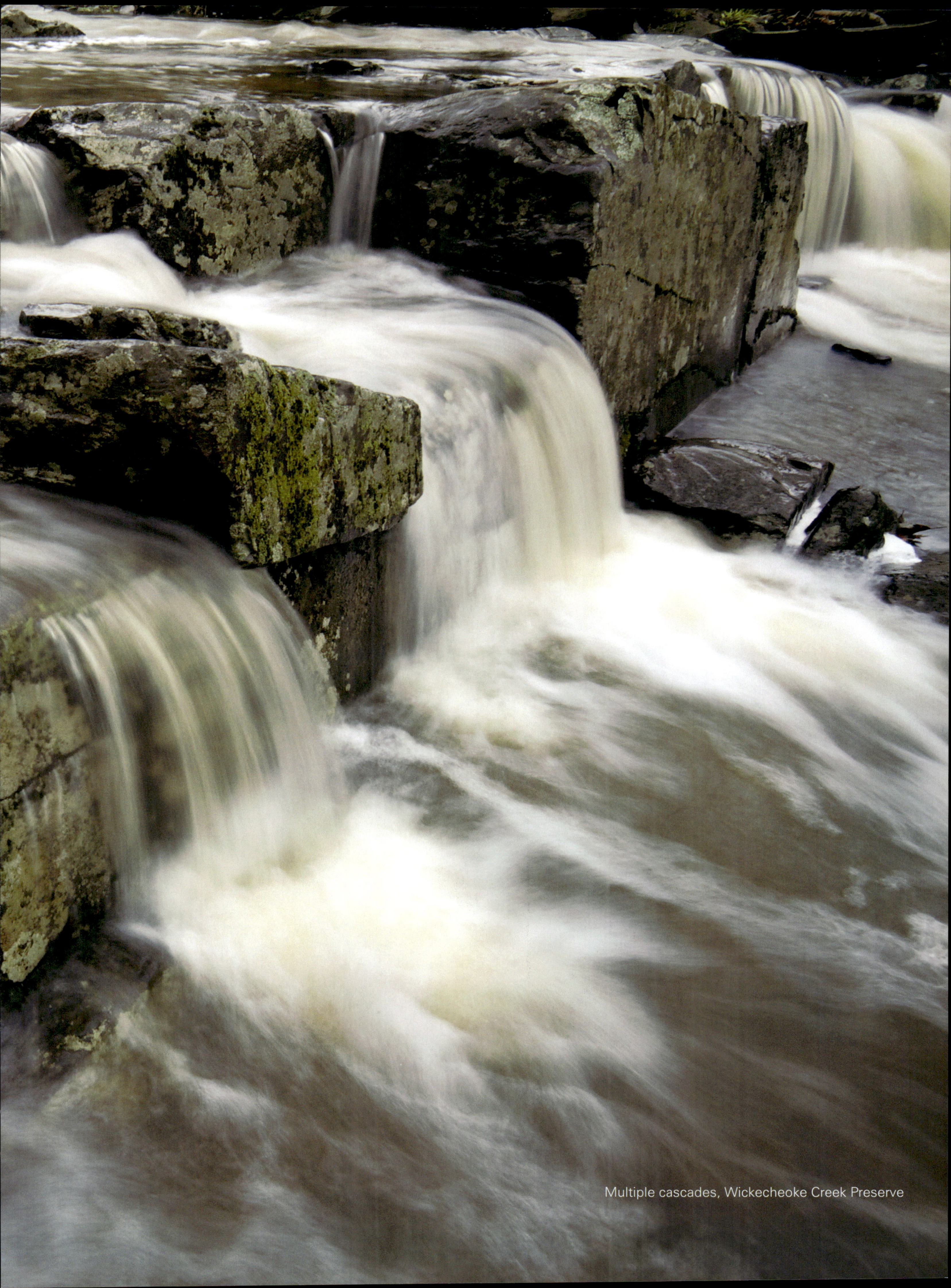

Multiple cascades, Wickecheoke Creek Preserve

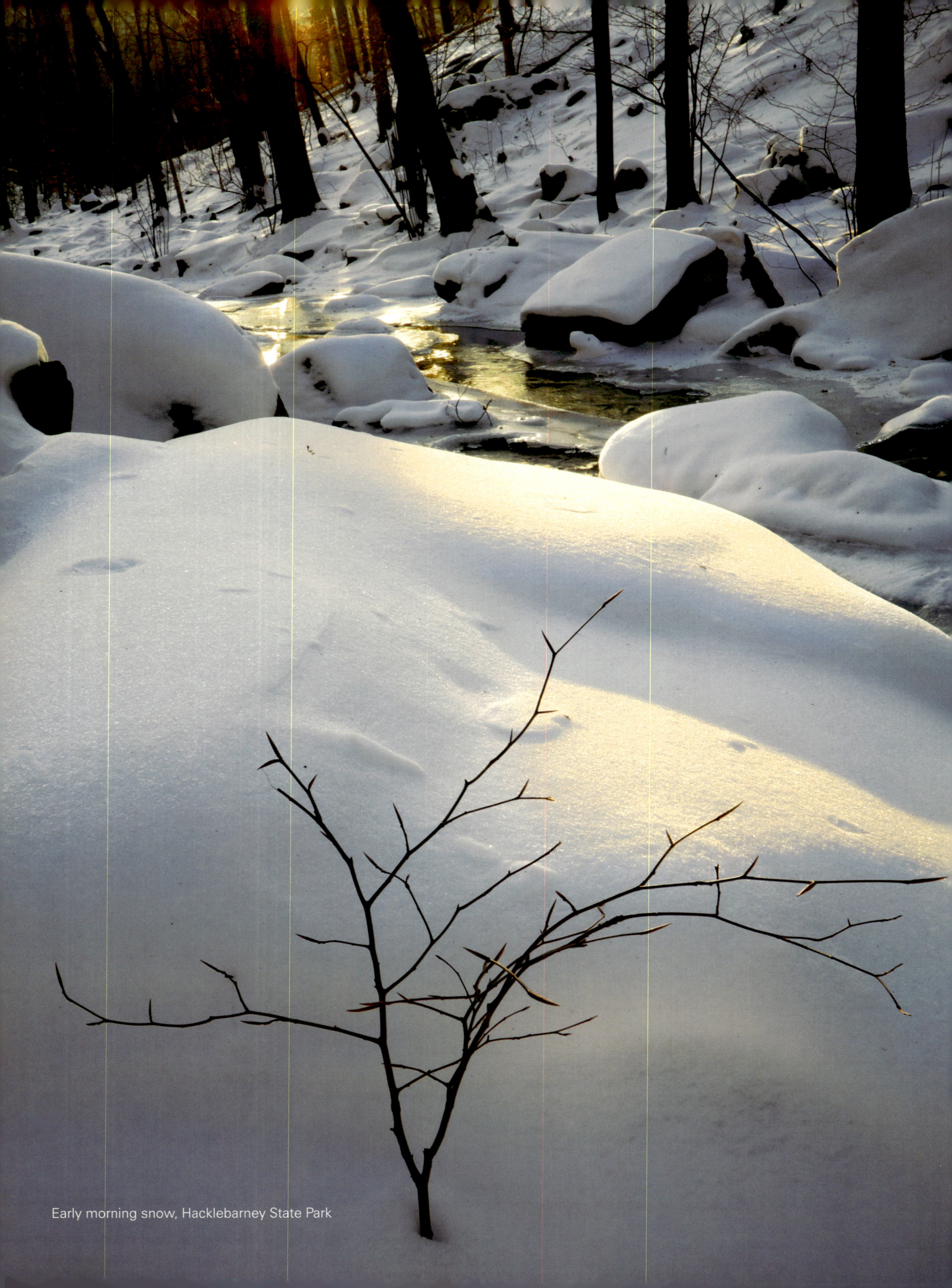

Early morning snow, Hacklebarney State Park

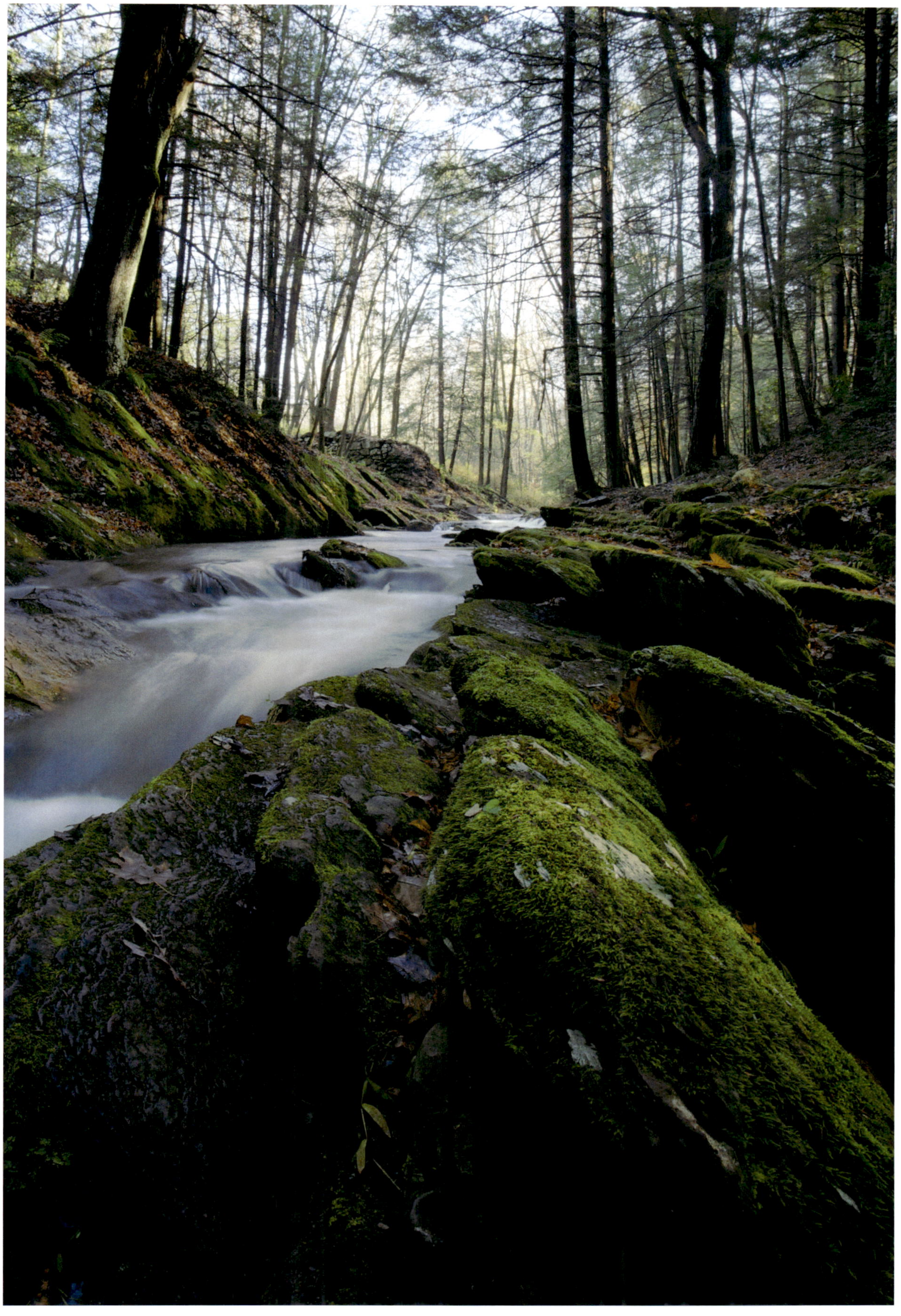

Van Campens Creek, Delaware Water Gap National Recreation Area

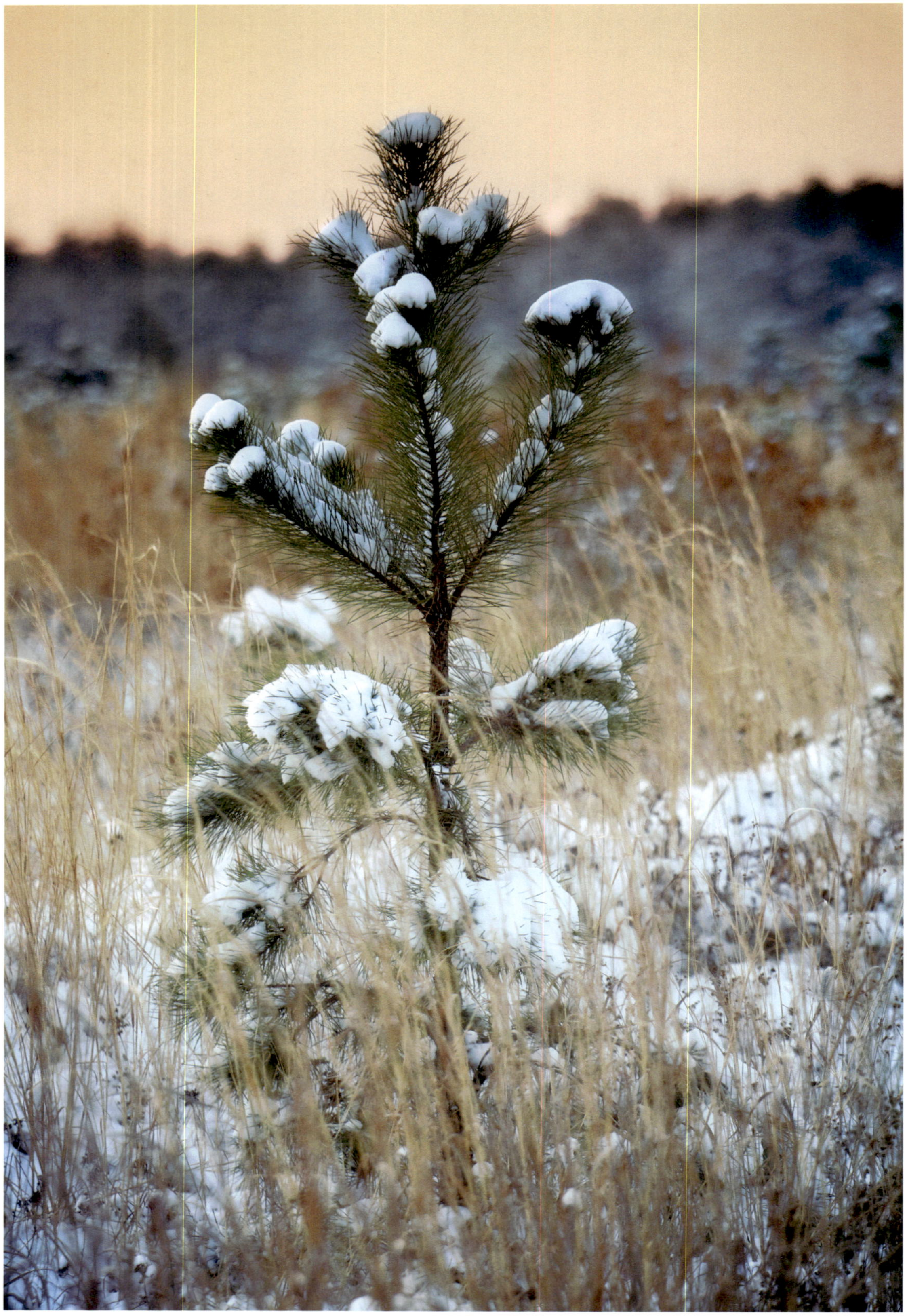

Snowy pine, Franklin Parker Preserve

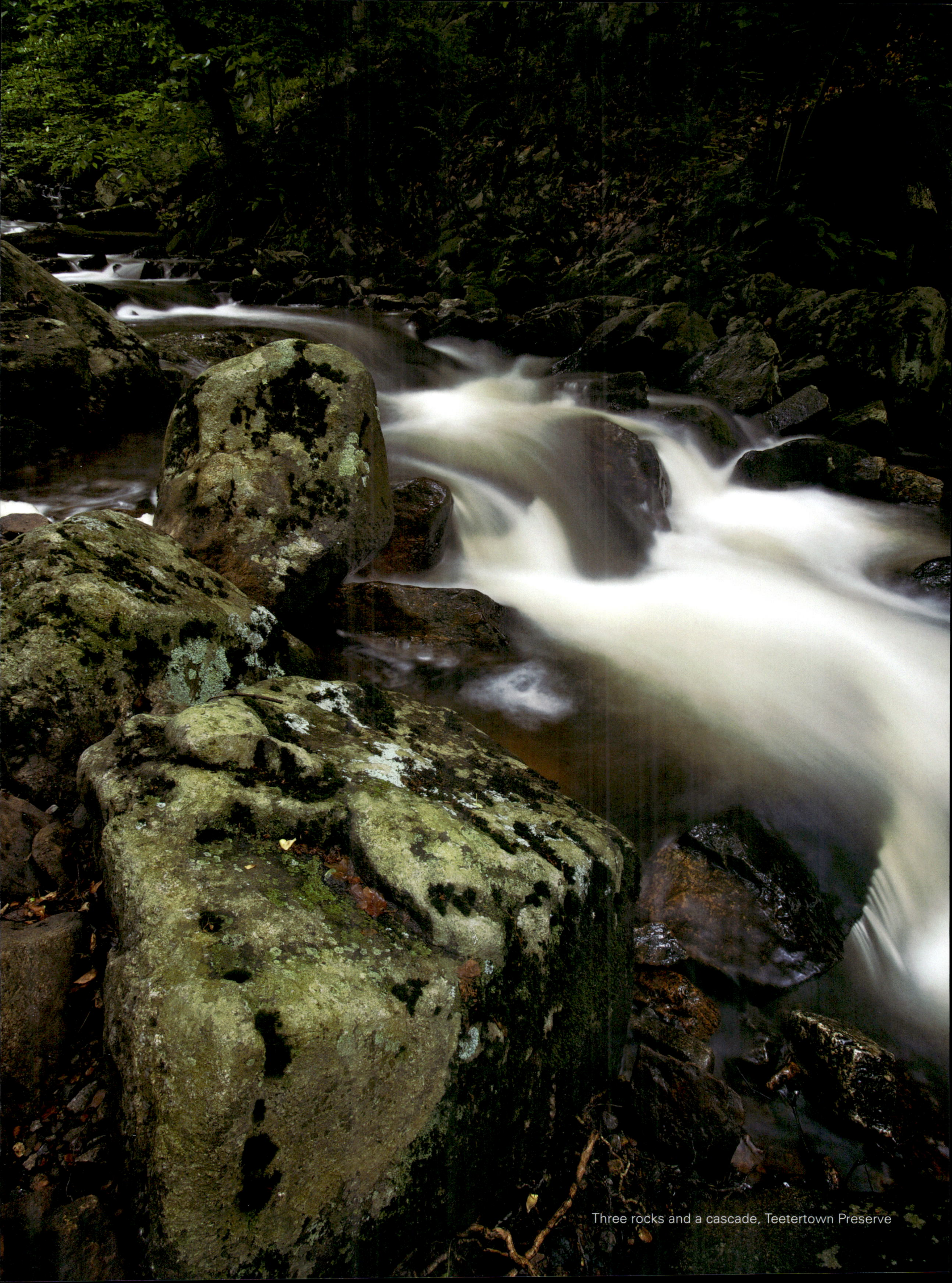

Three rocks and a cascade, Teetertown Preserve

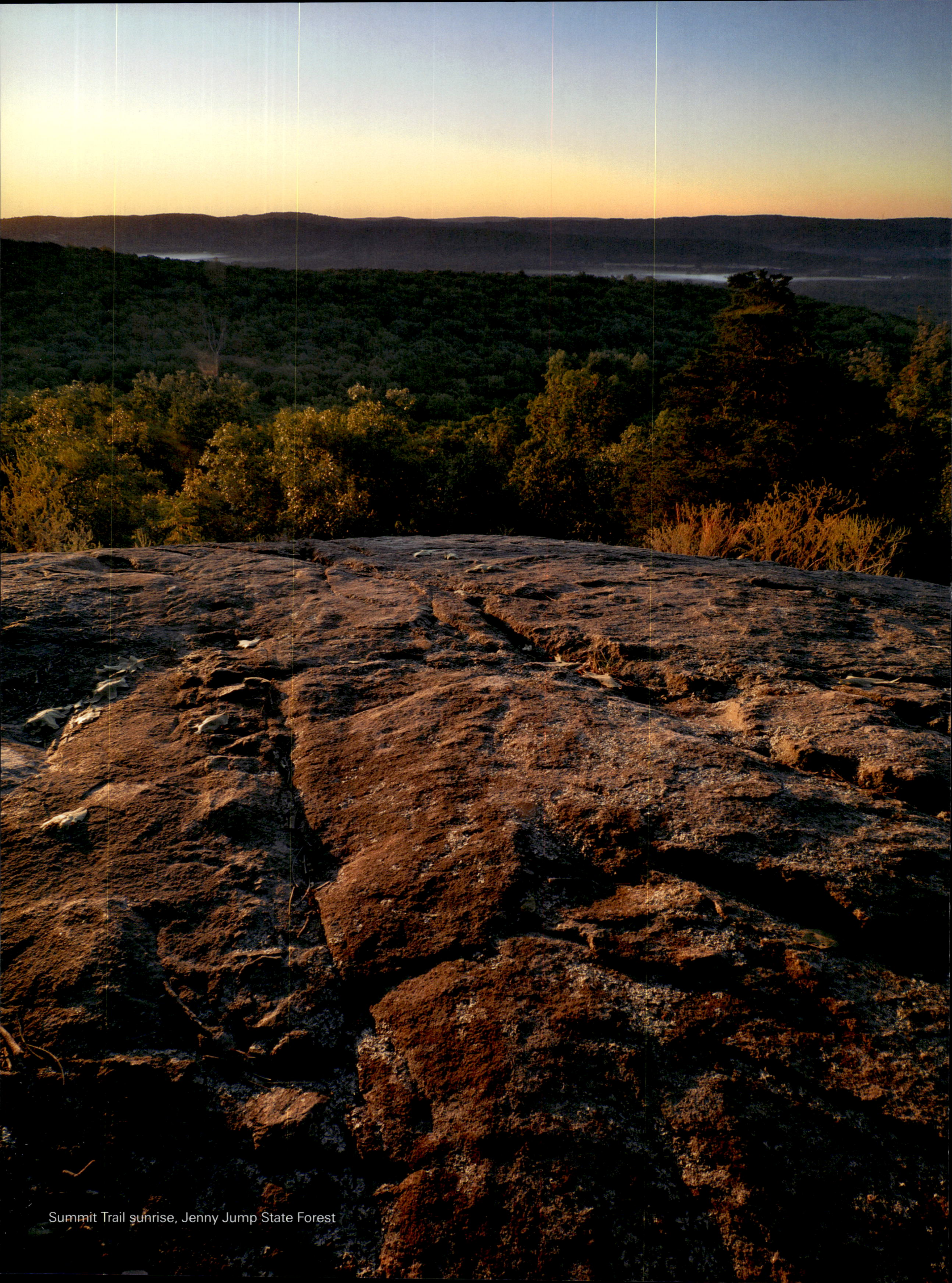

Summit Trail sunrise, Jenny Jump State Forest

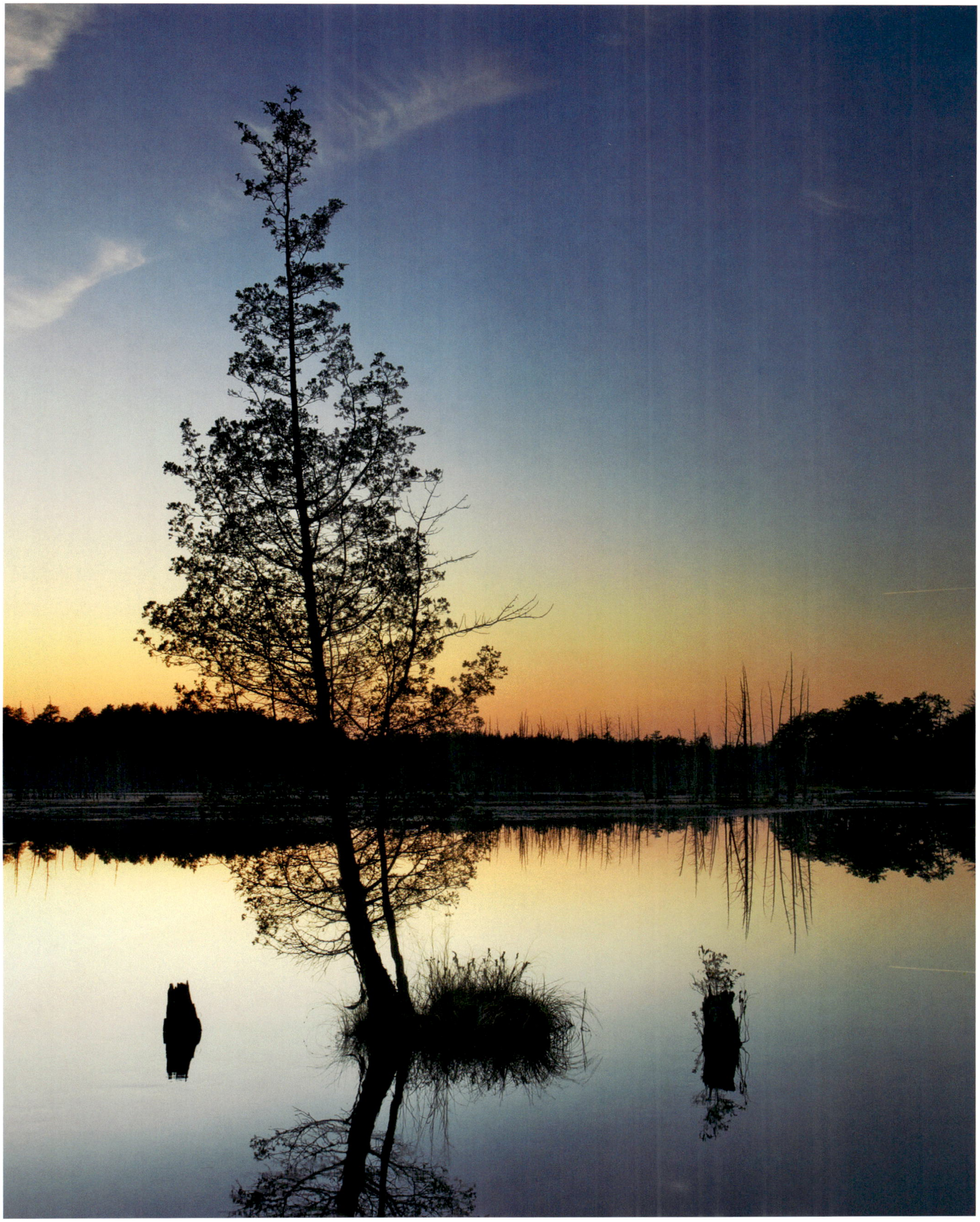

Sunset at a pond, Wharton State Forest

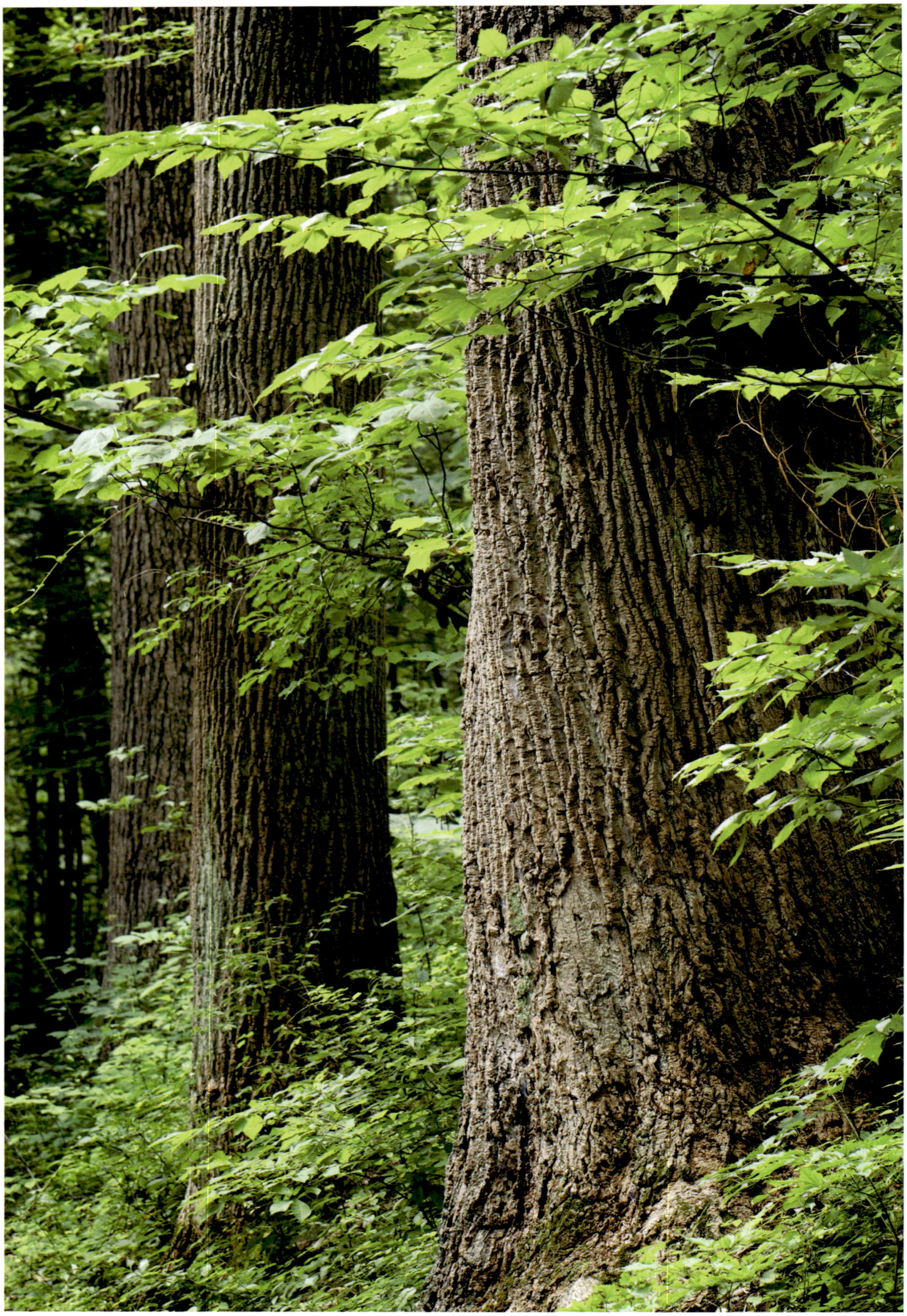

Three trees, Hacklebarney State Park

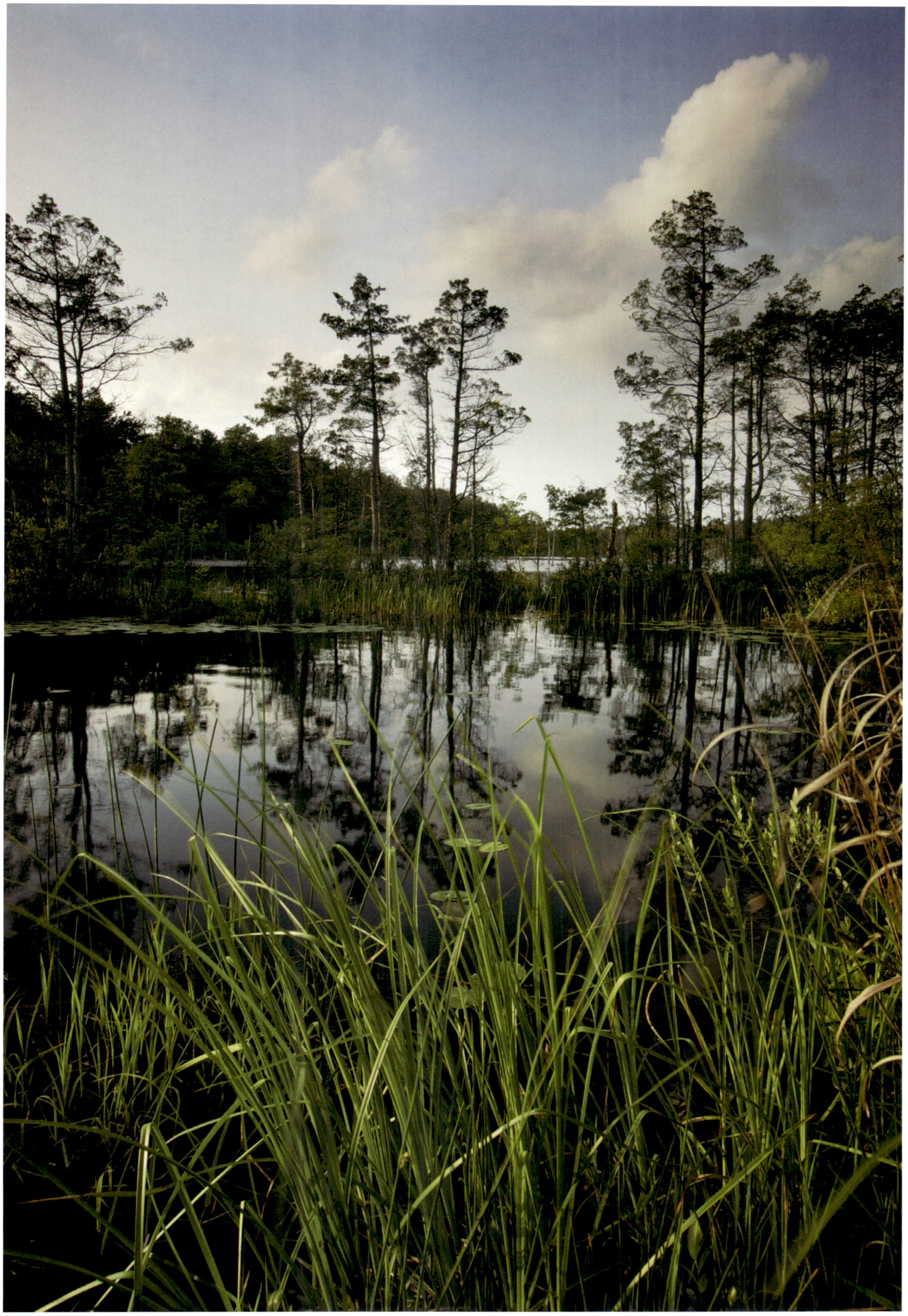

Oswego Lake, Penn State Forest

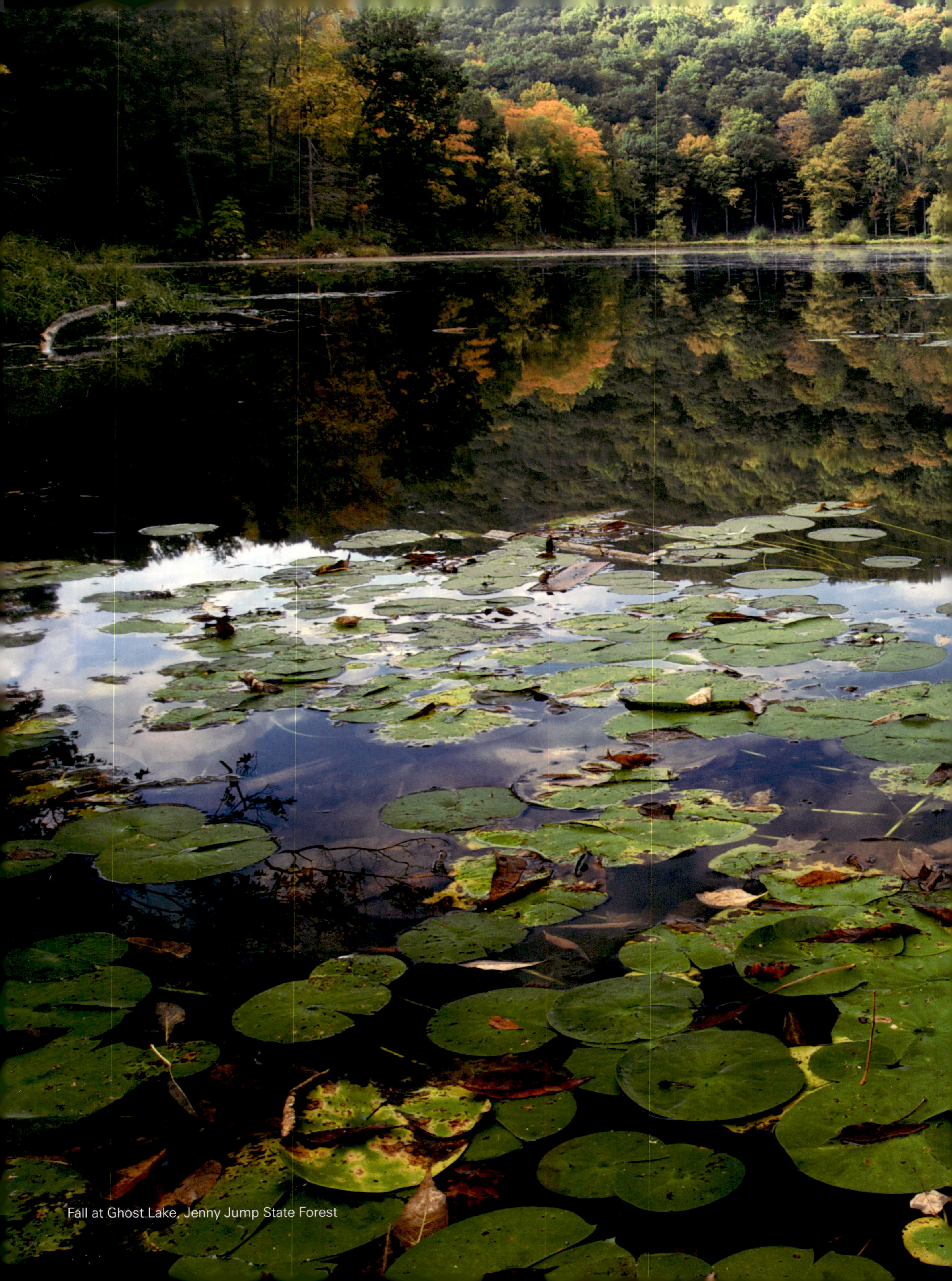

Fall at Ghost Lake, Jenny Jump State Forest

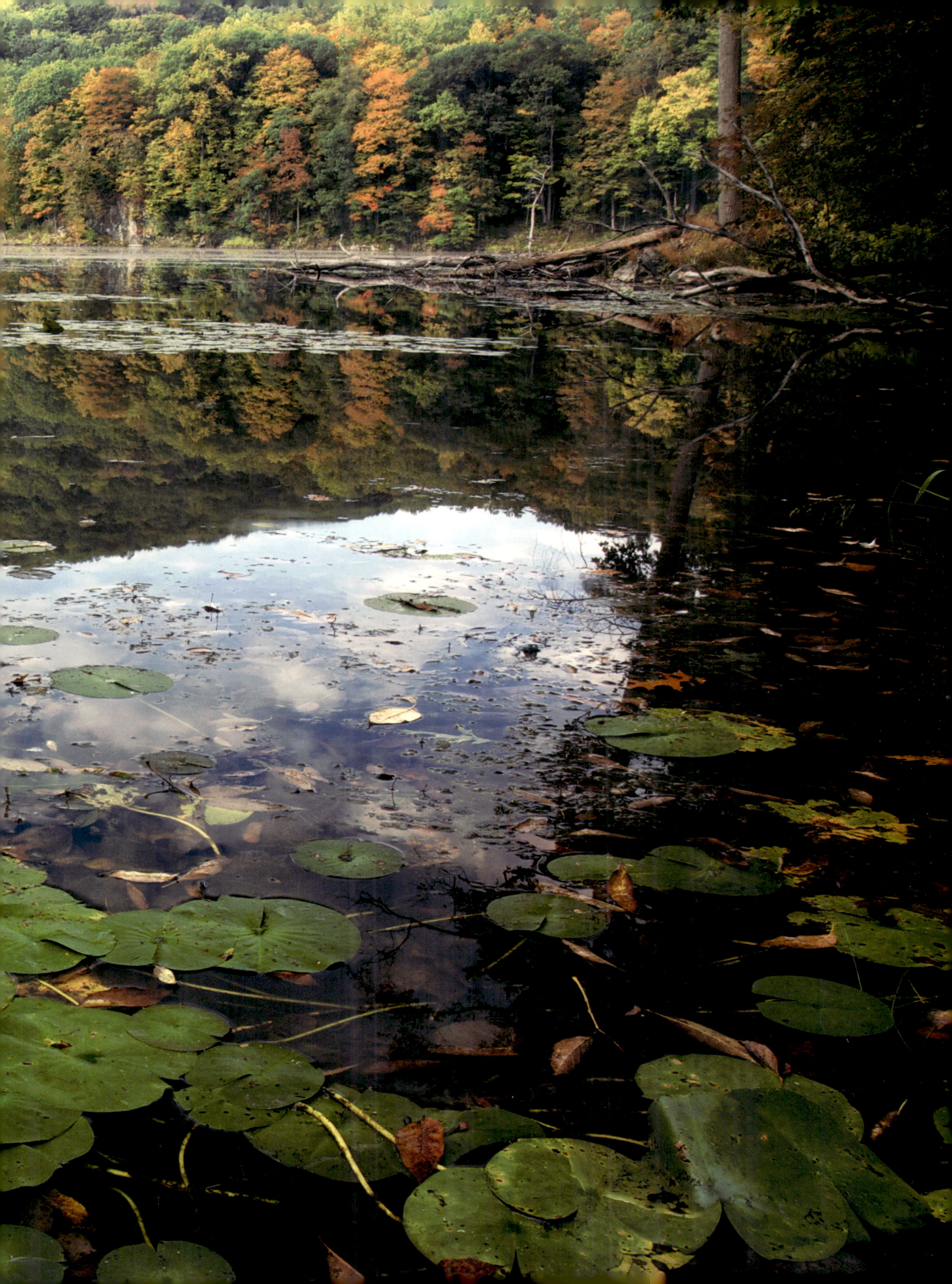

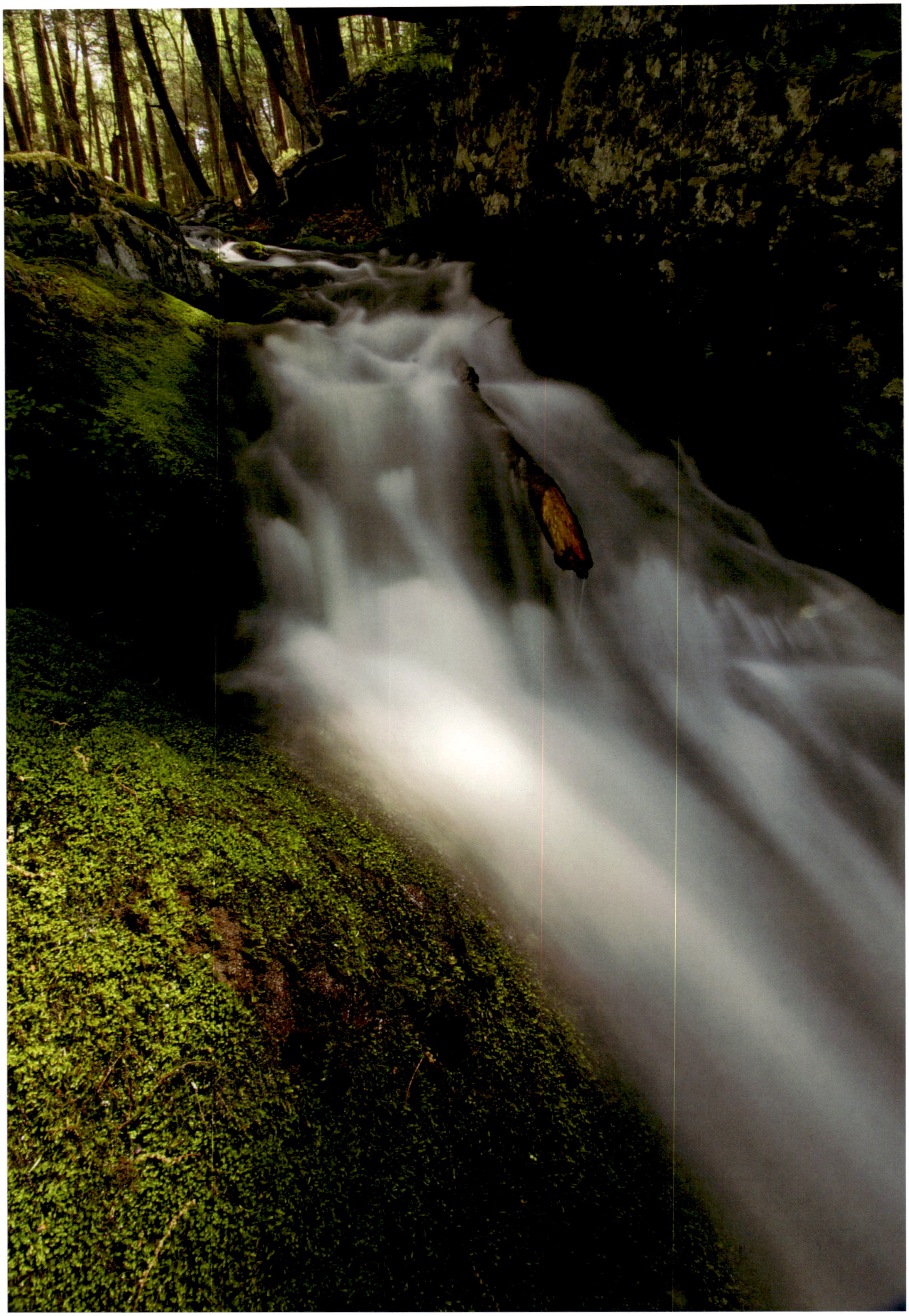

Dripping branch, Stokes State Forest

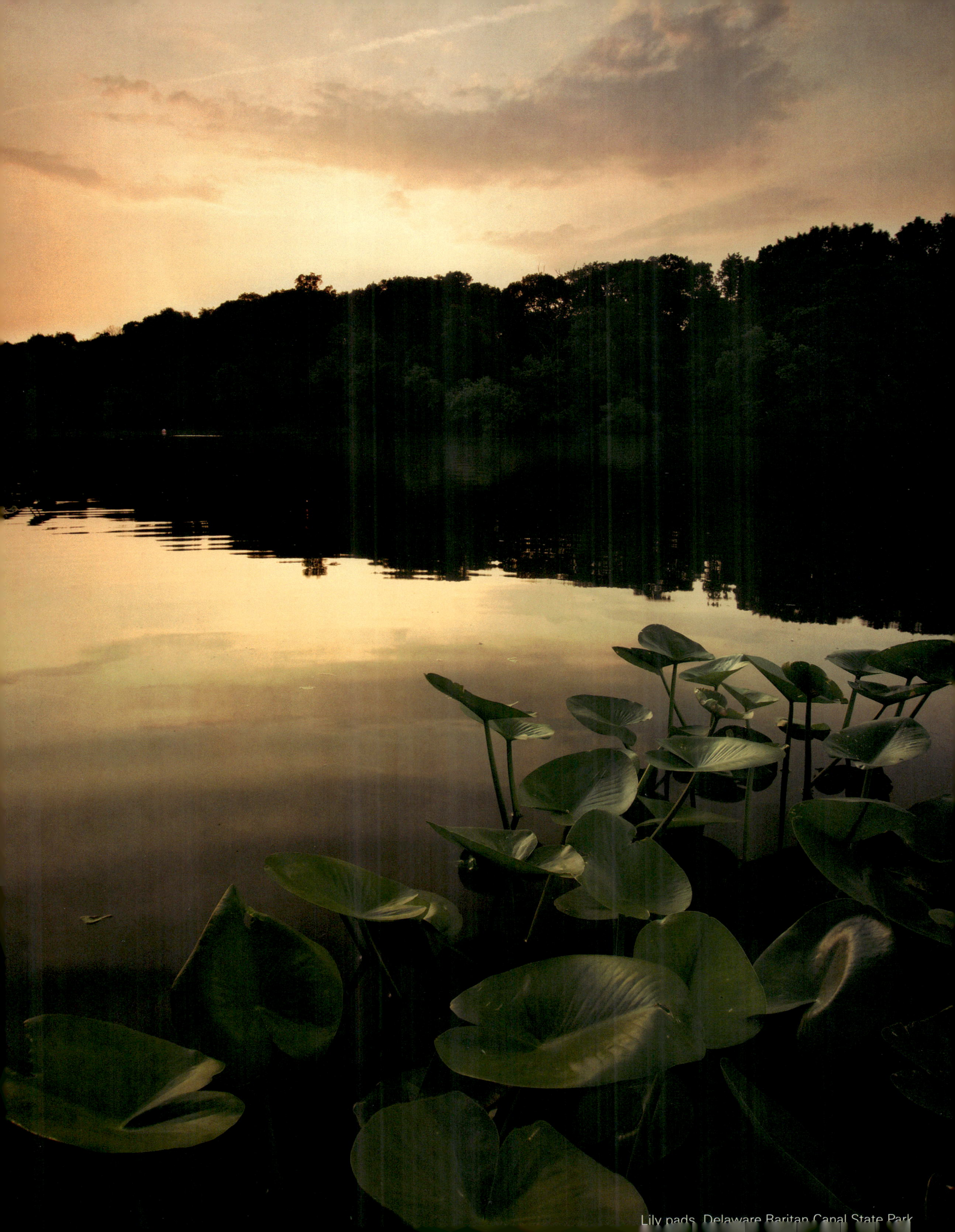

Lily pads, Delaware Raritan Canal State Park

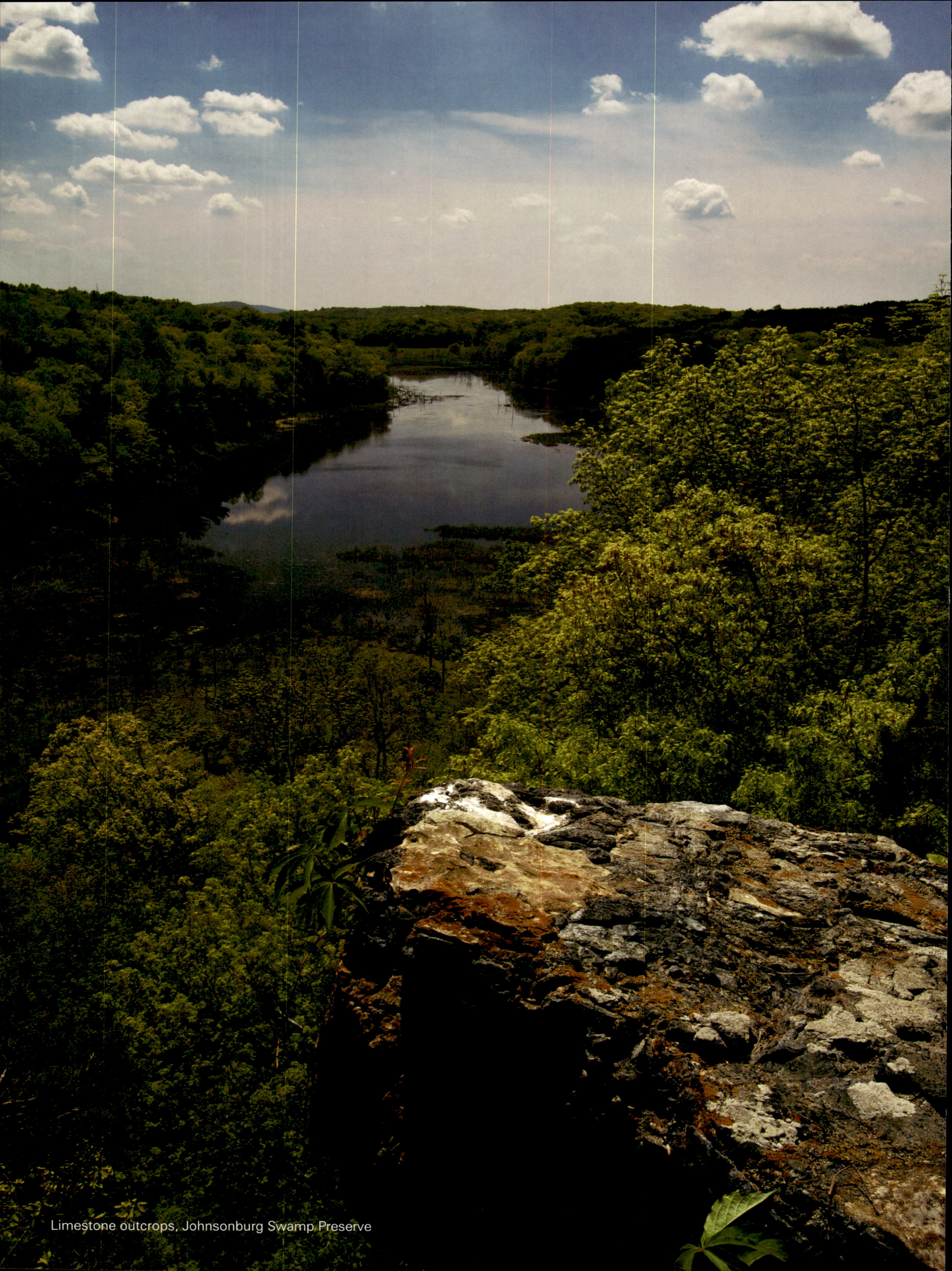
Limestone outcrops, Johnsonburg Swamp Preserve

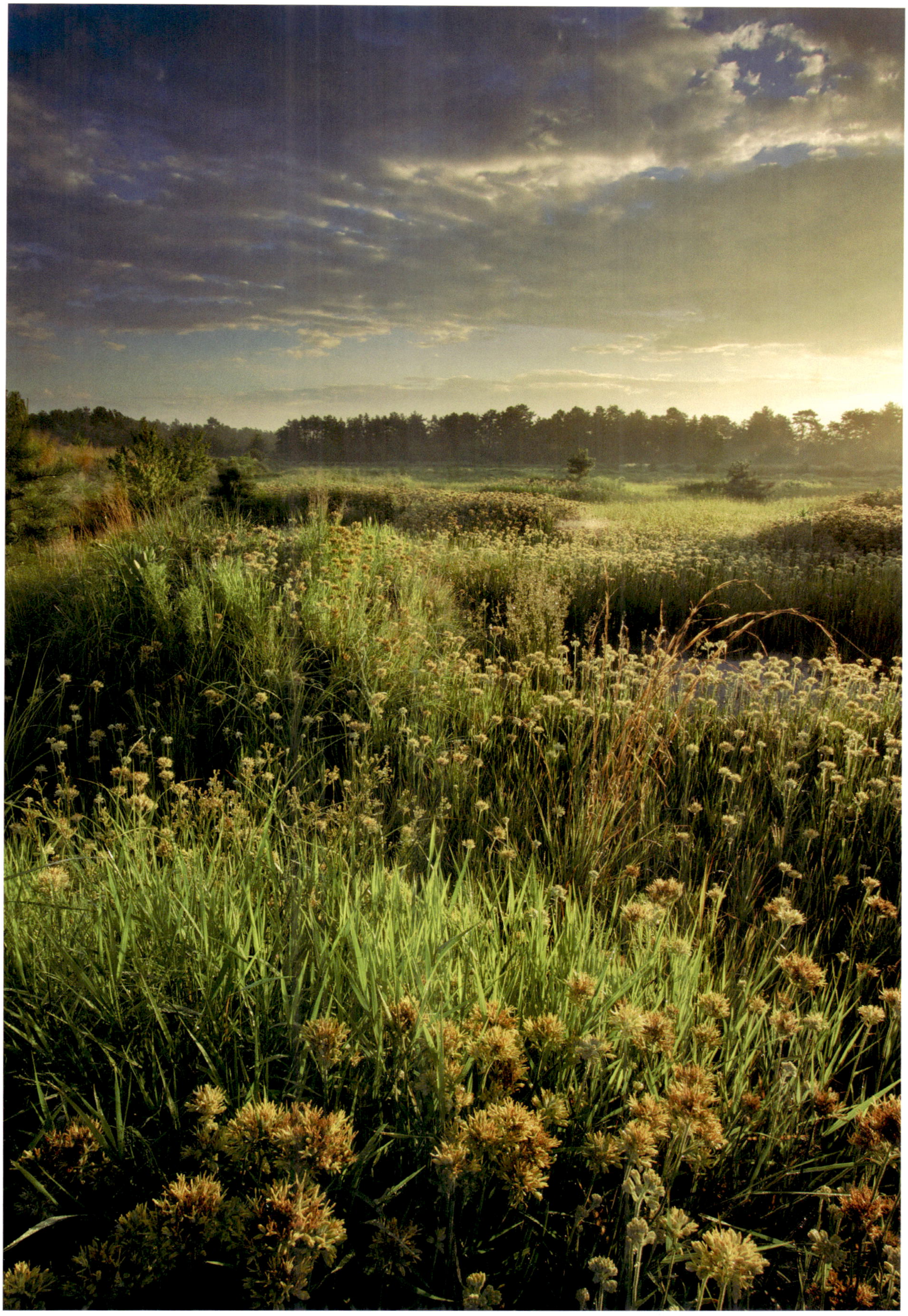

Summer flowers, Franklin Parker Preserve

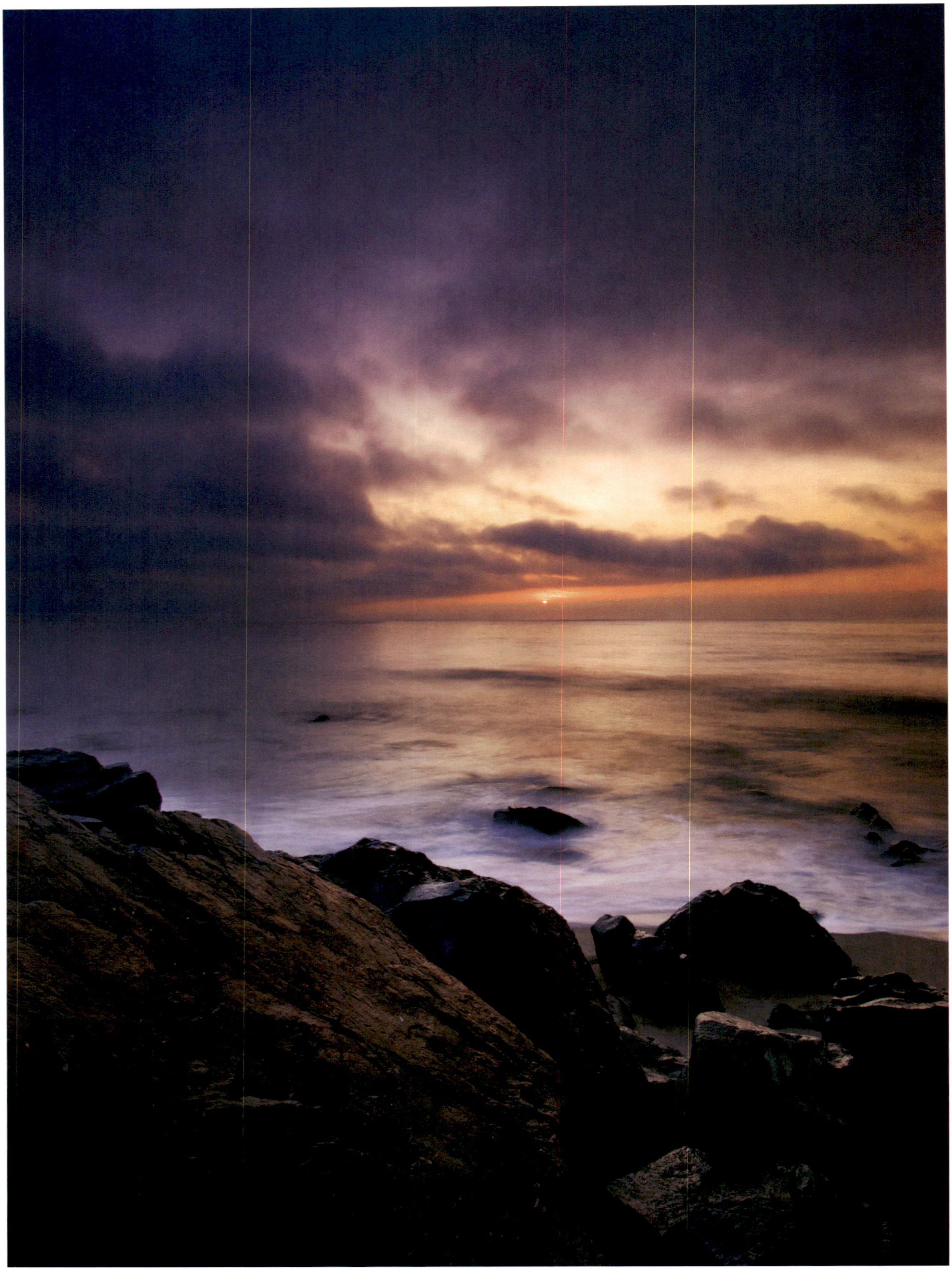

Atlantic Ocean, Sandy Hook/Gateway National Recreation Area

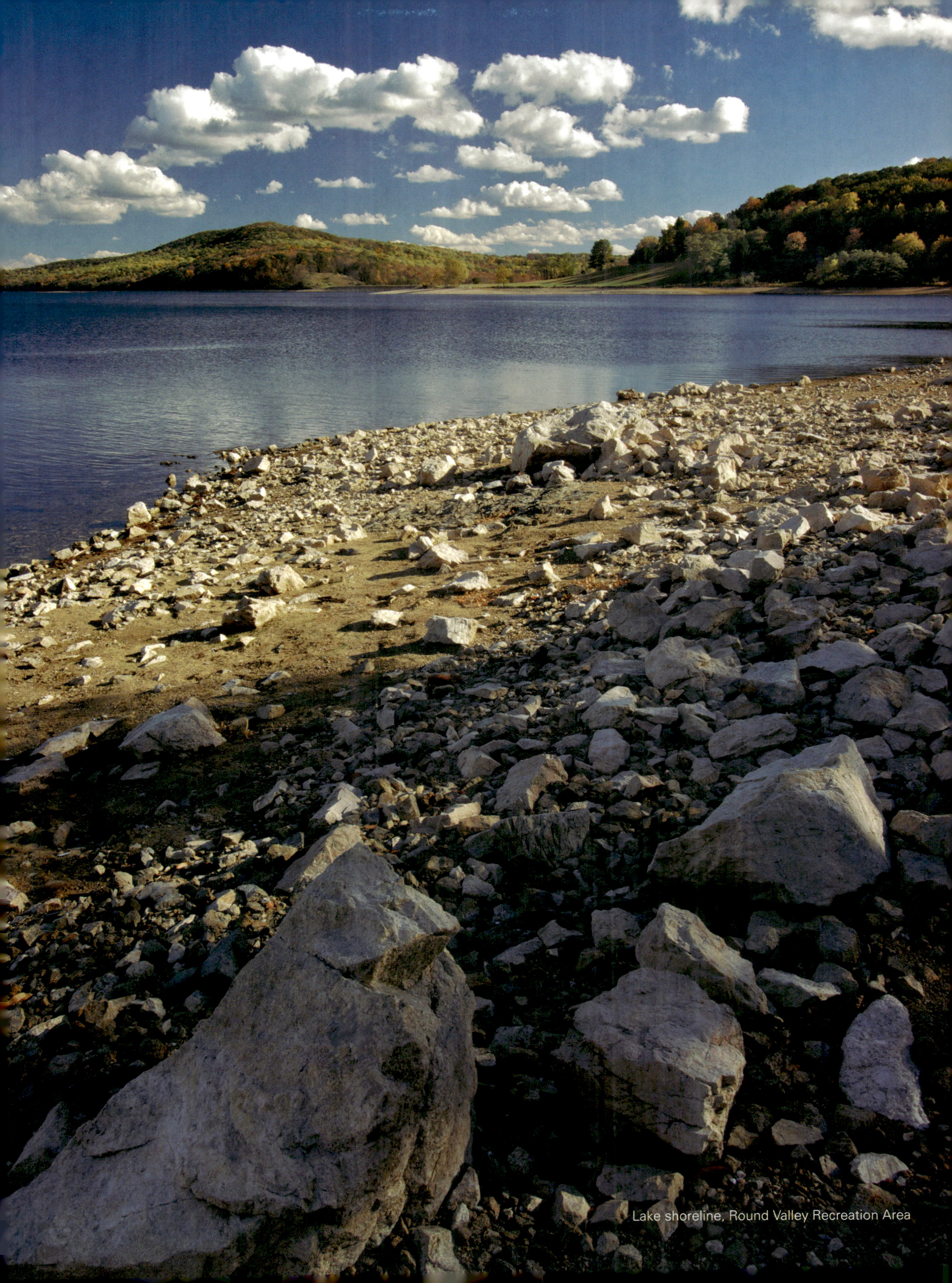

Lake shoreline, Round Valley Recreation Area

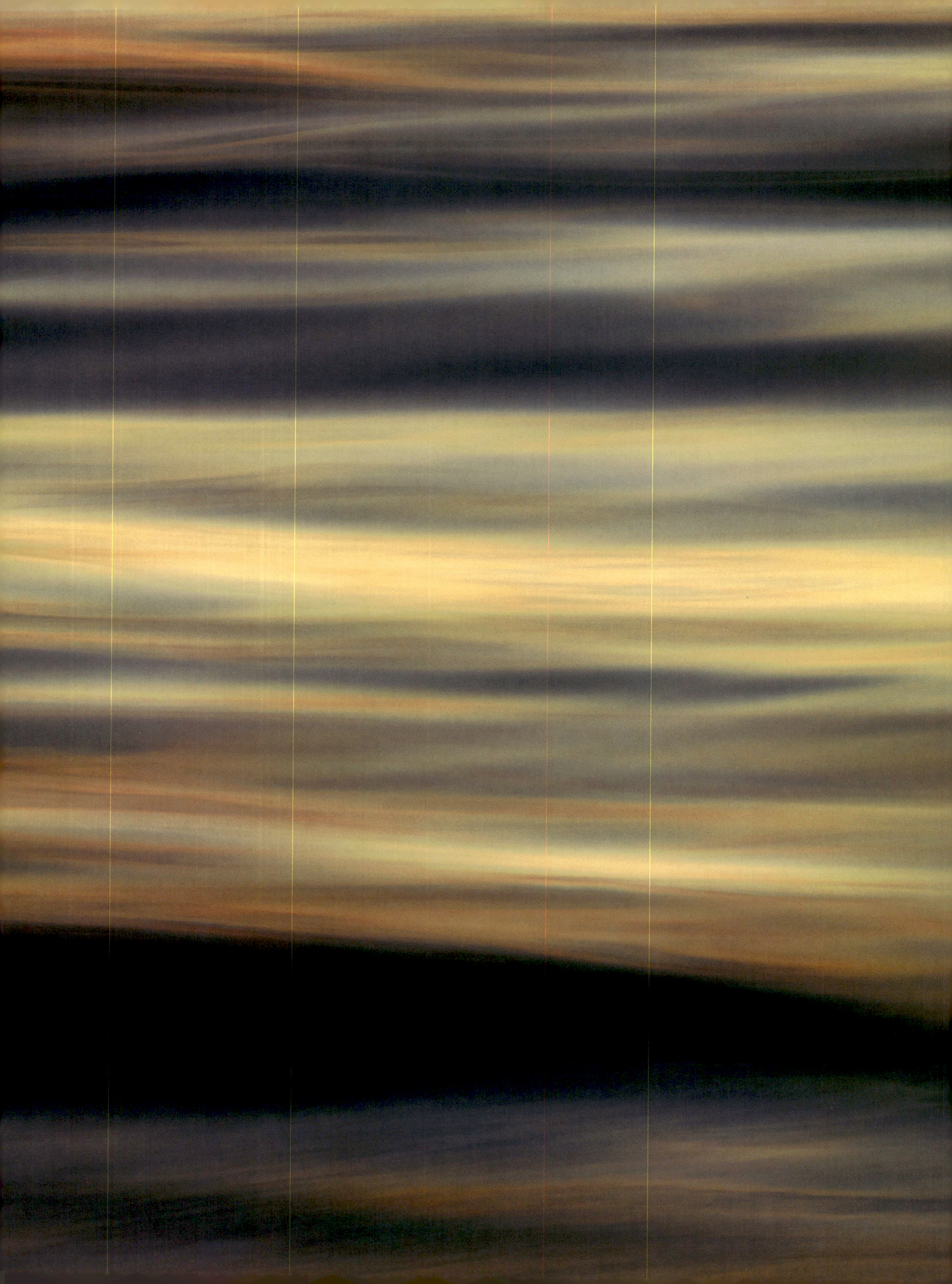

Bayside abstract, Sandy Hook/Gateway National Recreation Area

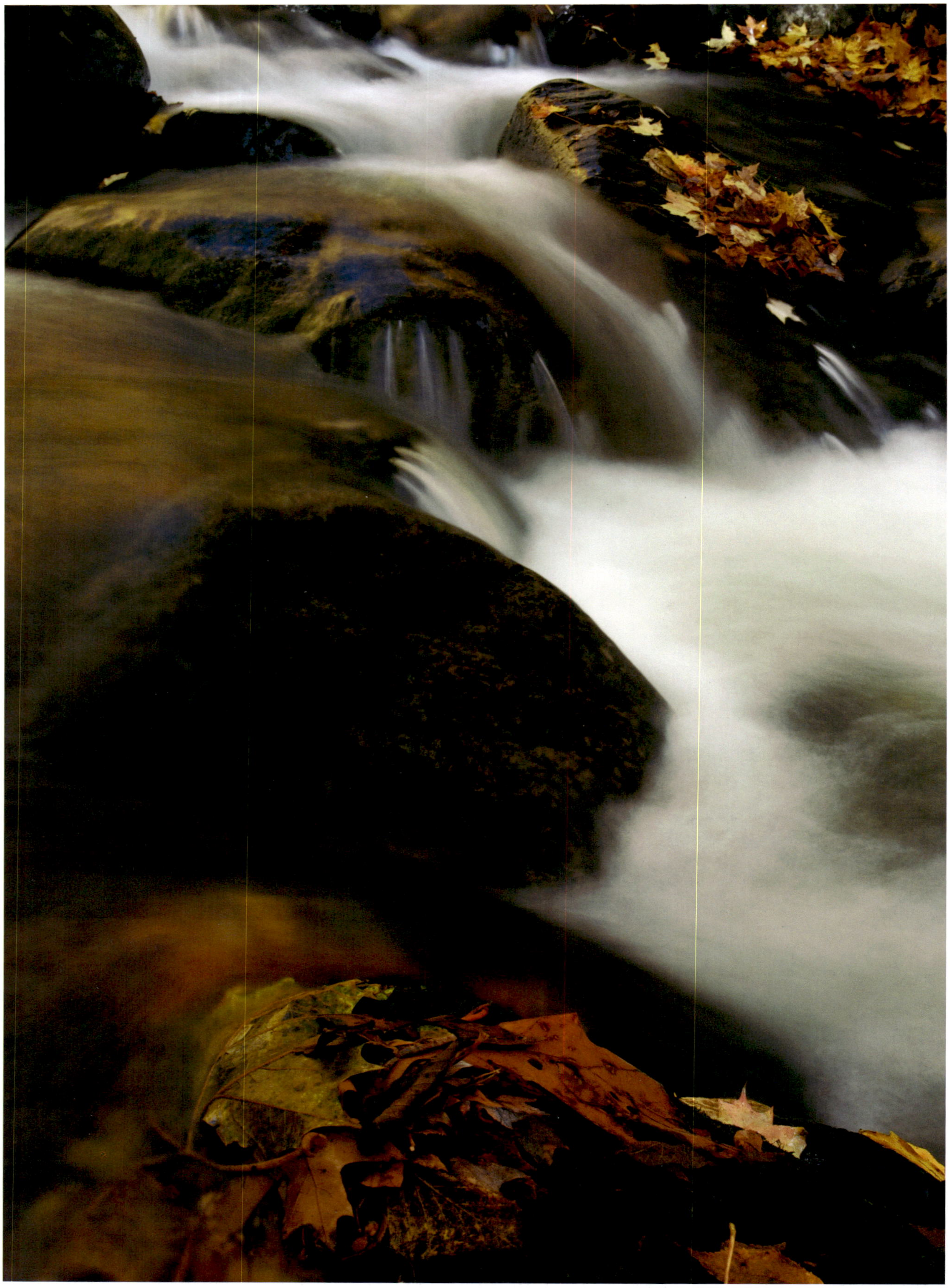

Dunnfield Creek, Worthington State Forest

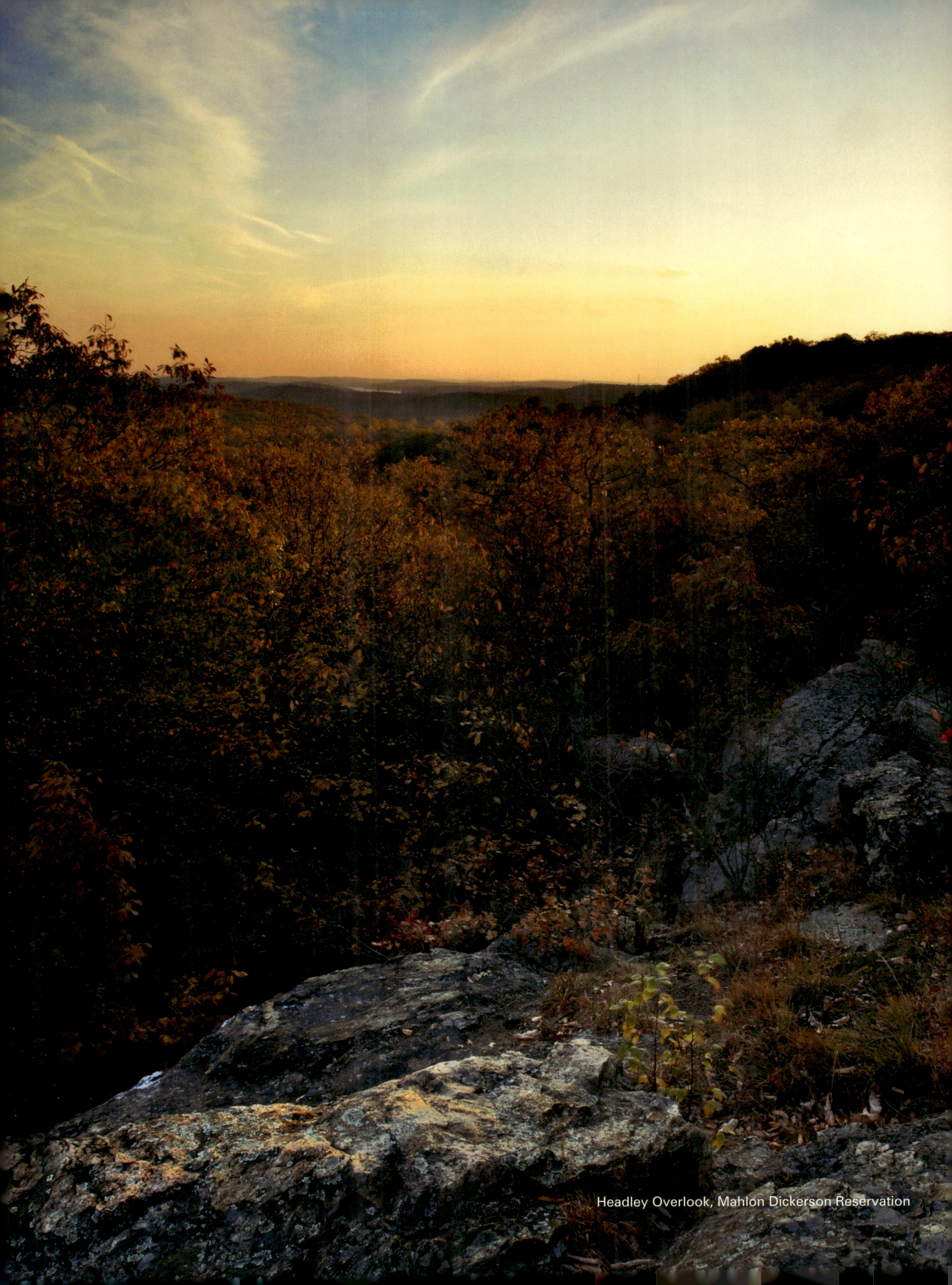

Headley Overlook, Mahlon Dickerson Reservation

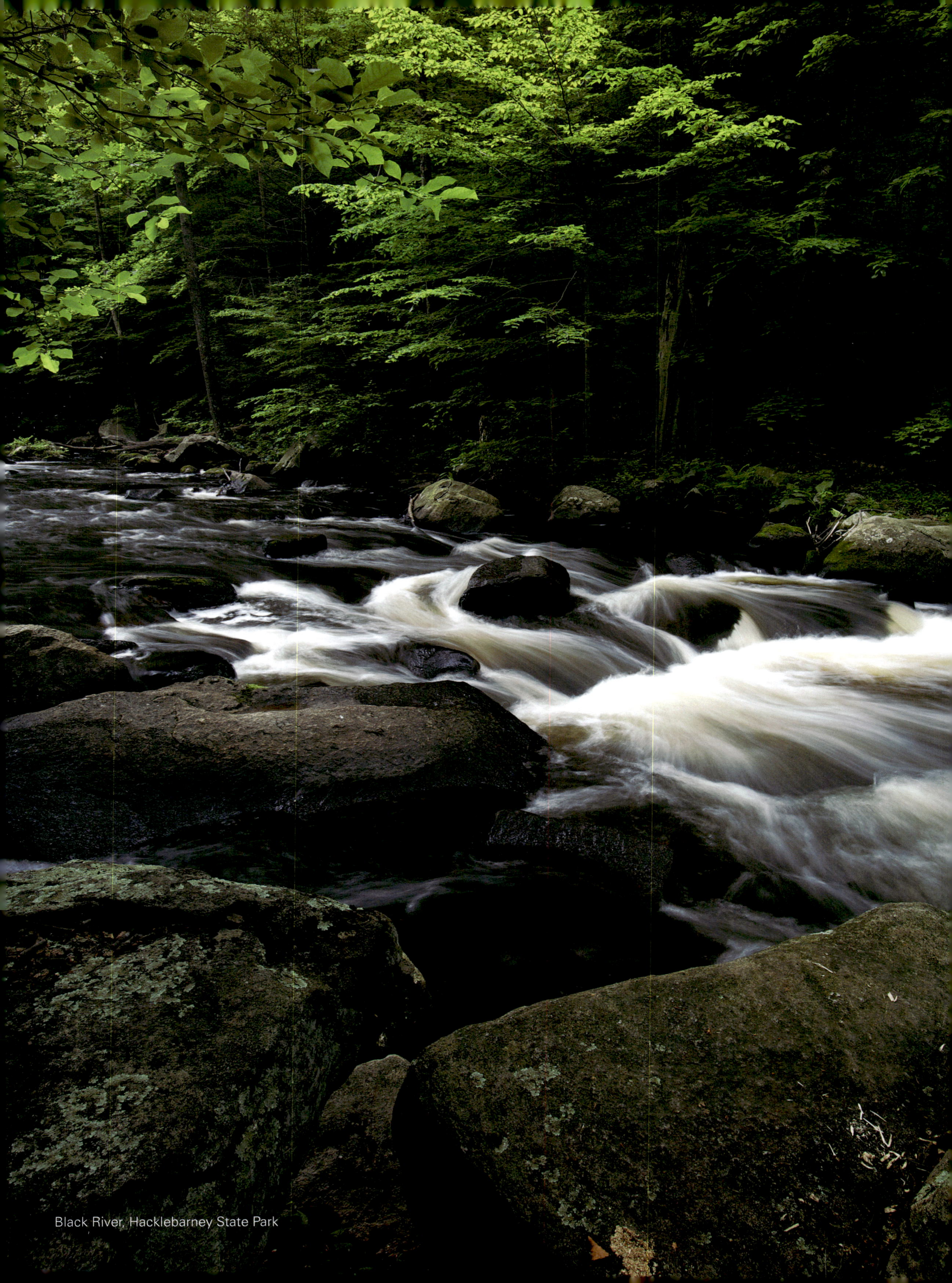

Black River, Hacklebarney State Park

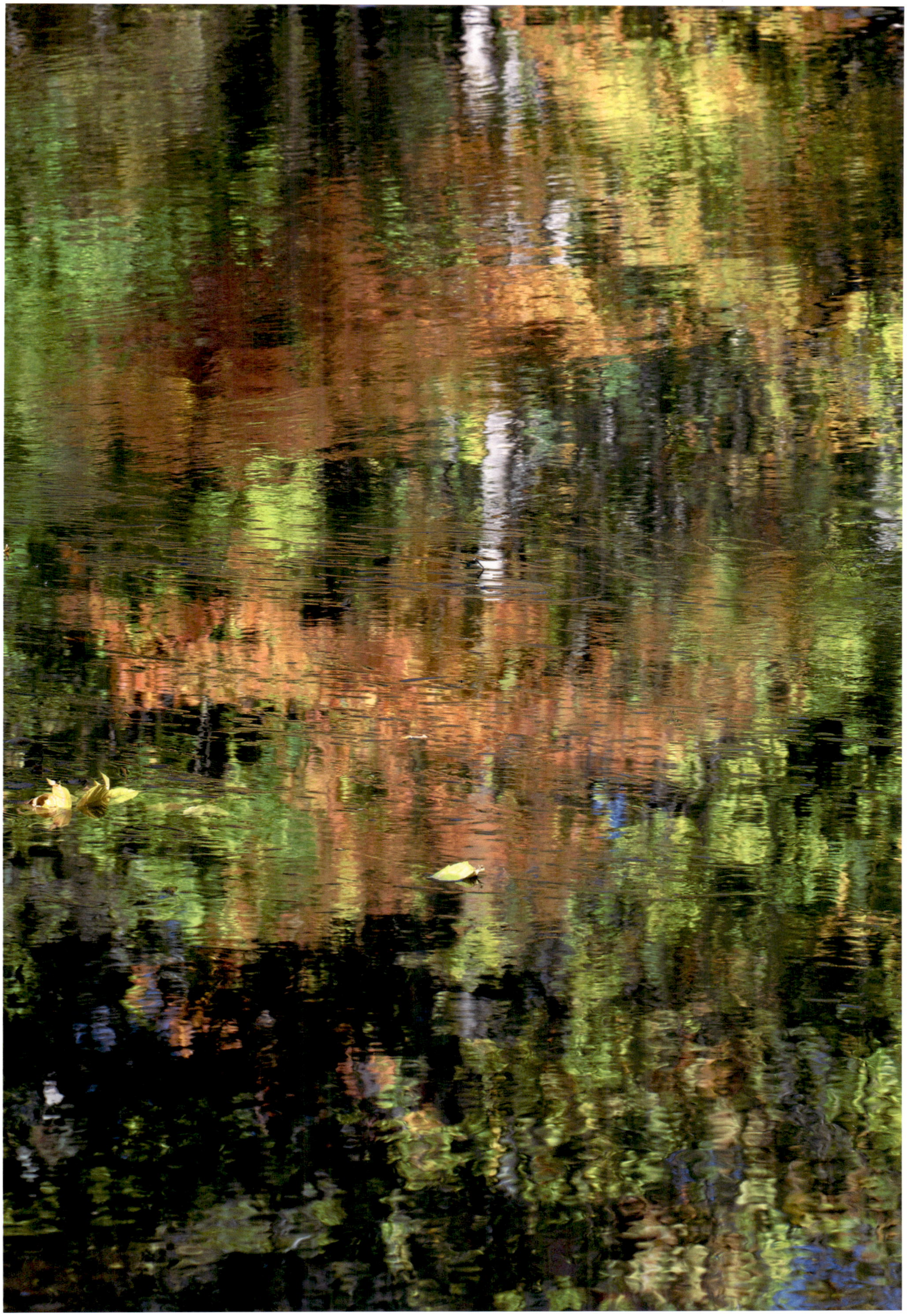

Canal reflections, Delaware Raritan Canal State Park

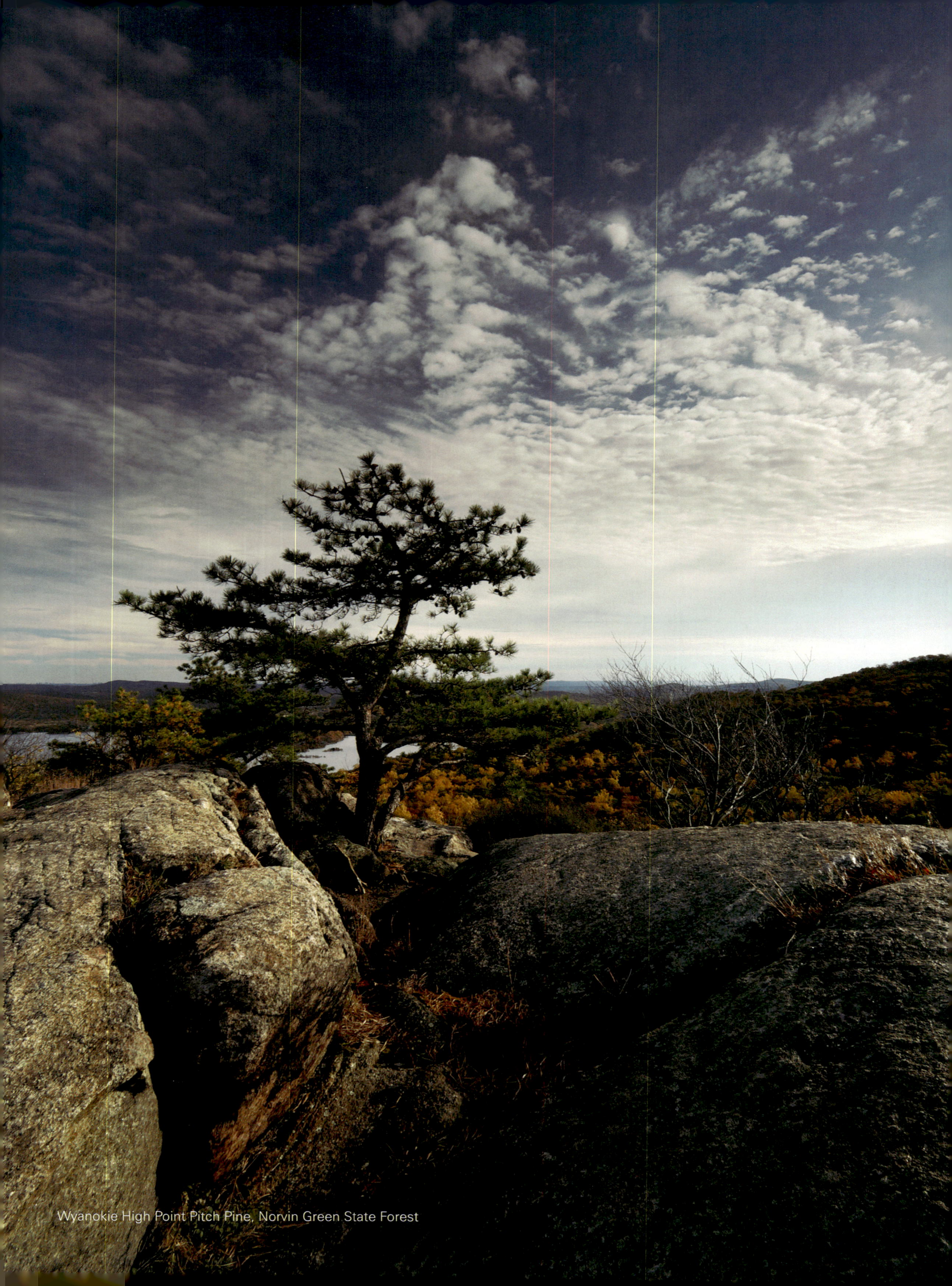

Wyanokie High Point Pitch Pine, Norvin Green State Forest

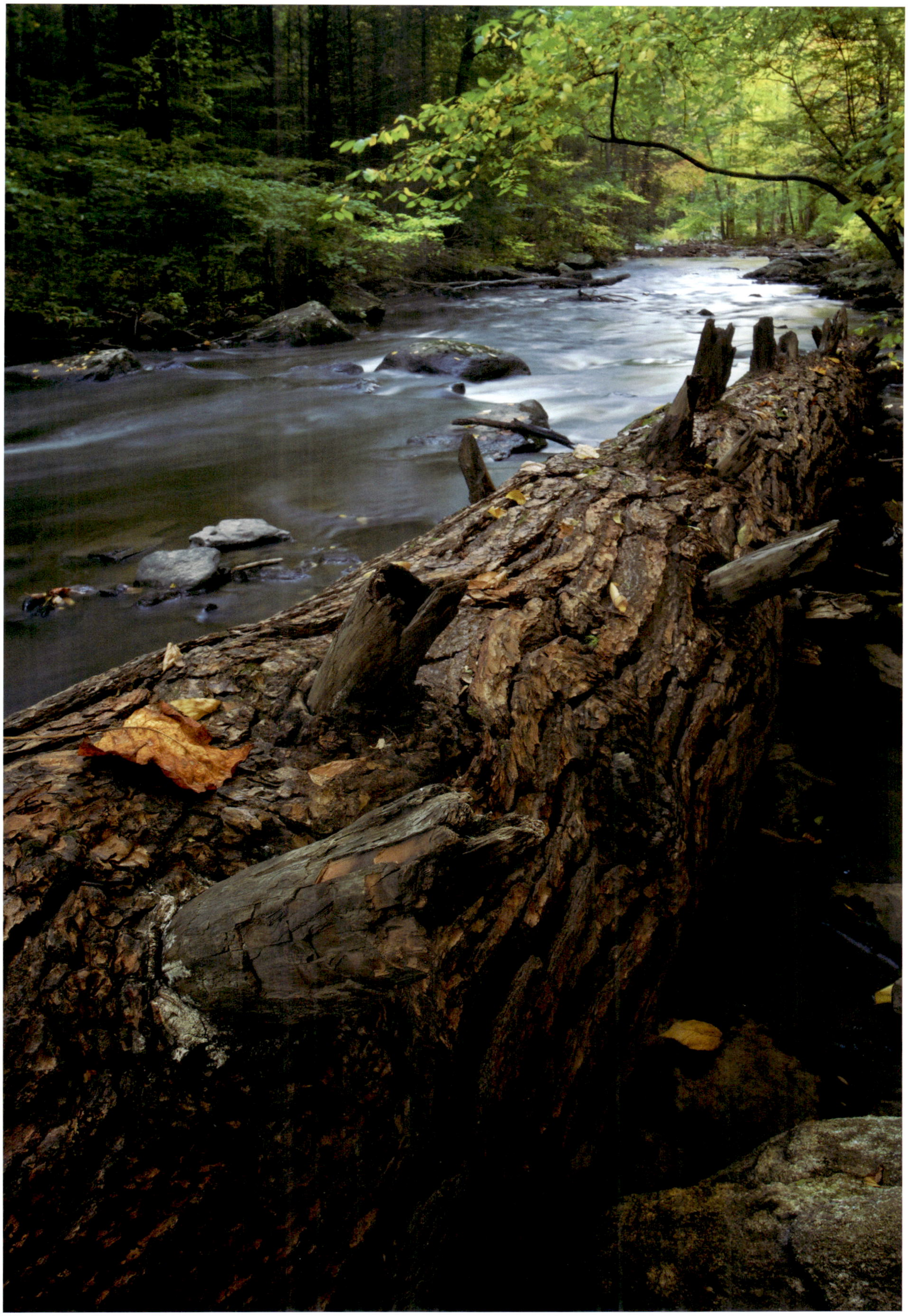

Fallen tree, Hacklebarney State Park

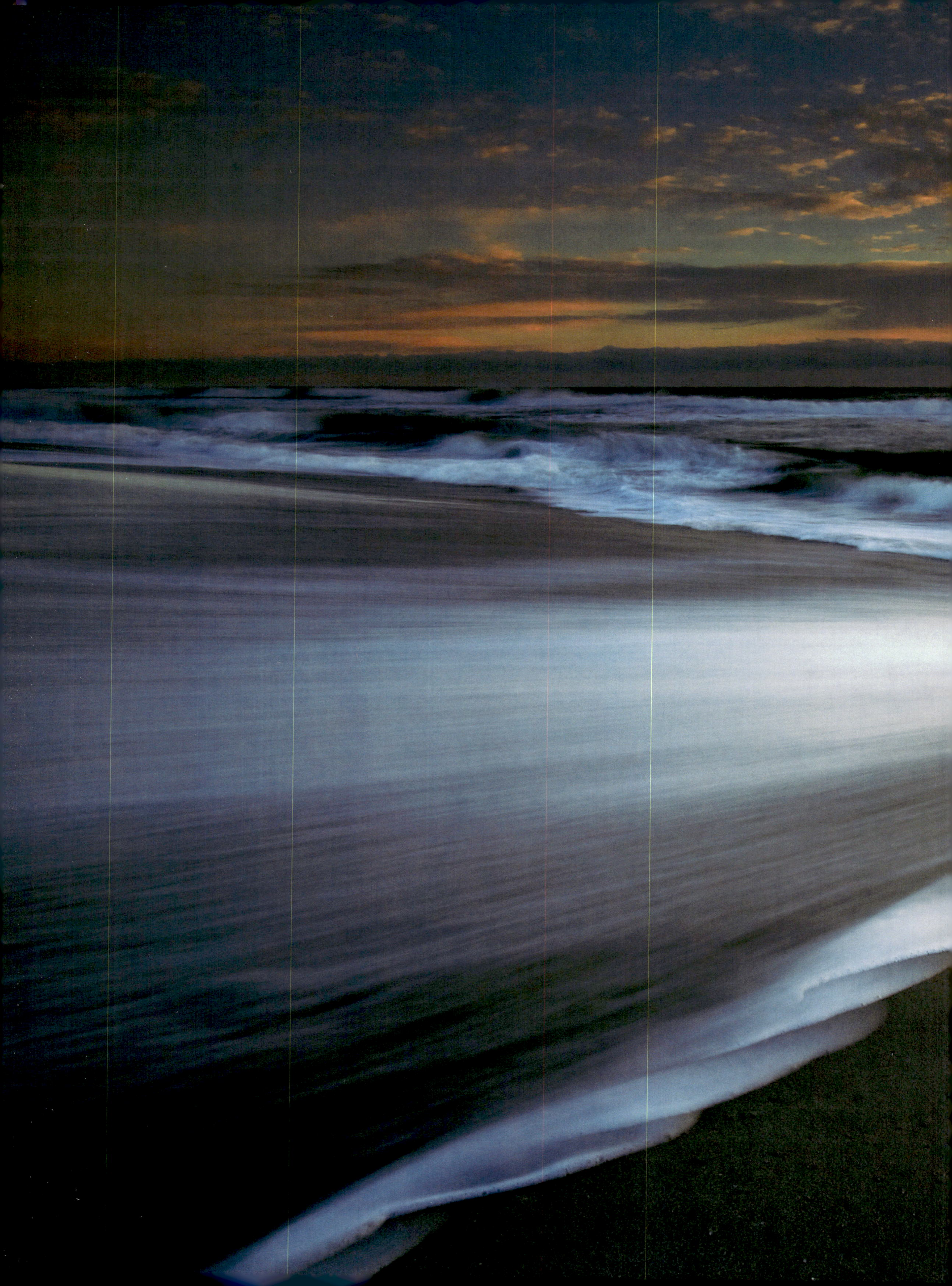

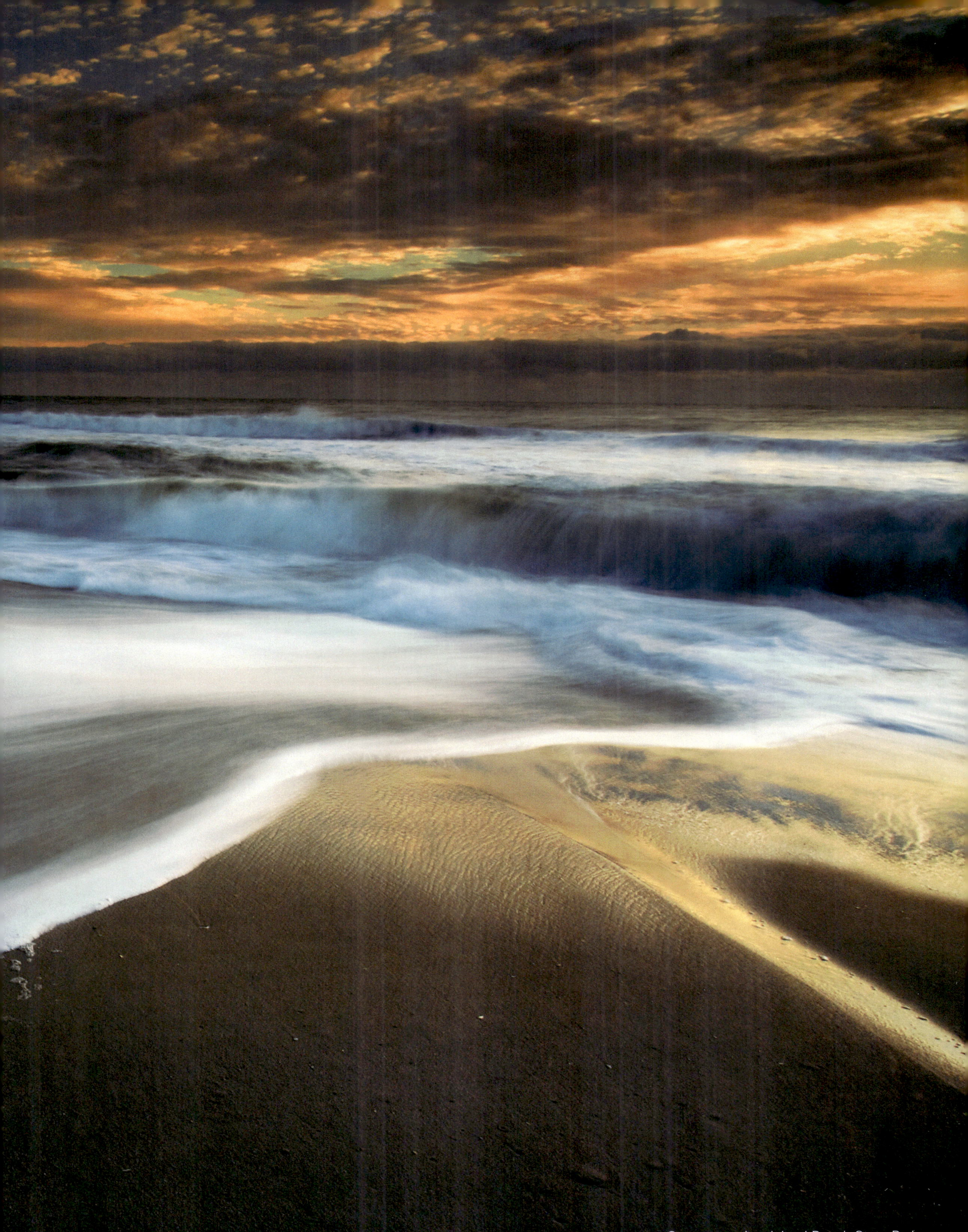

Orange sunrise, Island Beach State Park

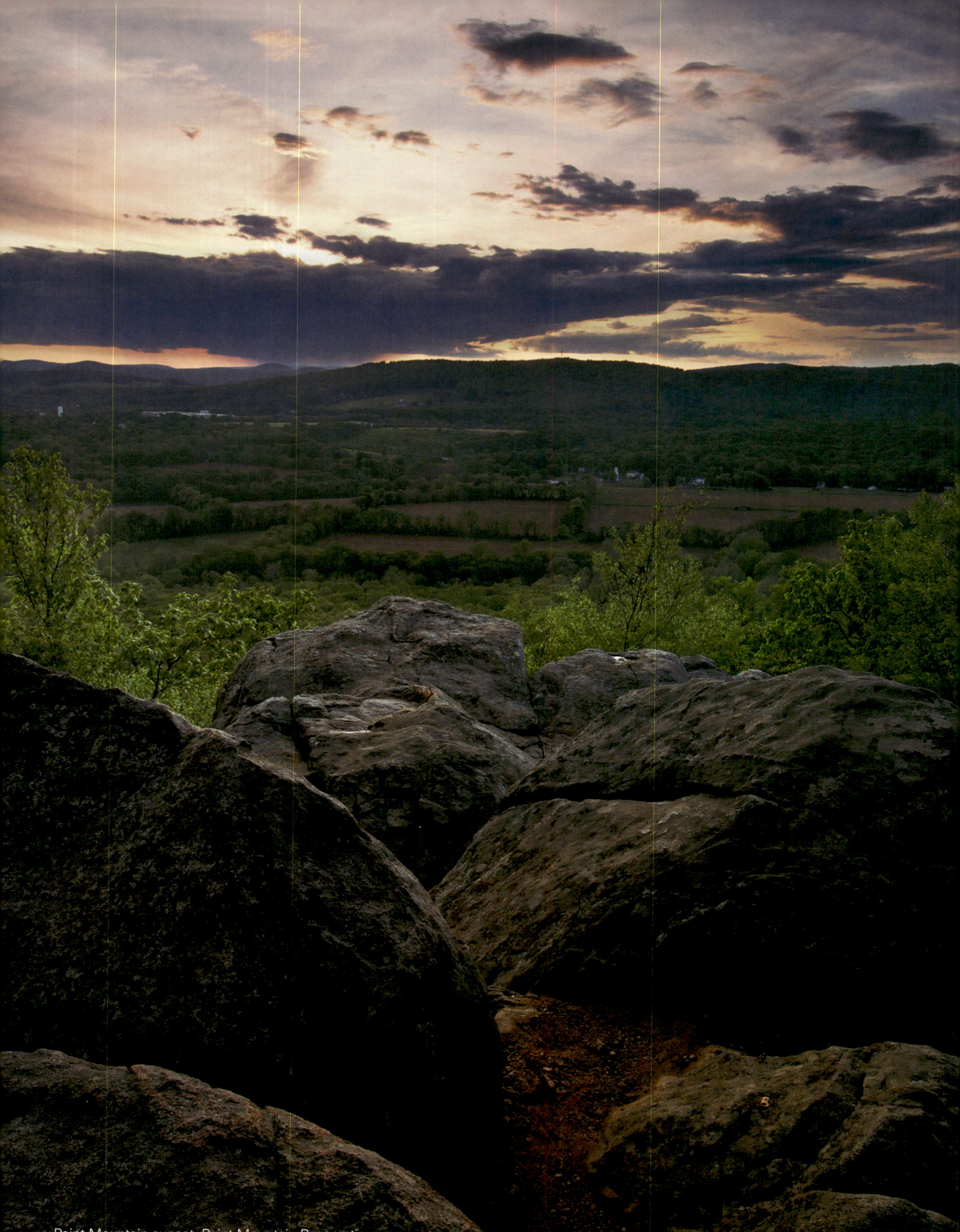

Point Mountain sunset, Point Mountain Reservation

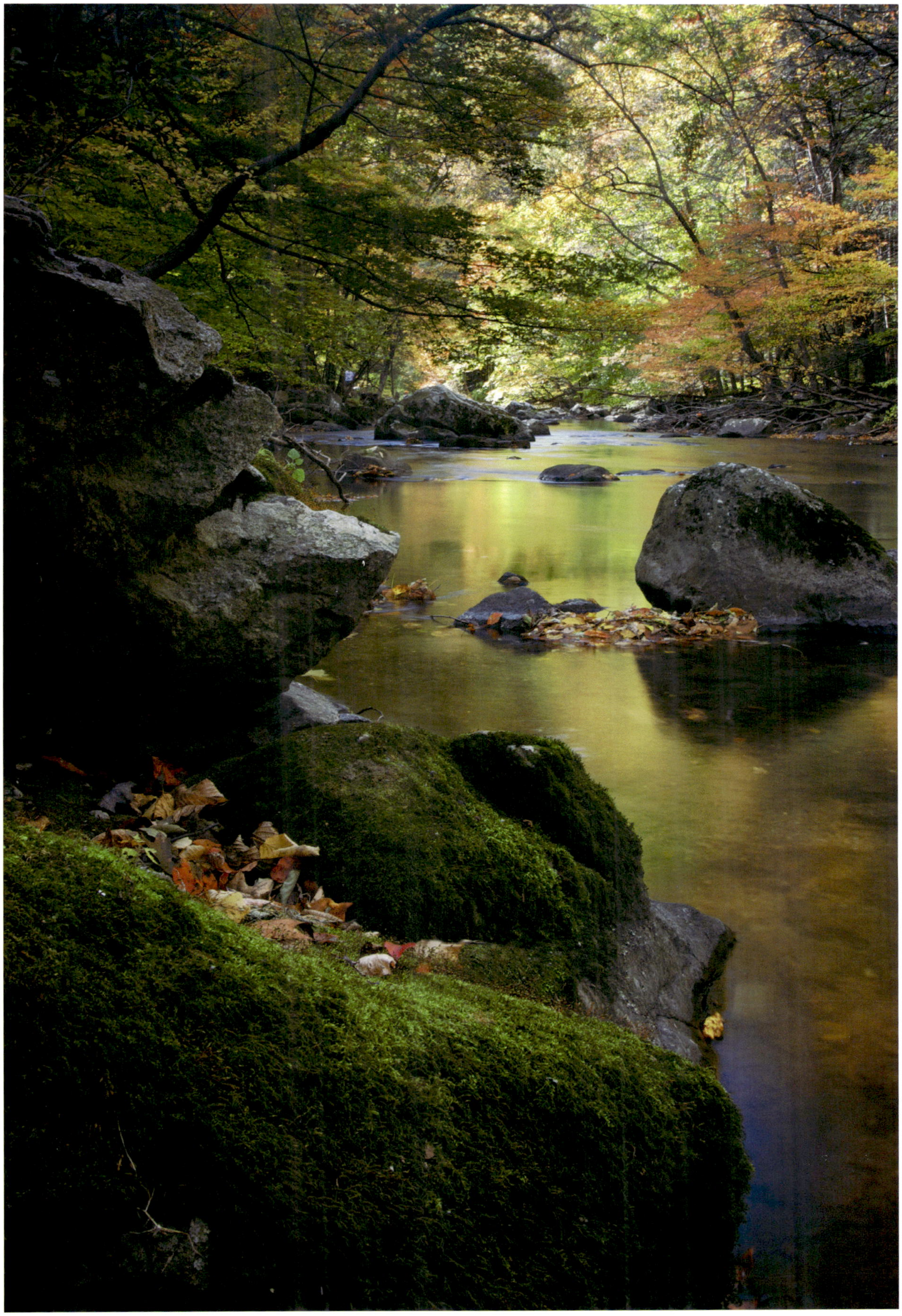

Raritan River, Ken Lockwood Gorge Wildlife Management Area

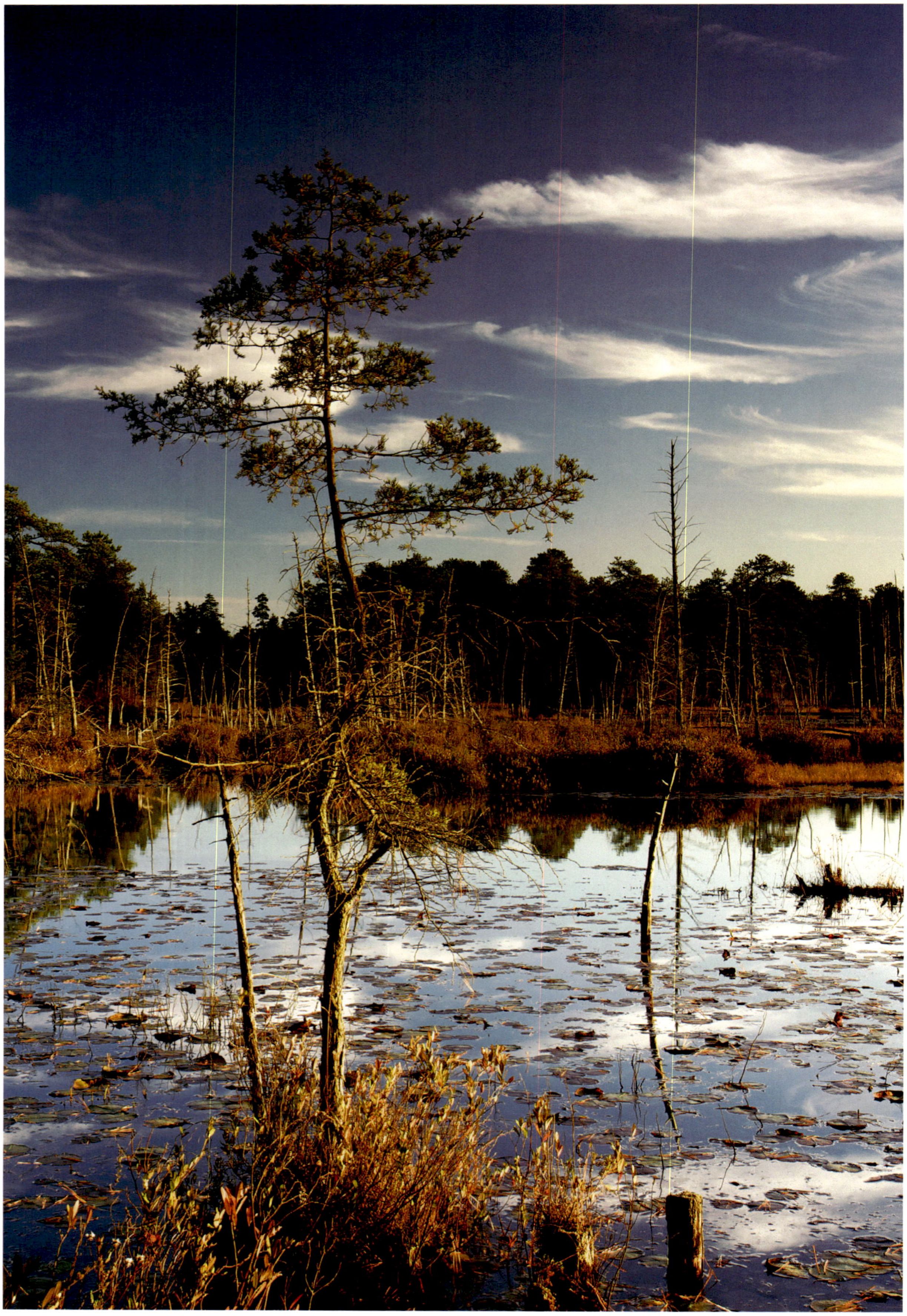

Goshen Pond, Wharton State Forest

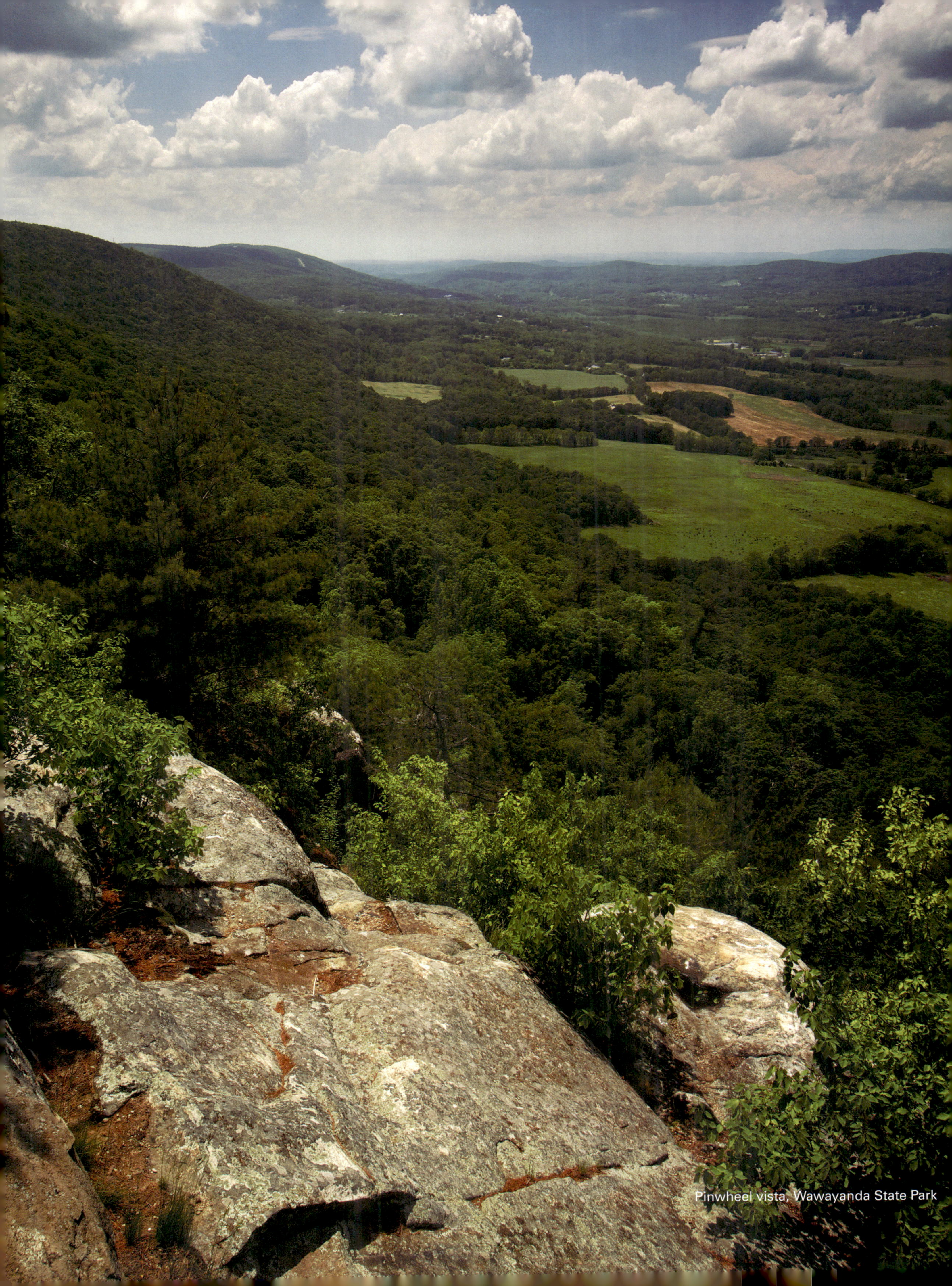

Pinwheel vista, Wawayanda State Park

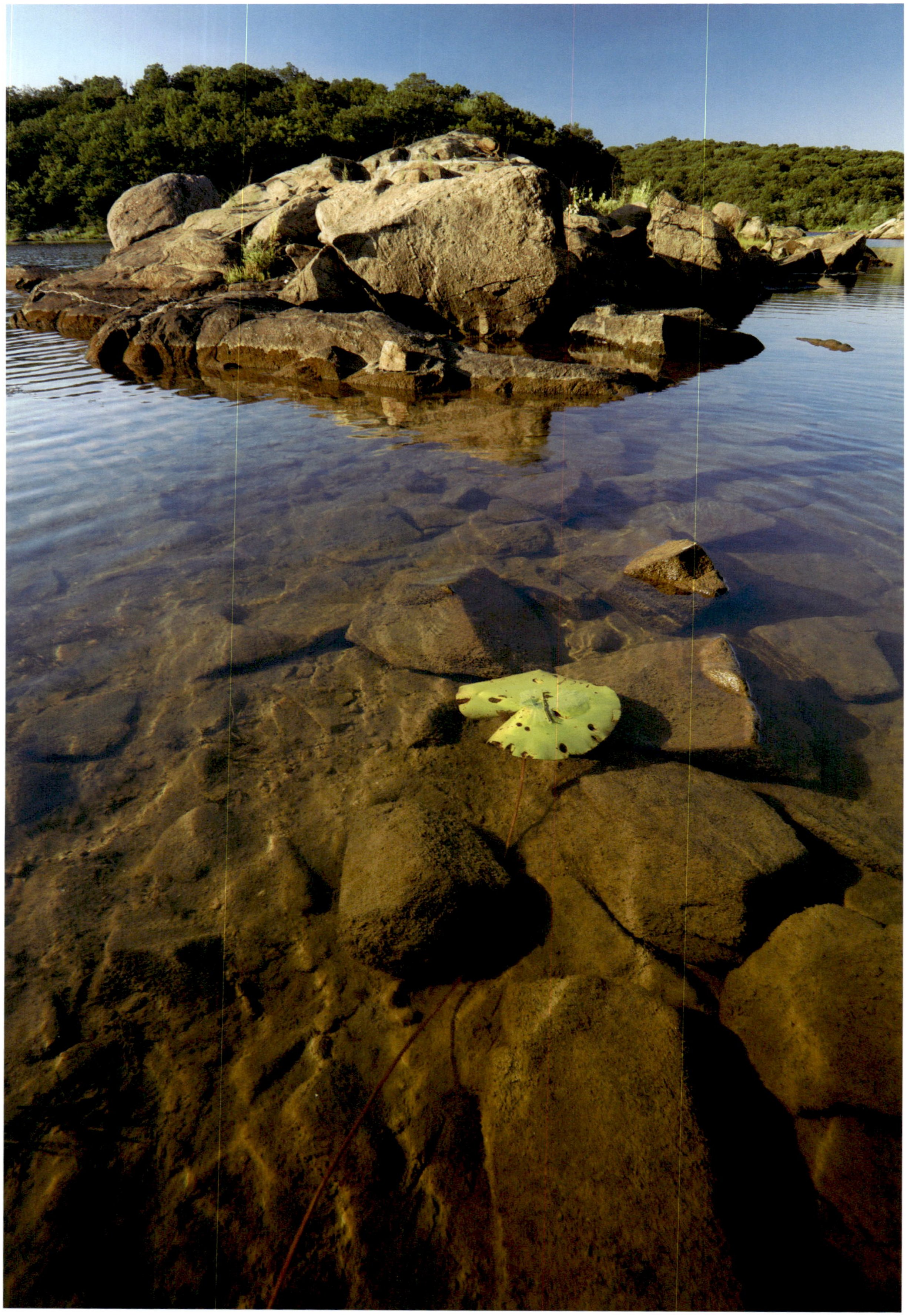

Rock islands, Apshawa Preserve

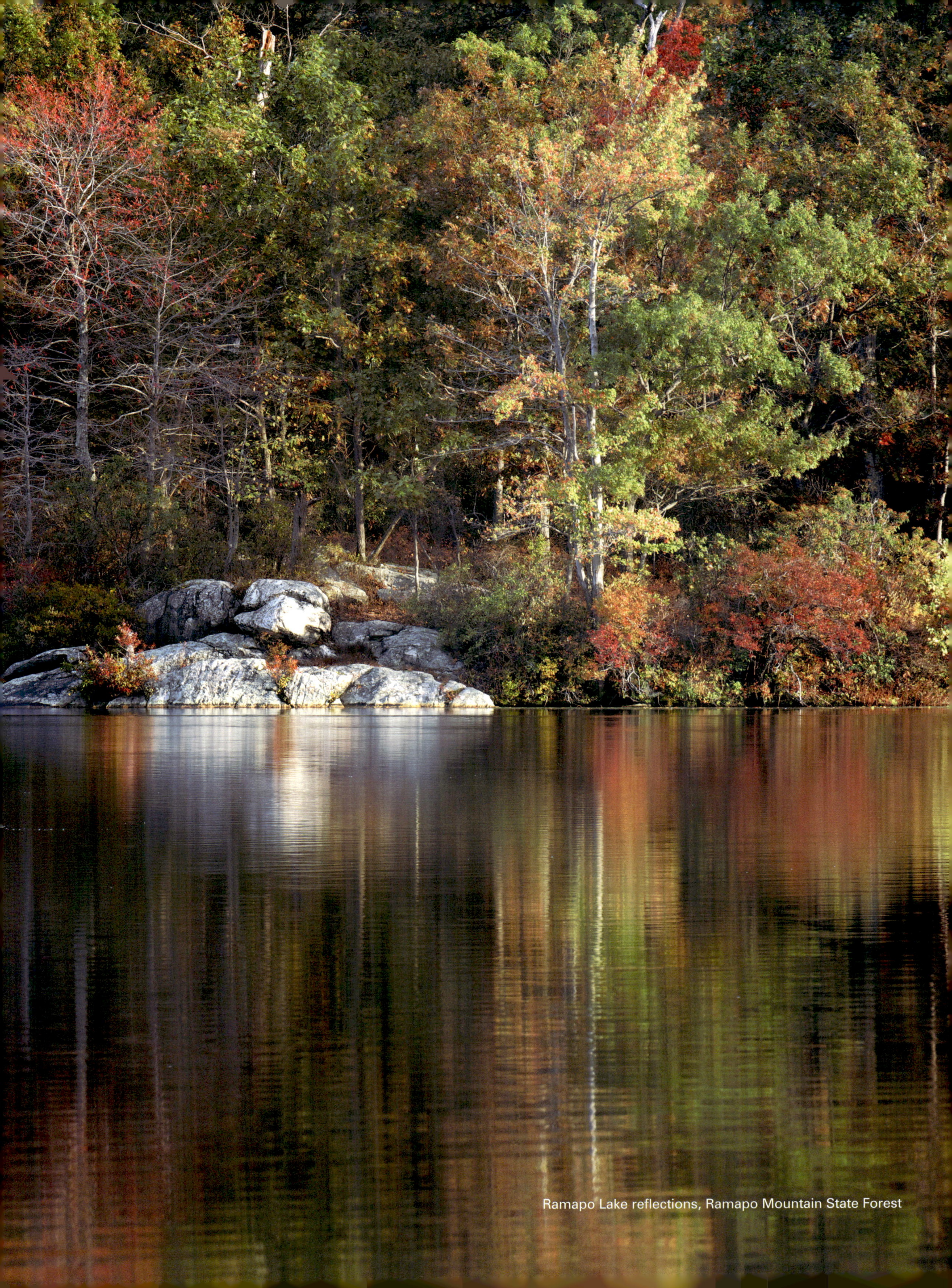

Ramapo Lake reflections, Ramapo Mountain State Forest

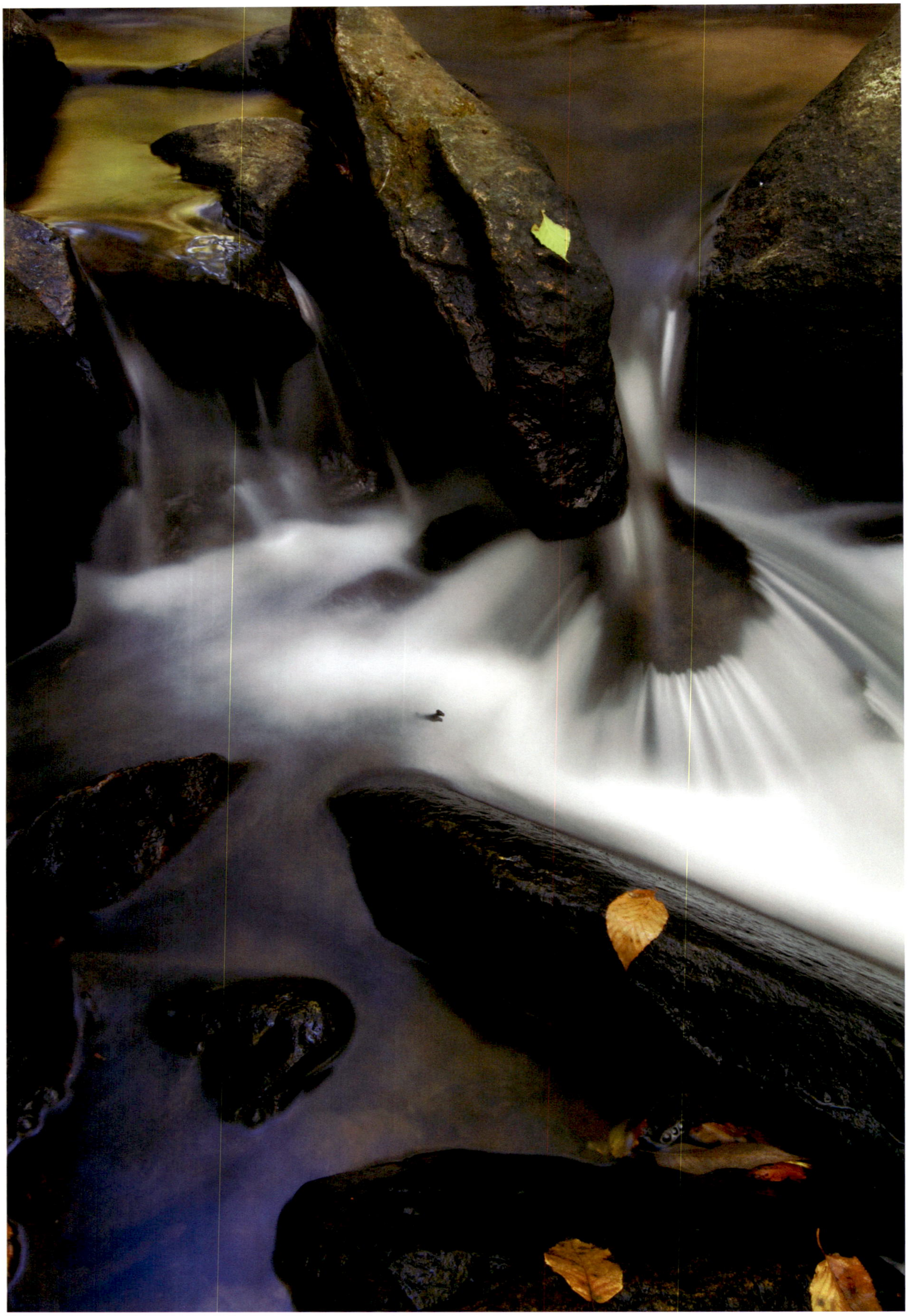

Delicate cascade, Hacklebarney State Park

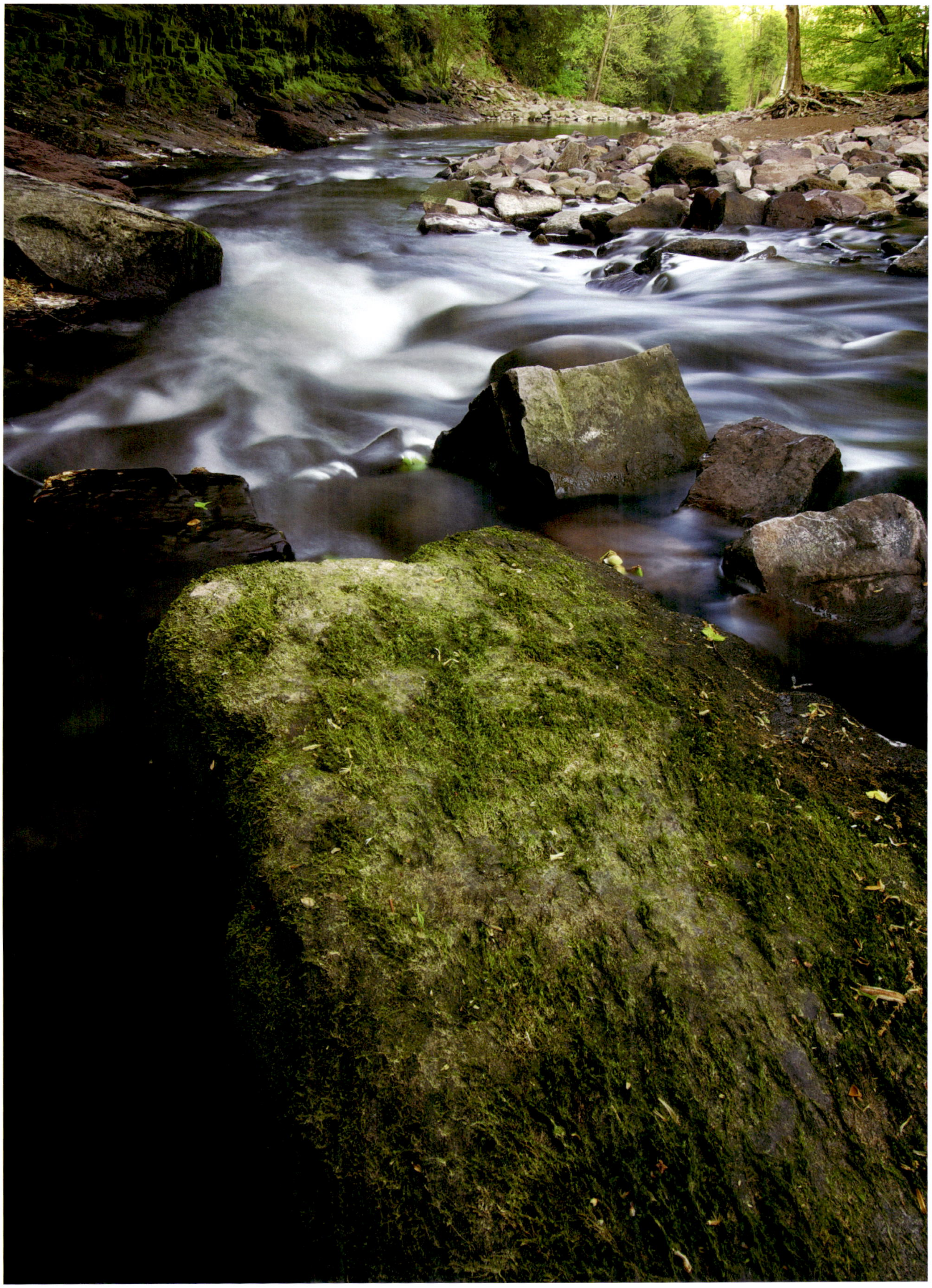

Wickecheoke Creek, Wickecheoke Creek Preserve

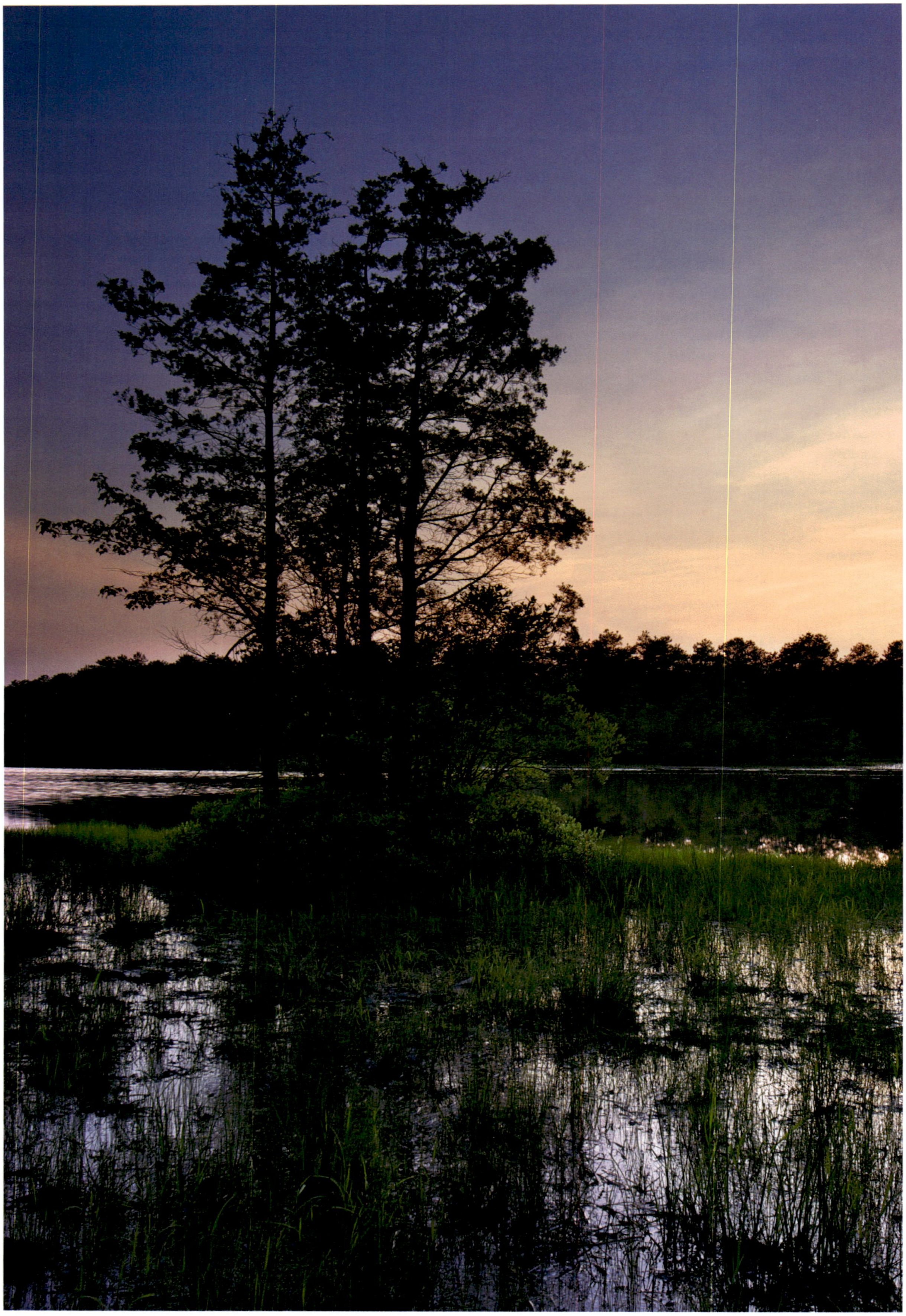

Sunset at Oswego Lake, Penn State Forest

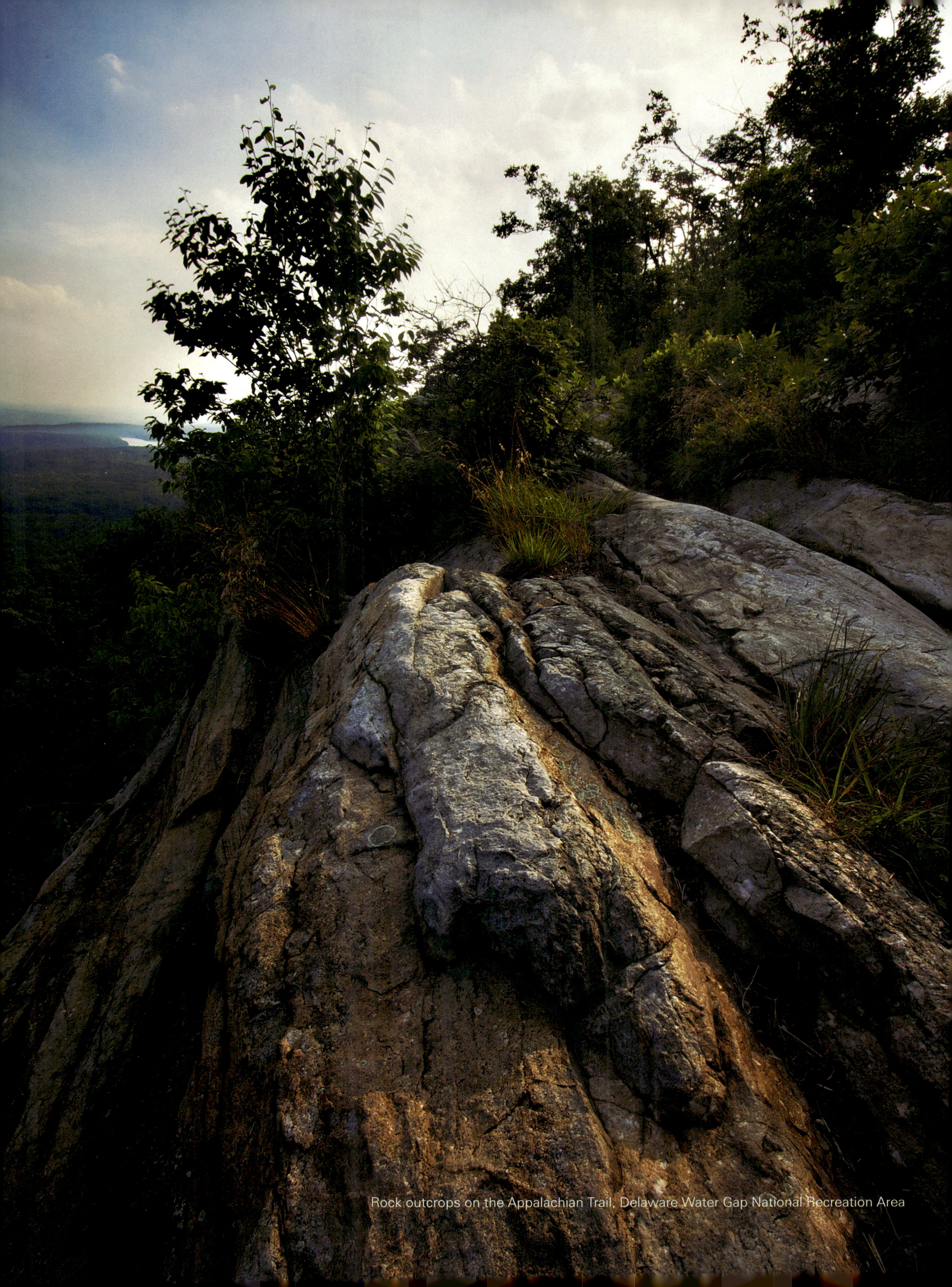

Rock outcrops on the Appalachian Trail, Delaware Water Gap National Recreation Area

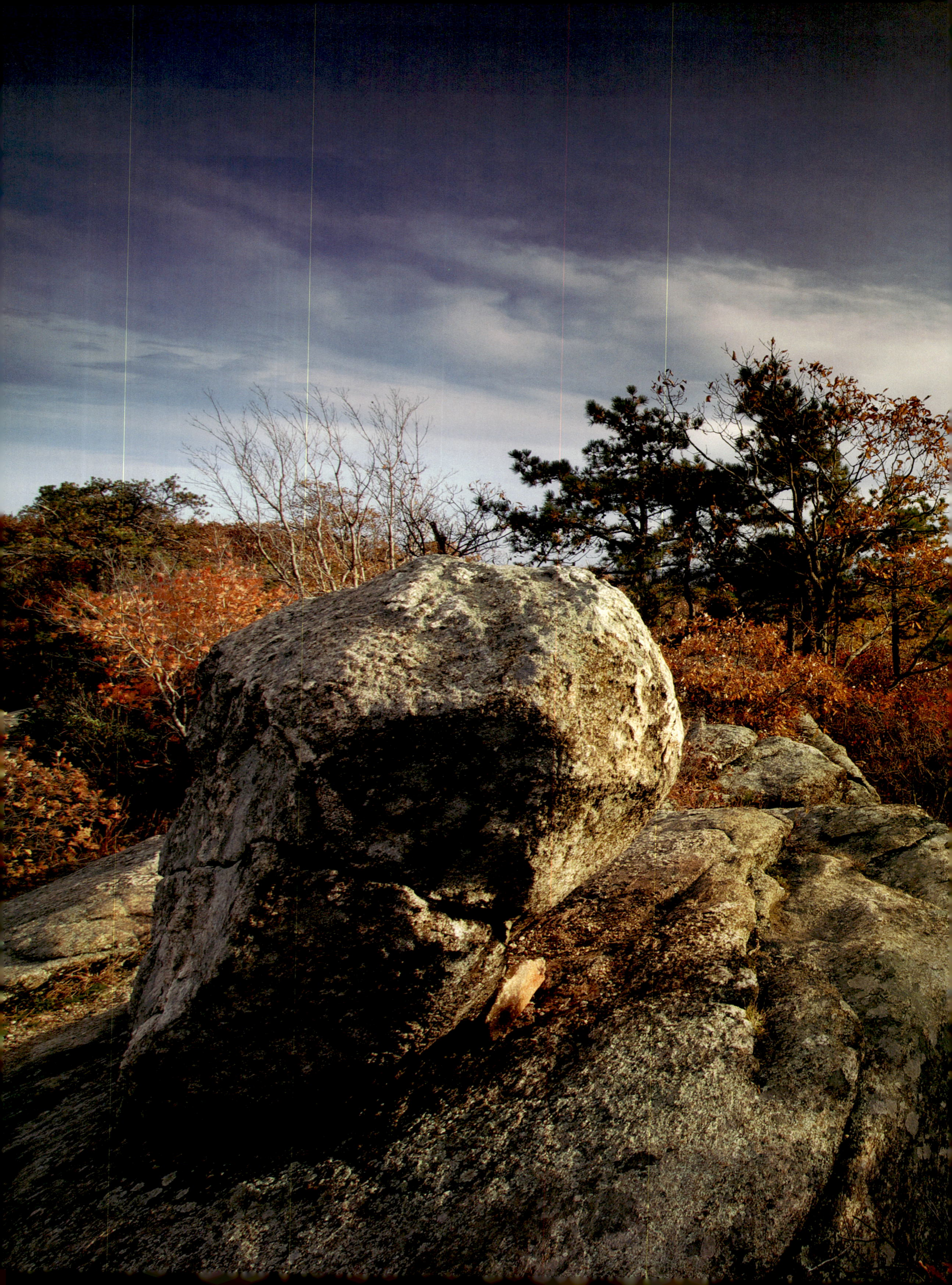

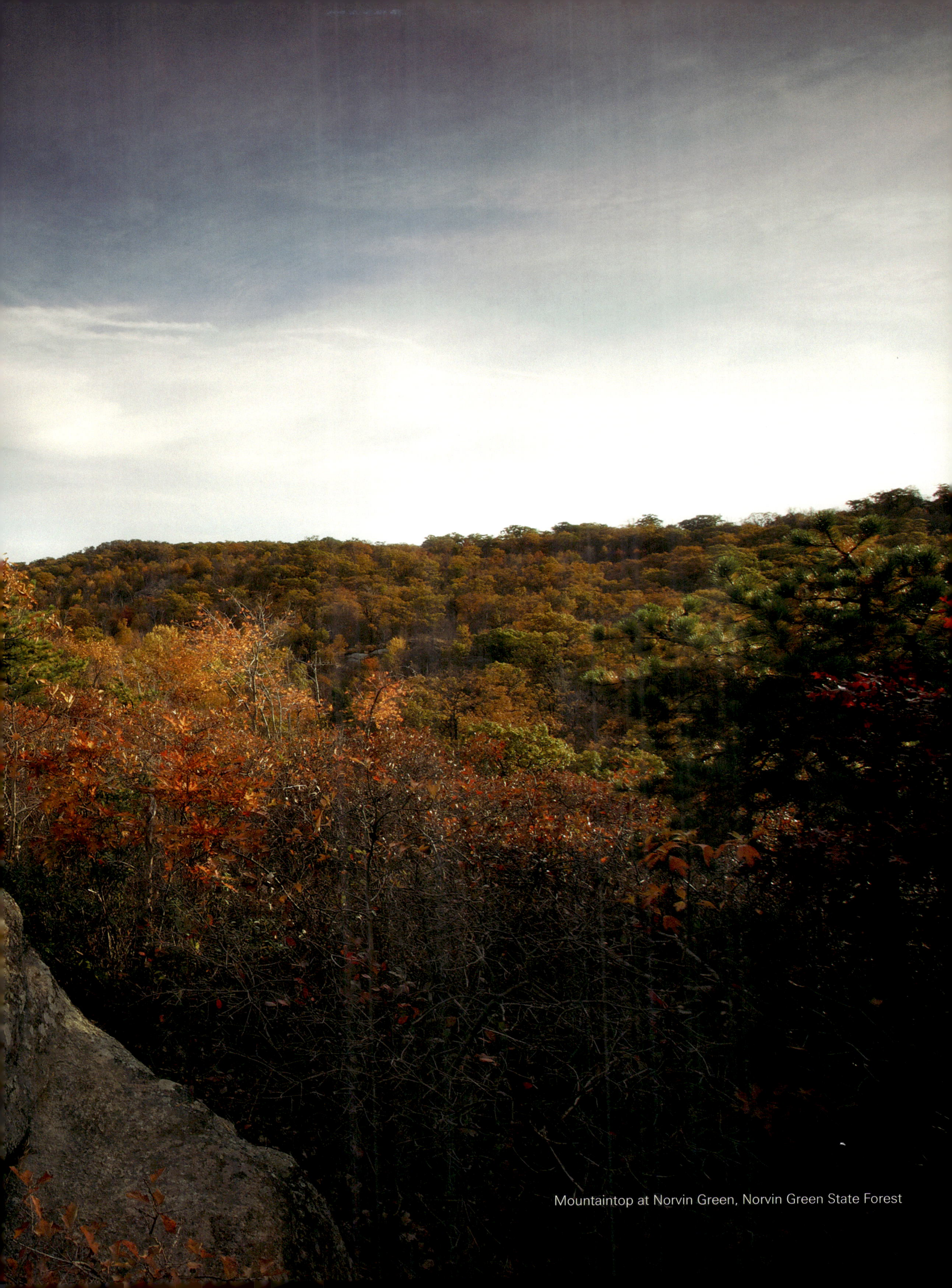

Mountaintop at Norvin Green, Norvin Green State Forest

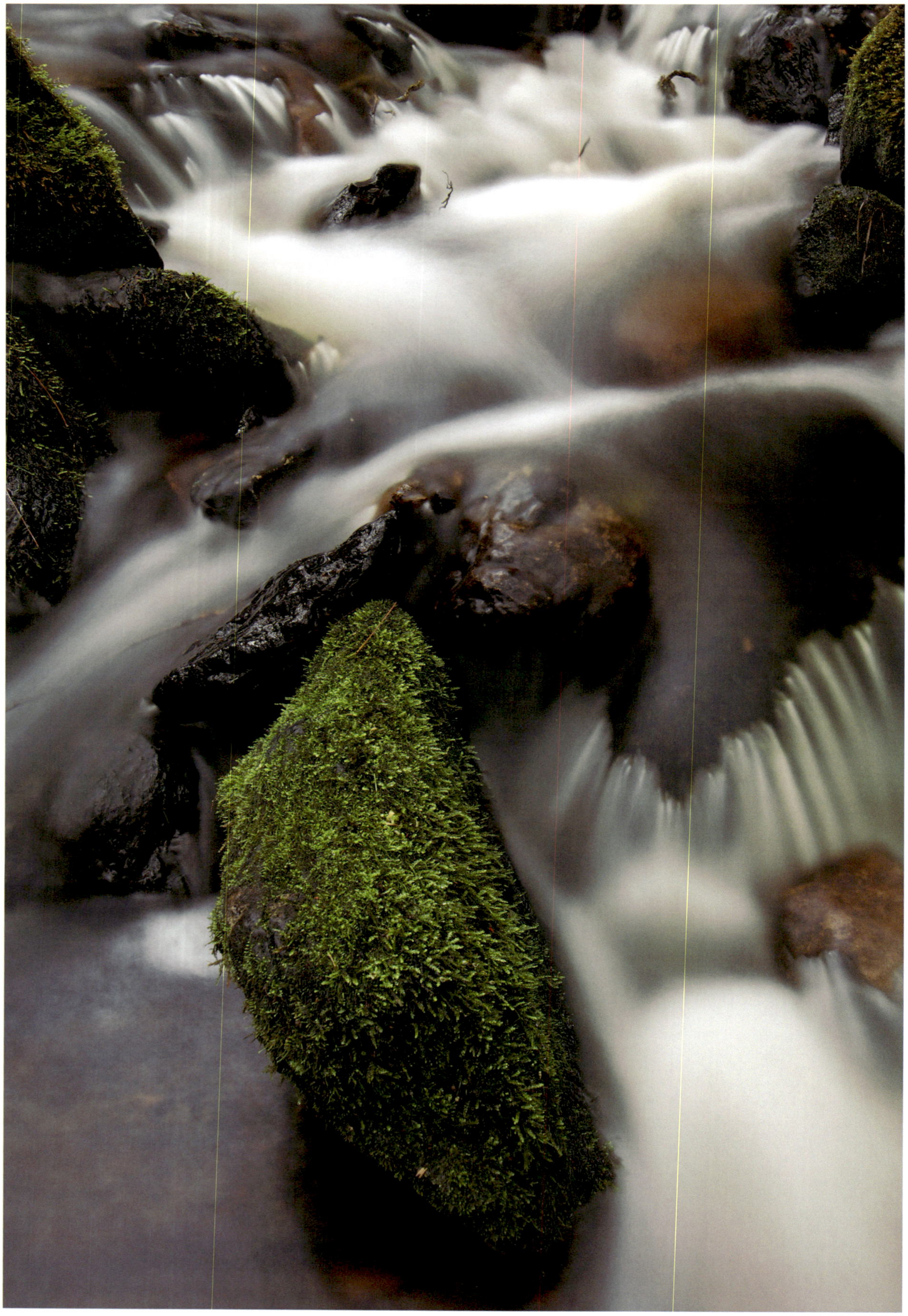

Mossy cascades, Stokes State Forest

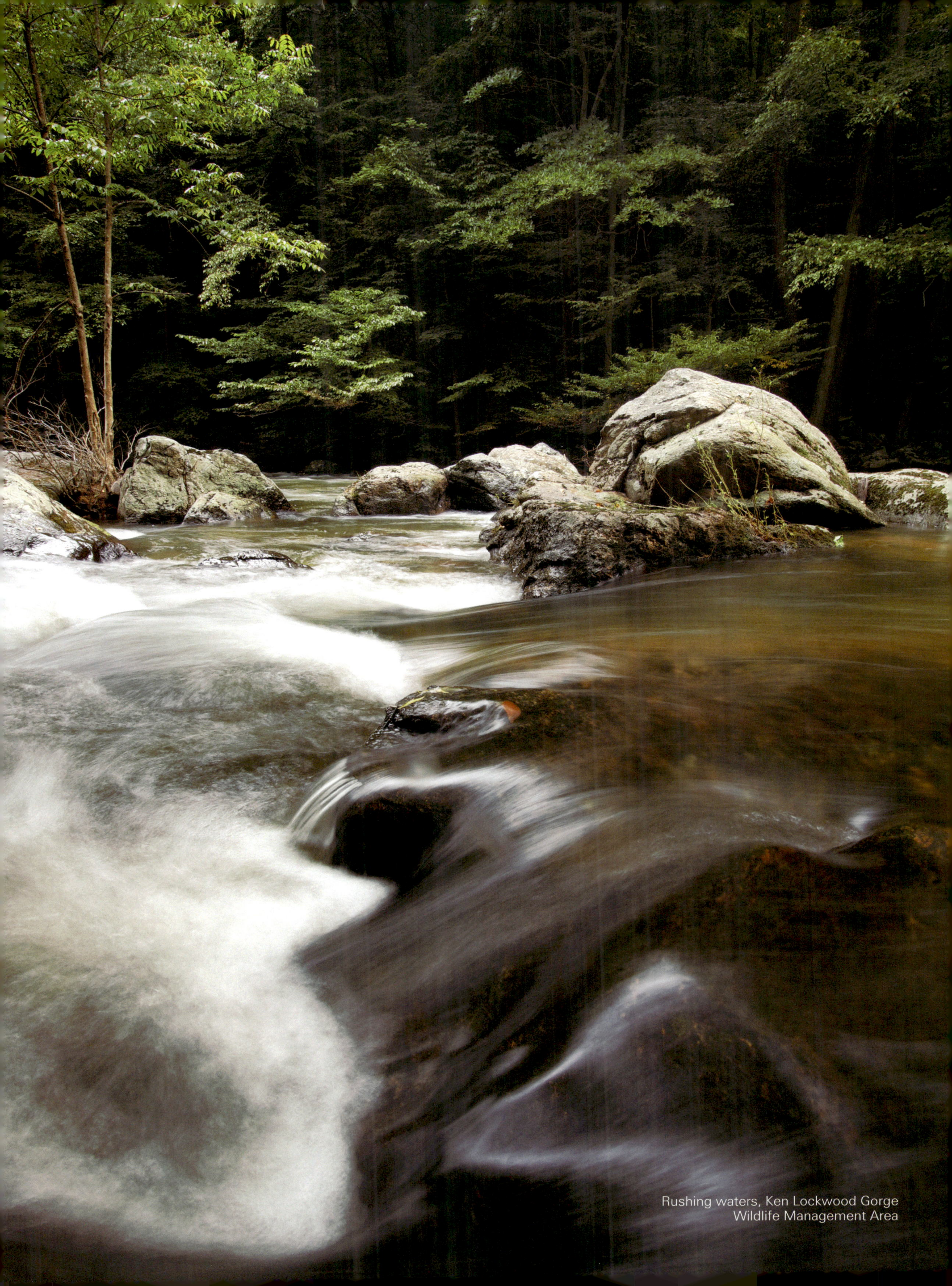

Rushing waters, Ken Lockwood Gorge
Wildlife Management Area

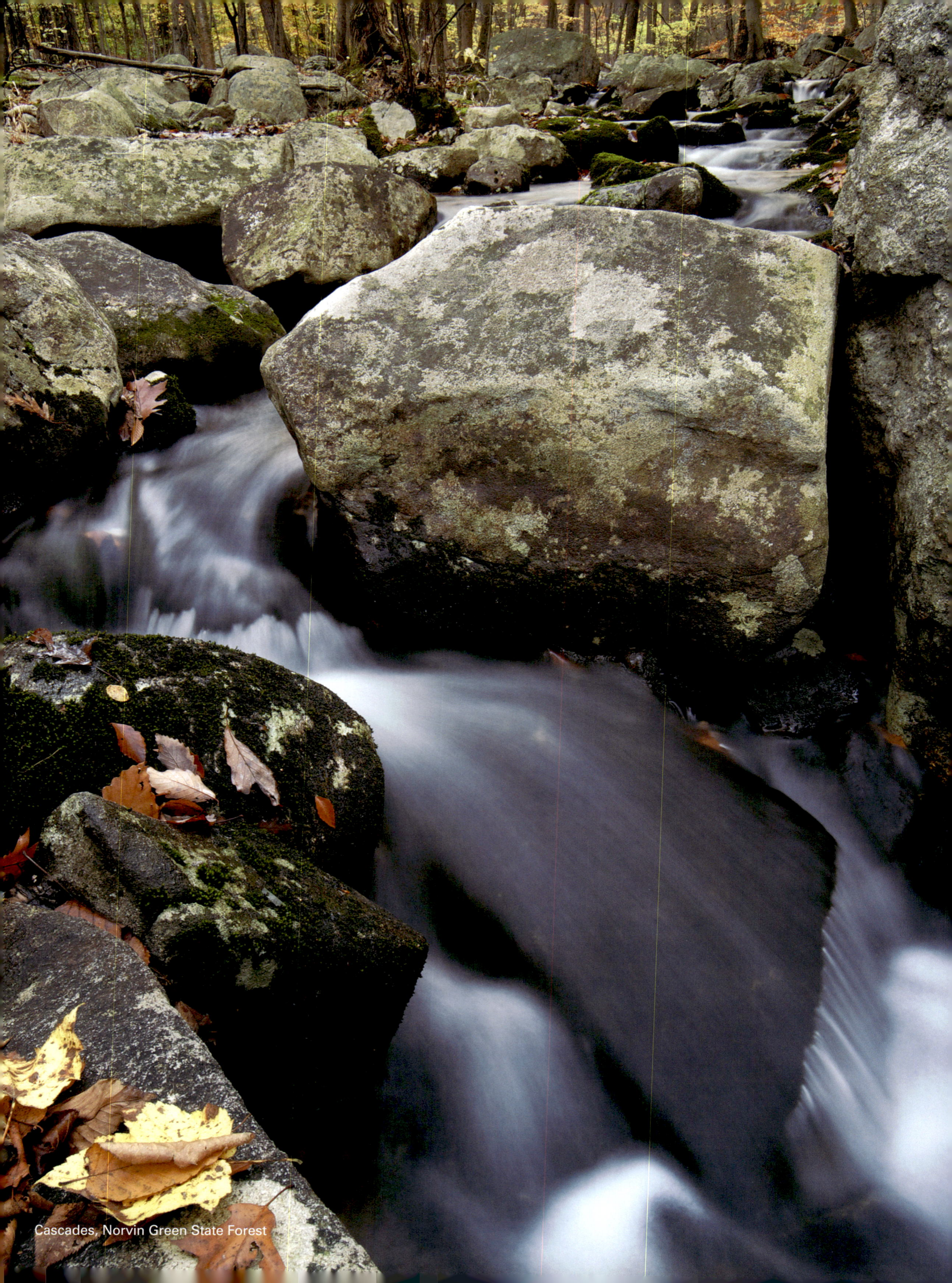

Cascades, Norvin Green State Forest

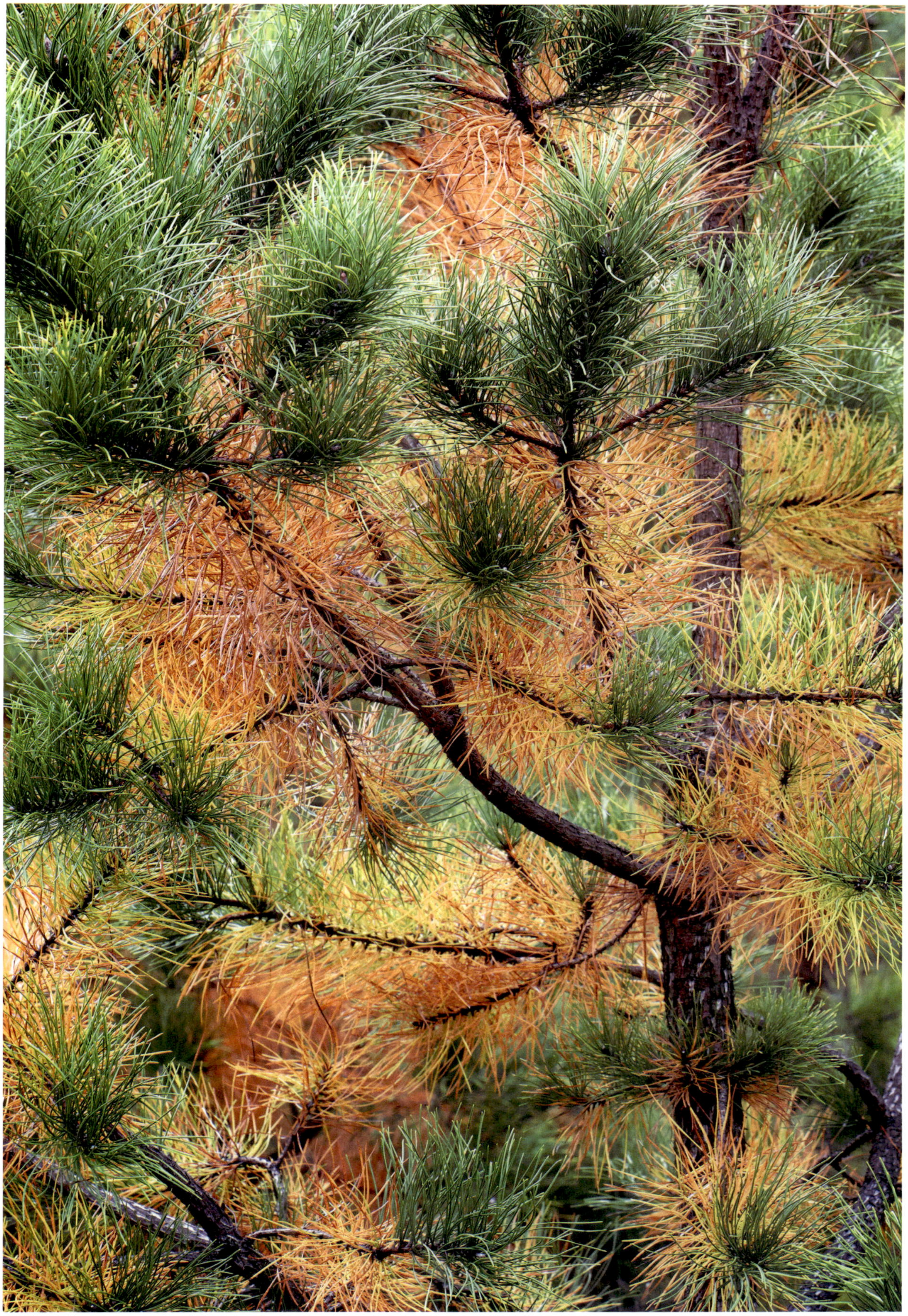

Pines, Franklin Parker Preserve

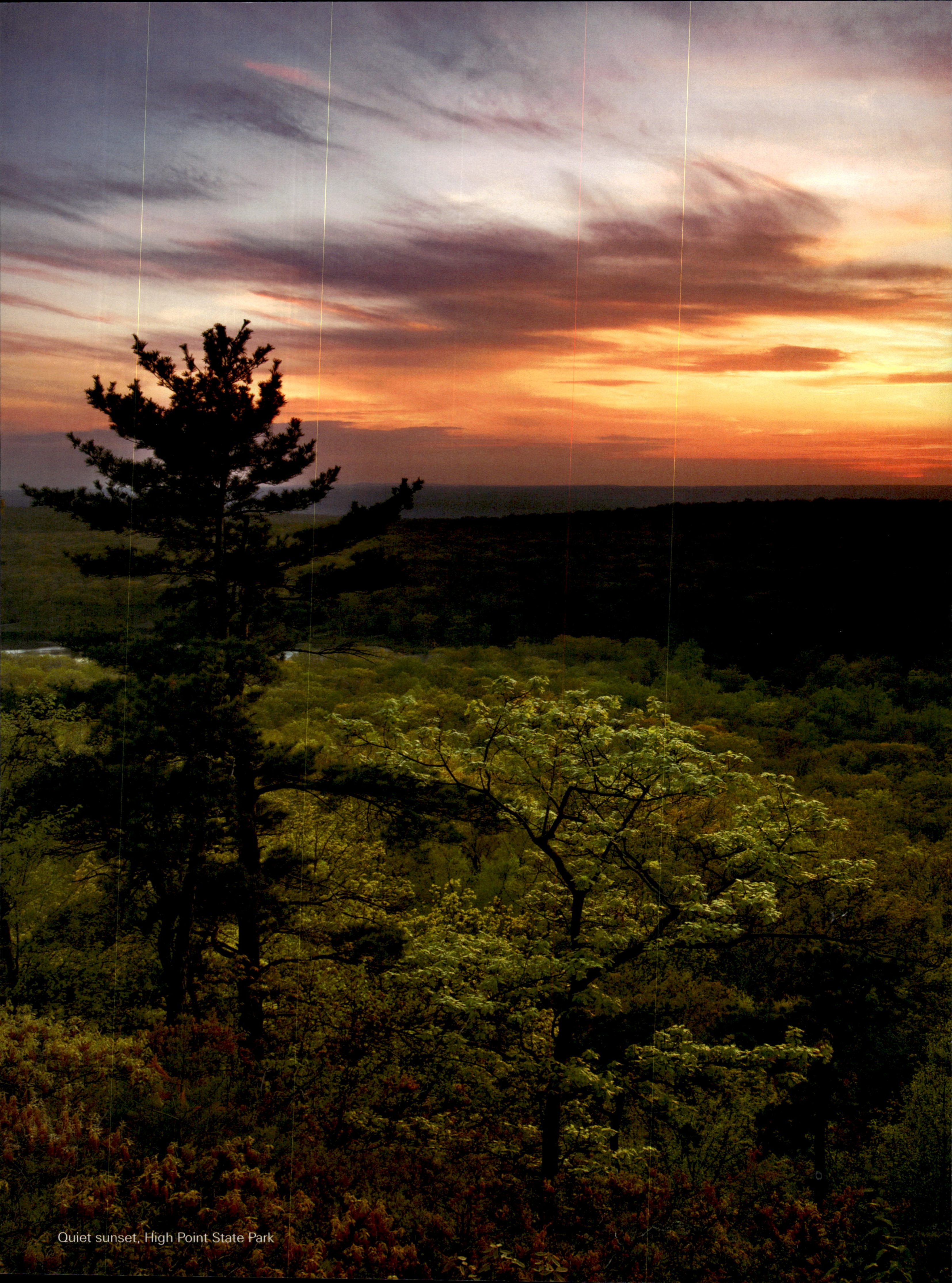

Quiet sunset, High Point State Park

A Visual Index to the Parks and the Photographs

Apshawa Preserve

Situated in the Highlands Region of New Jersey, the Apshawa Preserve is a cooperative venture between the New Jersey Conservation Foundation and the County of Passaic. The Preserve covers 576 acres with its main scenic attraction being the 40 acre Butler Reservoir. Even though it is in the middle of a populated area, Apshawa is a real treasure. It has 7 miles of hiking trails that wind through the hills with their overlooks, past waterfalls and streams, and around a beautiful lake. The lake is visually interesting because there are islands of rocks throughout that make it fun for a photographer or a hiker passing through.

For more information: ***www.njconservation.org/apshawapreserve.htm***

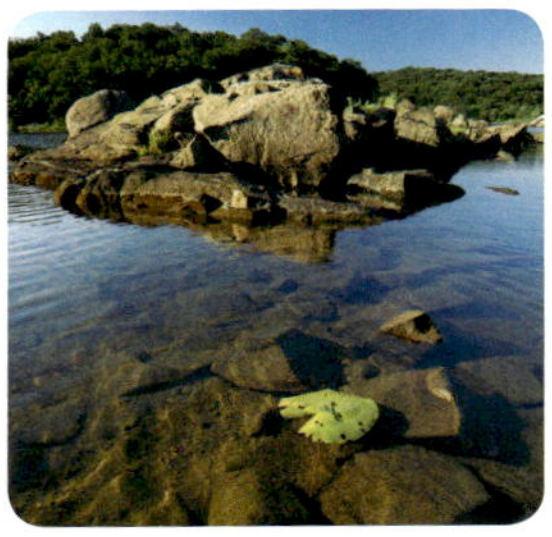

Page 100

Brendan T. Byrne State Forest

At 34,000 acres, Brendan T. Byrne State Forest is the second largest state forest in New Jersey. Amidst the aroma of the beautiful pines lies 25 miles of hiking trails. The Batona Trail, a 50-mile stretch that connects Brendan T. Byrne Forest, Wharton State Forest, and Bass State Park, originates in the park. Smaller trails run throughout the park, winding through the unique Pinelands environment. Within the forest is Historic Whitesbog Village, the center of the cranberry and blueberry industry that, years ago, thrived in the Pinelands. While not at the levels it used to be, cranberries and blueberries are still harvested to this day. Trails go throughout the bogs and provide a window into the economic past and present.

For more information: ***www.state.nj.us/dep/parksandforests/parks/byrne.html***

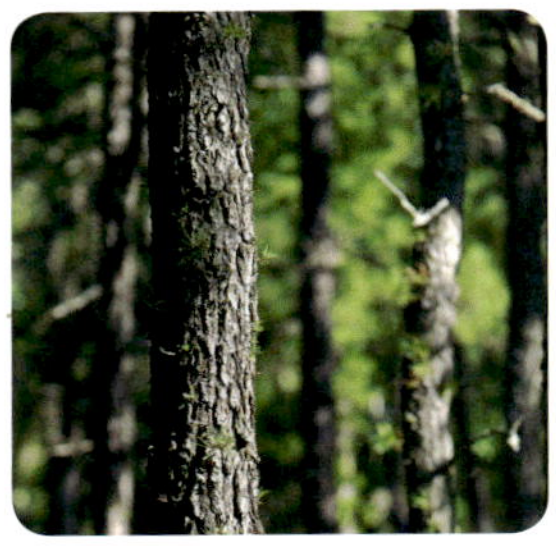

Page 24

Cape May National Wildlife Refuge

Established in 1989, The Cape May National Wildlife Refuge is an important wildlife habitat along the Delaware Bay. The refuge accounts for 11,000 acres of preserved bay front, salt marshes, and forests. These environments play an important role for migrating birds. The entire Cape May coast line is one of the most significant stops for migrating birds in the country. The most well known bird is the Red Knot. These little birds fly non-stop from South America to Cape May to gorge themselves on horseshoe crab eggs. They will continue on to the Arctic to breed and begin the entire process all over again. Many of the beaches within the Cape May National Wildlife Reserve are perfect for viewing their arrival and departure. Synchronized with the arrival of Red Knots is the mating ritual of horseshoe crabs along the Delaware Bay beaches in May and June, which is heaviest around full moons. This phenomenon has been happening for millions of years and the importance of horseshoe crab survival is critical not only for the Red Knots but also for the human population. Nearly every injected medication or medical device used in the human body has been tested using the blood from the horseshoe crab. Their survival is critically important for all concerned.

For more information: ***www.fws.gov/northeast/capemay***

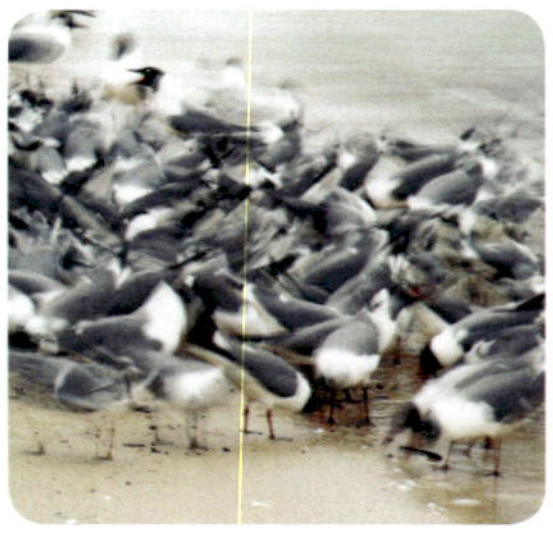

Page 58

Delaware Raritan Canal State Park

The Delaware Raritan Canal State Park cuts a straight path through central New Jersey. Much of its storied history remains intact today. Some of its many bridges, historic homes, bridgetender houses, and locks can be seen at almost any point along its 70-mile length. The canal passes by towns such as New Brunswick, Stockton, Griggstown, Kingston, and Princeton along the route. Hiking, jogging, and mountain biking along the tow path is a staple. Canoeing and kayaking in the canal brings back a lost era, as you pass by the historical sites and quaint towns.

For more information: ***www.dandrcanal.com/park_index.html***

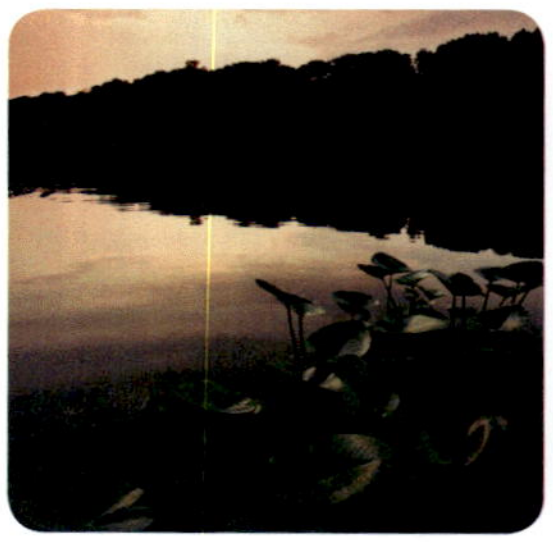

Page 81

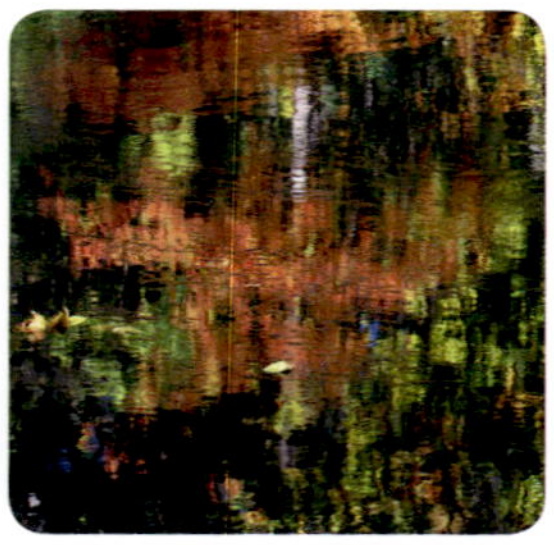

Page 91

Delaware Water Gap National Recreation Area

Arguably, the Delaware Water Gap National Recreation Area is the best known park in the state. The park runs parallel to the Delaware river and covers two states, New Jersey and Pennsylvania. Its dominant feature is a large gap in the mountains allowing the Delaware river to rush southward to empty into the Delaware Bay. Within the park are an array of waterfalls, challenging hikes, and the Appalachian trail. Beautiful glacier lakes abound and a variety of mammals and birds are always around to see and enjoy. Some parts of the park are very popular, so plan on being there early to avoid the crowds. If you are looking for a little peace and solitude, venture further into the park and hike the smaller trails. There are spots where you really feel isolated from everything and you'll feel like the only person enjoying the beauty.

For more information: ***www.nps.gov/dewa***

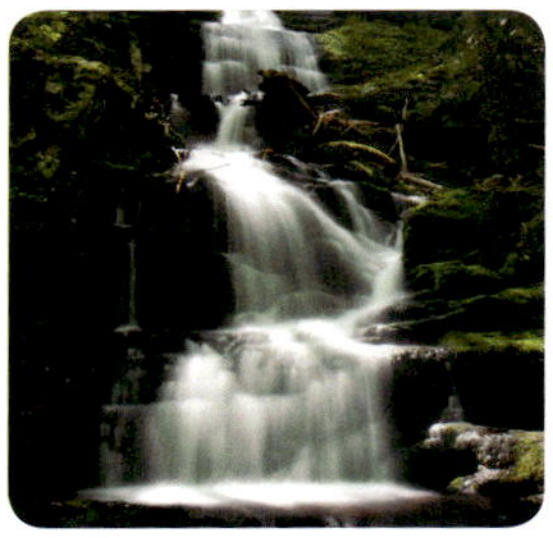
Page 28

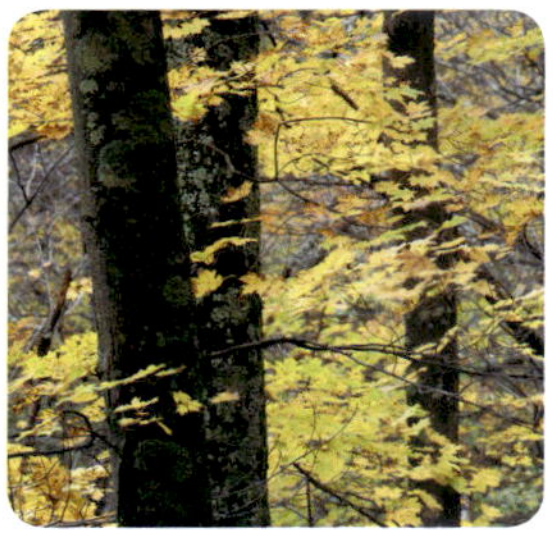
Page 36

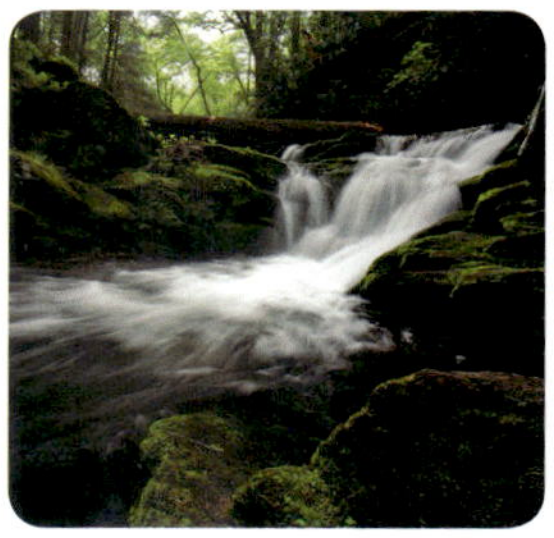
Page 48

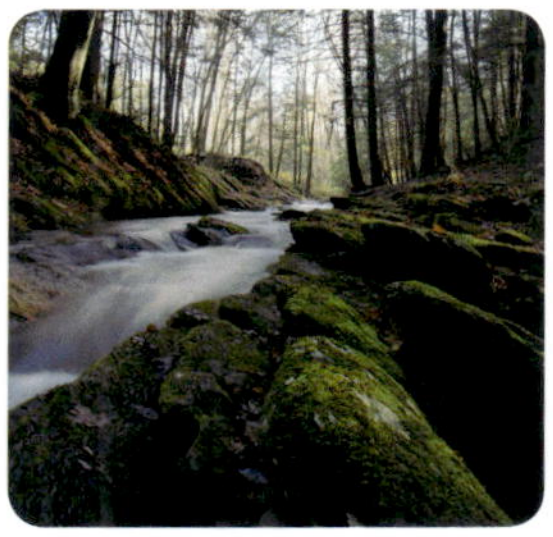
Page 71

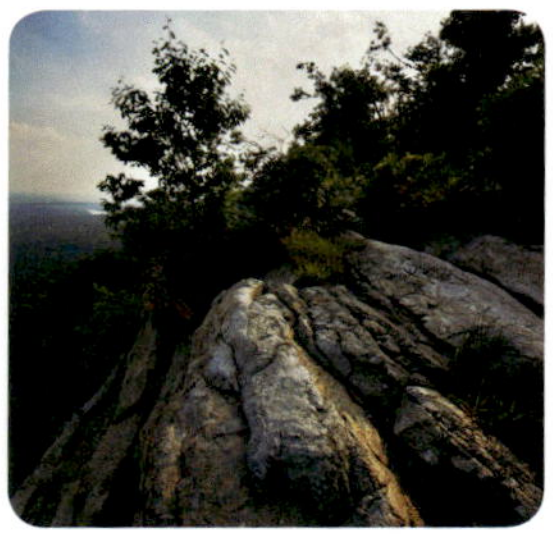
Page 105

Franklin Parker Preserve

In the heart of the Pine Barrens, a stone's throw from its unofficial capital Chatsworth, is a unique property known as Franklin Parker Preserve. The preserve is 14 square miles and maintained by the New Jersey Conservation Foundation. There are over 4,000 acres of pine oak forest, 5,000 acres of wetlands, cedar swamps, and large lakes. A wide variety of wildlife calls this preserve home; among them are eagles, herons, deer, and bobcats. In addition, locally endangered animals can be found, including the Barred Owl, Pine Barrens Tree Frog, and Northern Pine Snakes. All year round visits to Franklin Parker Reserve are rewarded with wonderful views, spectacular colors, and great opportunities to take interesting photographs.

For more information: ***www.njconservation.org/franklinparkerpreserve.htm***

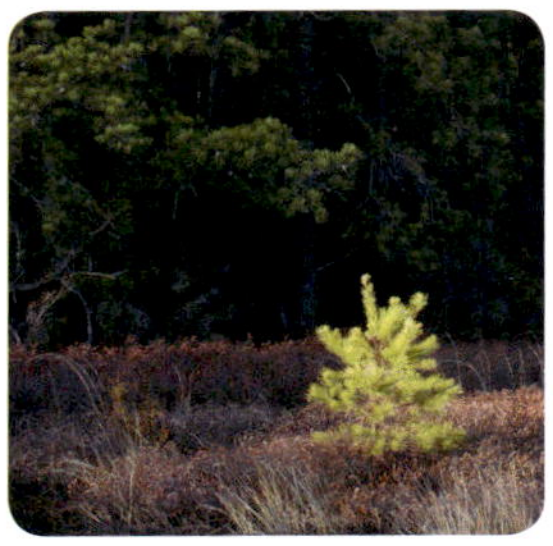
Page 31

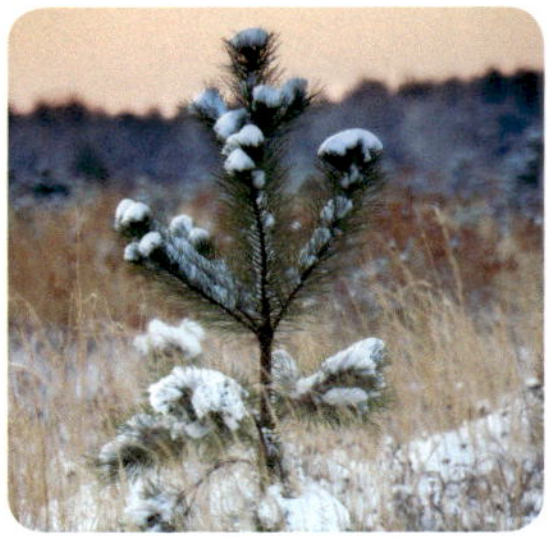
Page 72

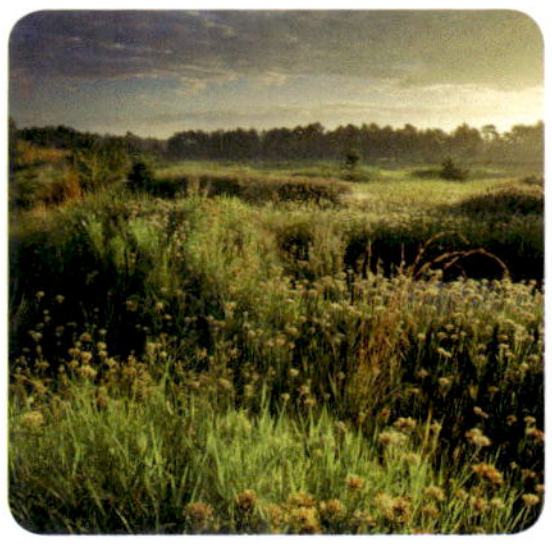
Page 83

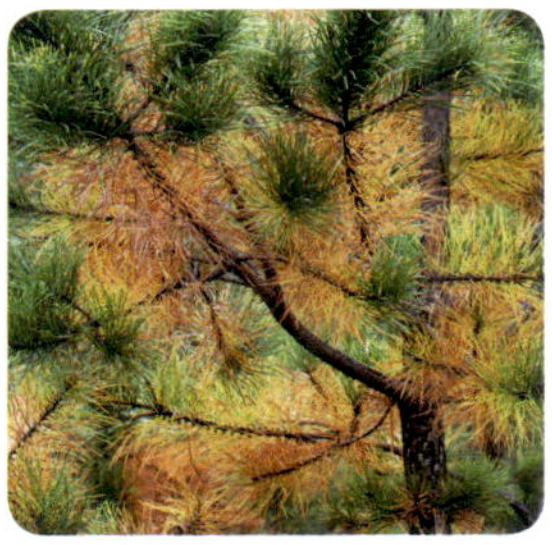
Page 111

Hacklebarney State Park

Hacklebarney State Park is a beautiful, forested park in Morris County. Of the parks in this volume, it is the most family friendly. Most of the hiking is along wide paved trails. Sections of the park were built by the Civilian Conservation Corps in the 1920s, adding to the nostalgic feel and beauty. What Hacklebarney Park lacks in opportunities for solitude, it more than makes up for with its natural beauty, especially as the trail winds towards the Black River. This beautiful river rushes through a hemlock-lined ravine. Small streams cascade down the ravine and feed into the clear water as the river courses its way through the park. Isolated park benches spring up unexpectedly on the trail, providing a place to rest and take in the terrific views and sounds of a beautiful space.

For more information: ***www.state.nj.us/dep/parksandforests/parks/hackle.html***

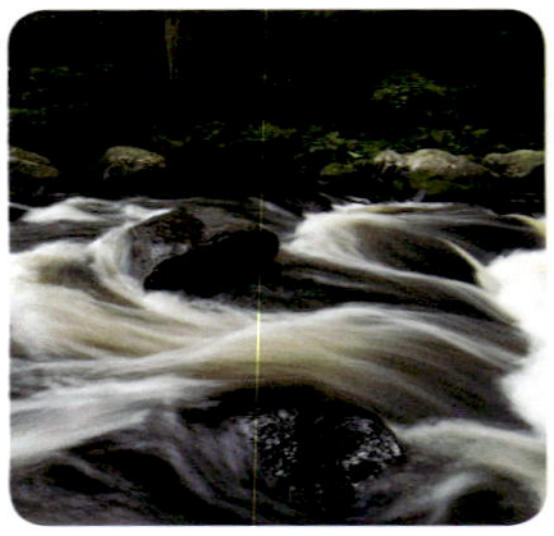

Page 32

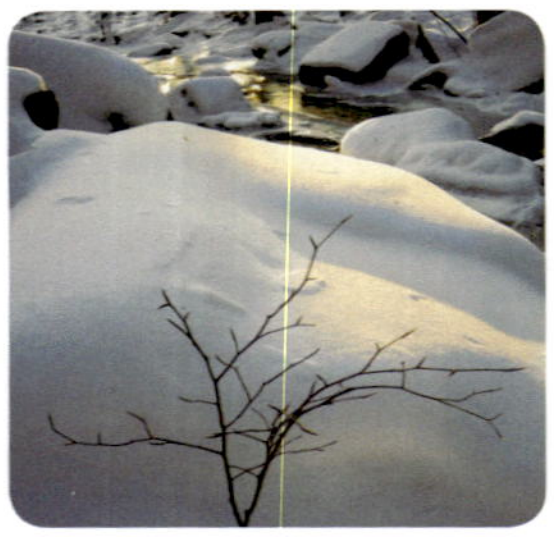

Page 70

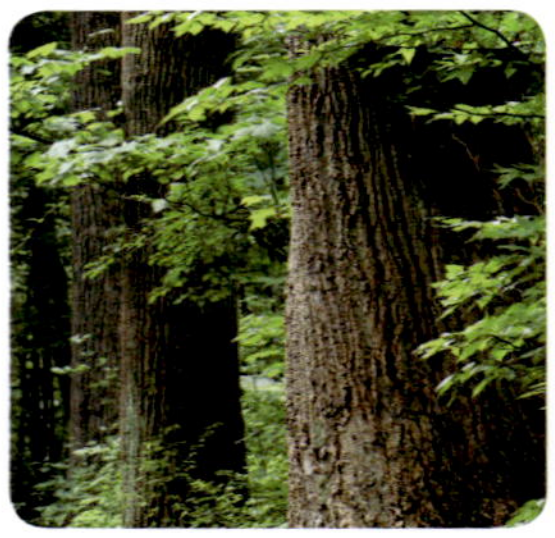

Page 76

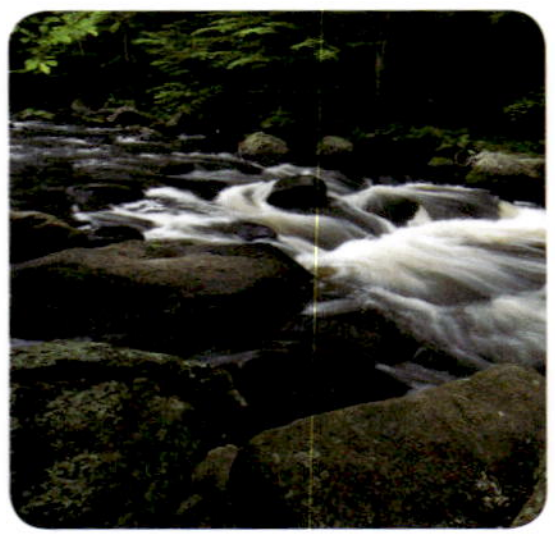

Page 90

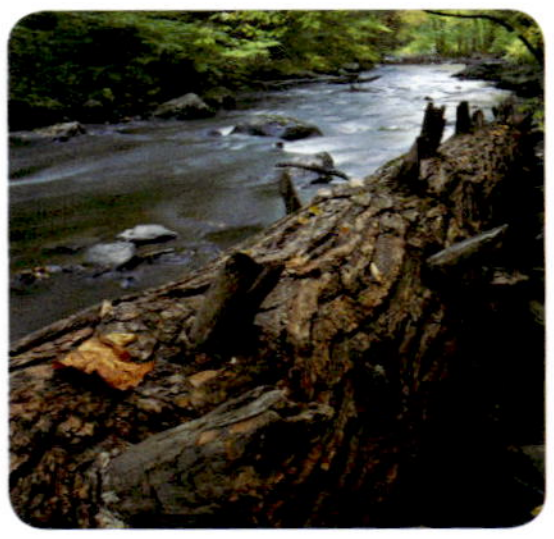

Page 93

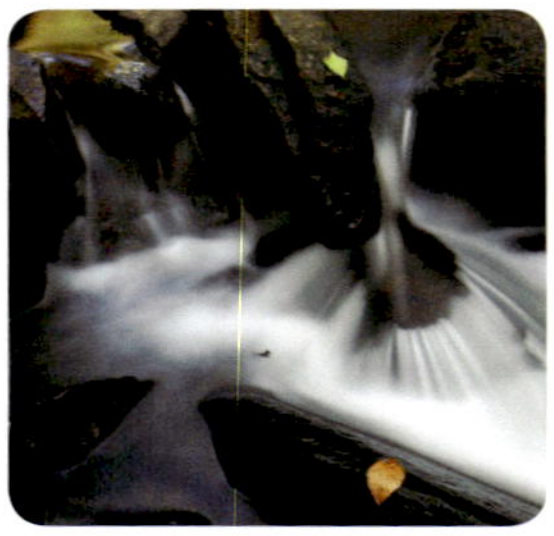

Page 102

Heislerville Wildlife Management Area

Located in Cumberland County bordering both the Delaware Bay and the Maurice River, the Heislerville Wildlife Management Area is about 45 minutes north of Cape May. It is popular for its wildlife diversity and overall beauty. As with most of the New Jersey shore line, this area is very popular for migrating shore birds, especially in the spring and fall. At high tide in May and June, horseshoe crabs work their way to the beach to spawn, creating an exciting event that has been happening for millions of years. Also located on the property is the beautifully restored East Point Lighthouse, which was built in 1849. The lighthouse is open to the public every third Sunday from April to October.

For more information: ***www.njwildlifetrails.org***

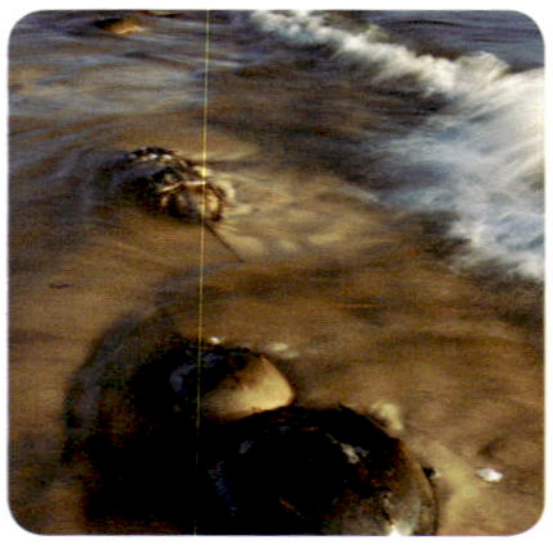

Page 13

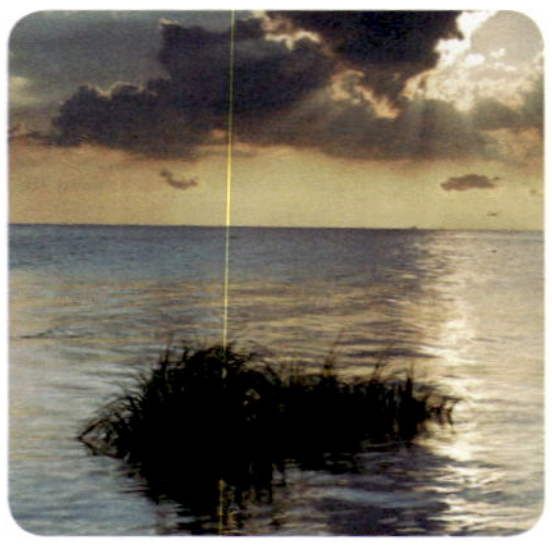

Page 45

High Point State Park

Located in Sussex County and residing at the highest point of the Kittatinny Ridge is High Point State Park. A large 14,000 acre park, it has views of Pennsylvania to the west, New York to the north, and New Jersey farmlands to the east. At its apex is a 220-foot monument honoring veterans that was built in 1930 and can be viewed from miles around. The park is a popular camping and swimming destination and, with the Appalachian trail cutting through the park, it attracts many visitors to enjoy its views. There are a great number and variety of activities and landscapes available for the visitor's enjoyment.

For more information: ***www.state.nj.us/dep/parksandforests/parks/highpoint.html***

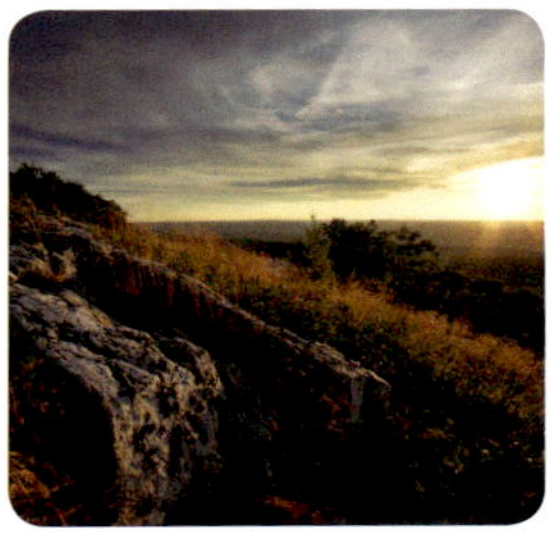

Page 14

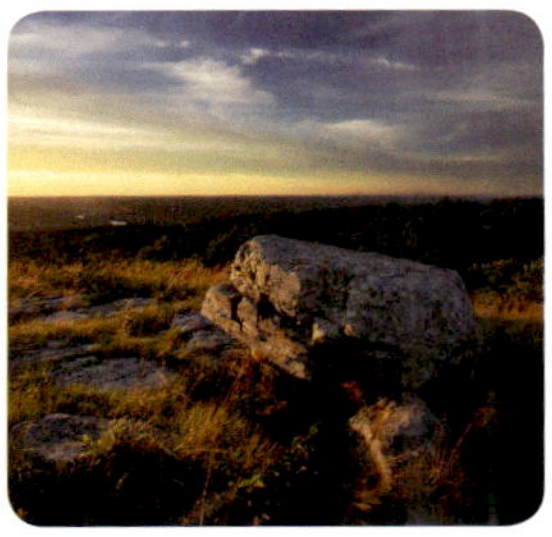

Page 29

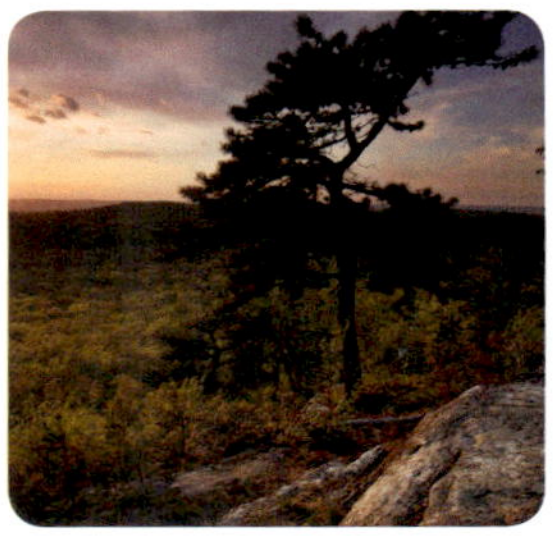

Page 33

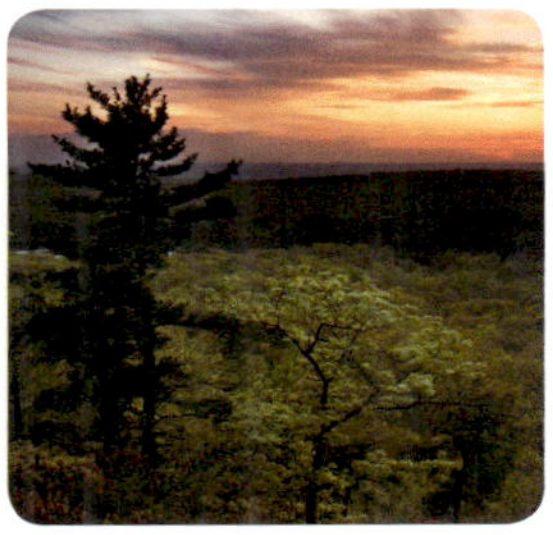

Page 112

Island Beach State Park

Island Beach State Park, located just south of Seaside Park, is a barrier island between the Atlantic Ocean and Barnegat Bay. Crucial to maintaining the safety of the mainland, the park offers beautiful sand dunes, clean sandy beaches, migrating birds, and small animals including Red Foxes. While much of New Jersey's coast is built up and enjoyed by millions, Island Beach State Park is an oasis of natural beauty. As with any protected shorelines it's important to stay on the paths and not destroy the dunes and plant life that inhabits the island.

For more information: ***www.state.nj.us/dep/parksandforests/parks/island.html***

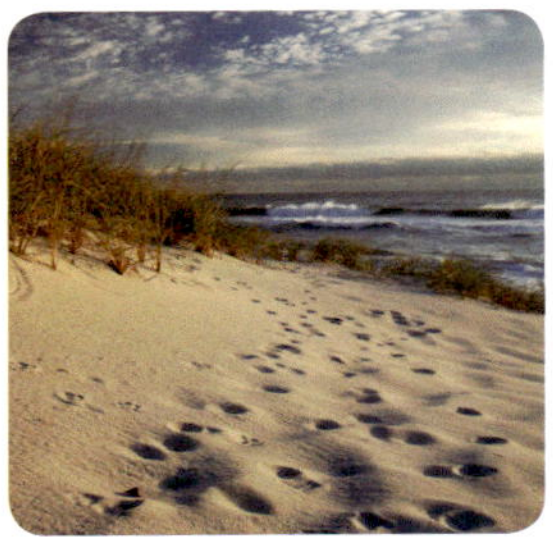

Page 11

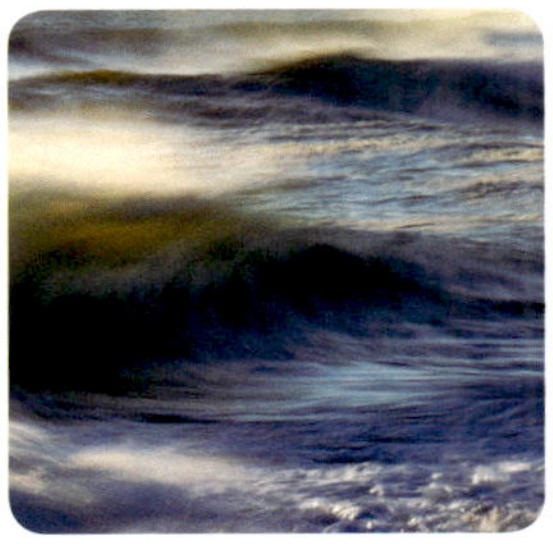

Page 34

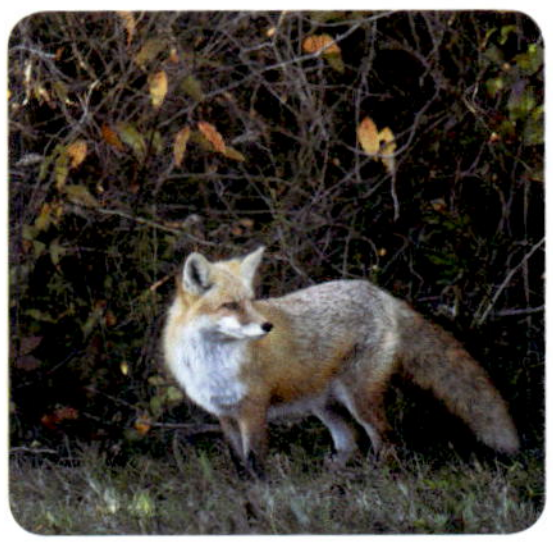

Page 46

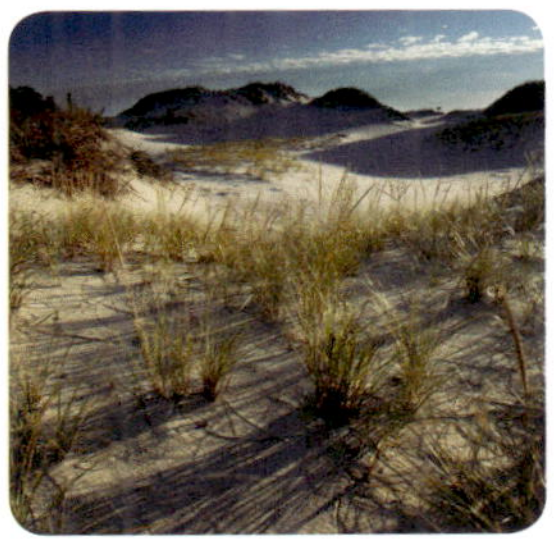

Page 52

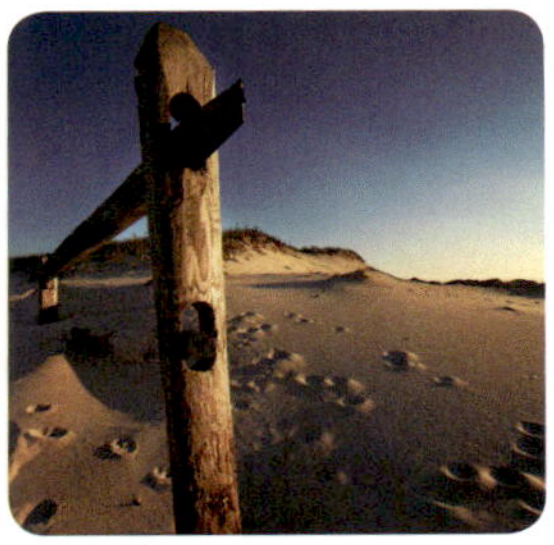

Page 62

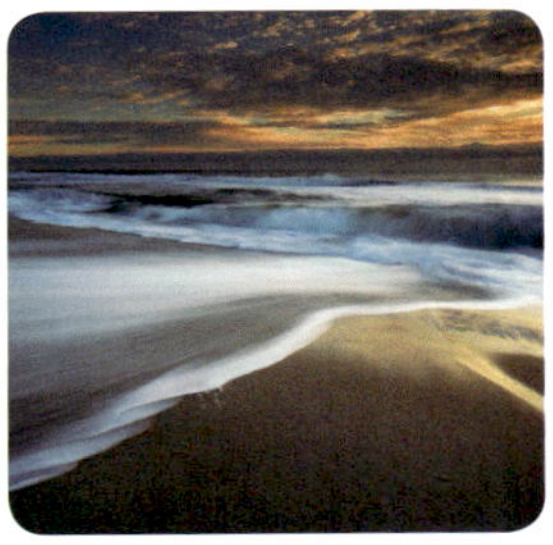

Page 94

Jenny Jump State Forest

Jenny Jump State Forest is located in Warren County near Hope, New Jersey. Legend has it that a young settler girl named Jenny jumped to her death while being chased by Indians, as her father yelled to her from the bottom of the mountain, "Jump Jenny, jump." Jenny jumped. The park has some of the oldest outcrop formations in the state, the scenic Ghost Lake, cabins, and camping facilities. This is a hidden jewel in the state parks system. There are 11 miles of hiking trails, including the Summit Trail, which overlooks the valley to the east and the Delaware Water Gap to the west.

For more information: ***www.state.nj.us/dep/parksandforests/parks/jennyjump.html***

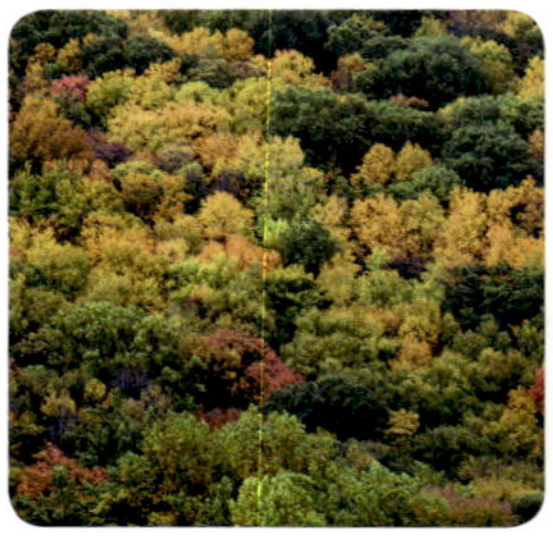

Page 42

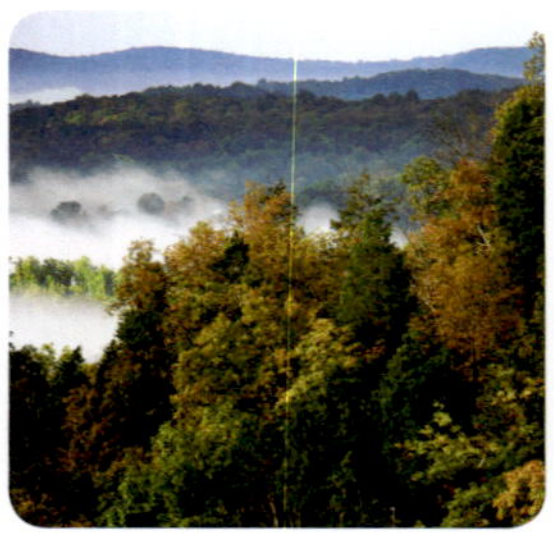

Page 64

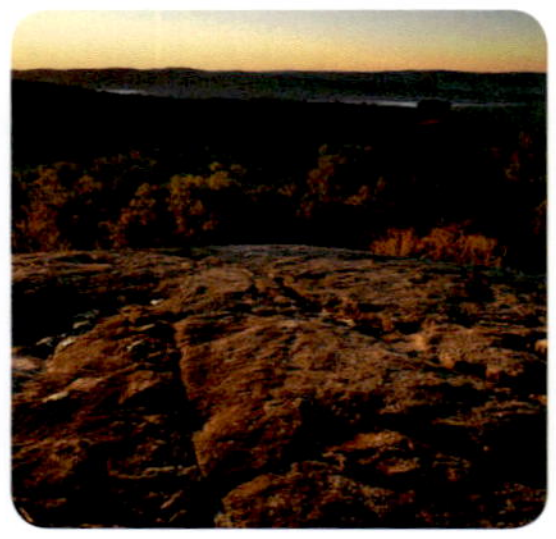

Page 74

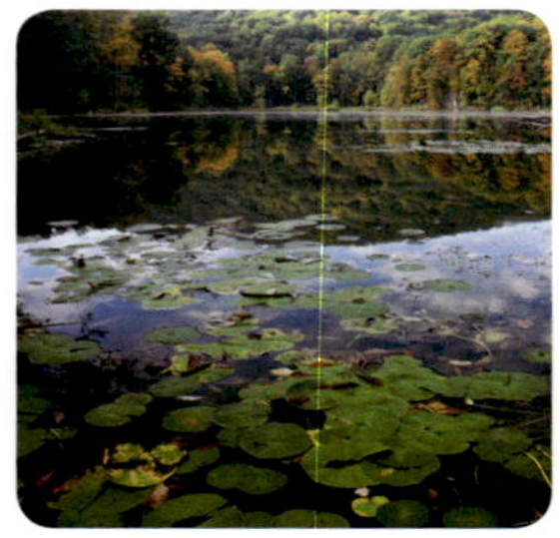

Page 78

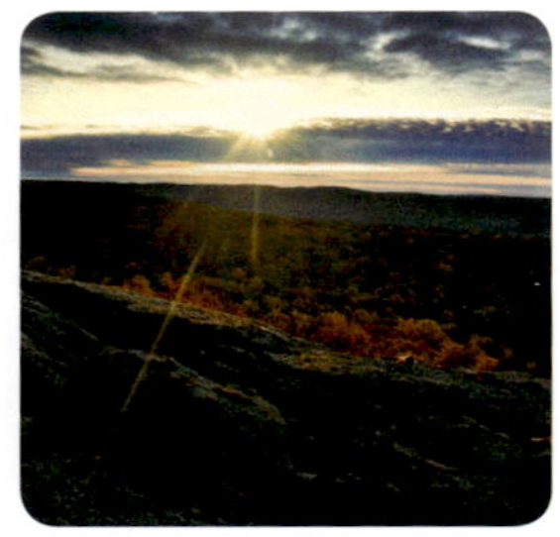

Page 128

Johnsonburg Swamp Preserve

Johnsonburg Swamp Preserve consists of 700 acres maintained by the Nature Conservancy in Sussex County, New Jersey. The hike begins at an open field, passes through a small wooded area, then enters another large open field. At the back end of the second open field the trail heads into the limestone forest. The main attraction of the Preserve is the limestone outcrops that overlook Mud Pond, a large wetland that is surrounded by the forest. An easy hike takes you to the cliffs, which provide an unobstructed, beautiful view of the pond and the local scenery. Many important plant species thrive within the boundaries of the Preserve, along with various animals and birds that call it home.

For more information: ***www.nature.org***

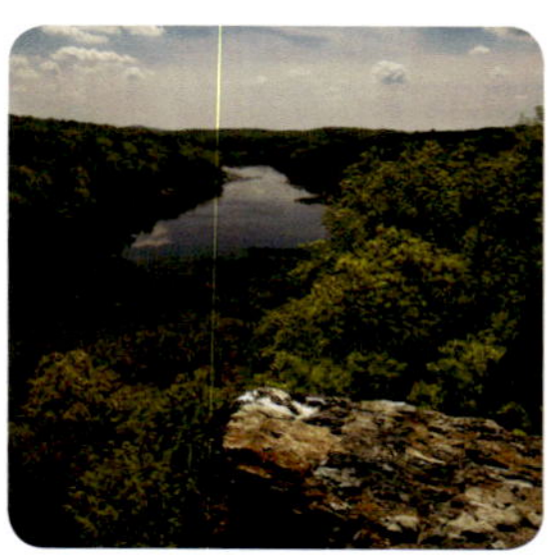

Page 82

Ken Lockwood Gorge Wildlife Management Area

Ken Lockwood Gorge Wildlife Management Area covers 445 acres in Hunterdon County. The property is named after Ken Lockwood, an outdoor journalist and conservationist, who worked for the *Newark Evening News*. The highlight of the park is the lower branch of the Raritan River that runs 2.5 miles through the park at the bottom of a beautiful gorge. Ken Lockwood Gorge is consistently rated as one of the top locations in the state for fly fishing, with beautiful rainbow and brown trout. In addition, hawks and blue herons can be found near the river and trees surrounding it. A wide path follows the river, where hikers, bikers, and fisherman mix company to enjoy one of the most picturesque places in the state.

For more information: ***www.nynjtc.org/park/ken-lockwood-gorge-wildlife-management-area***

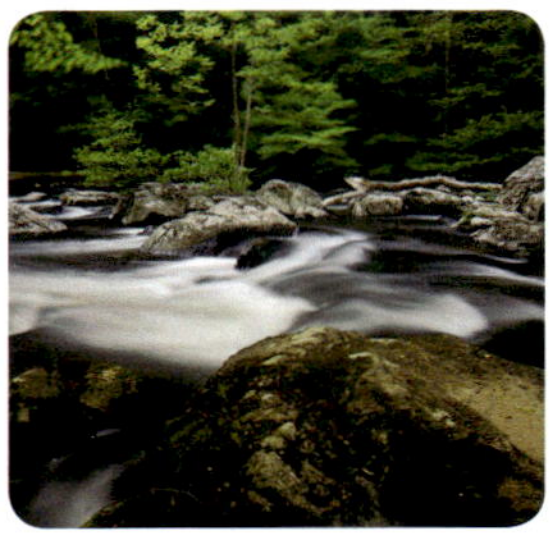

Page 20

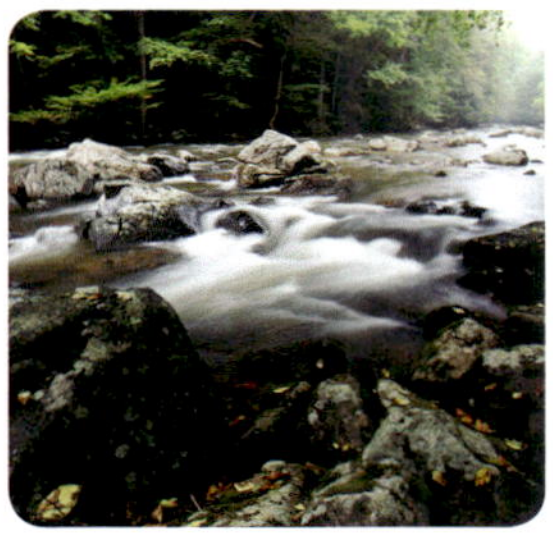

Page 30

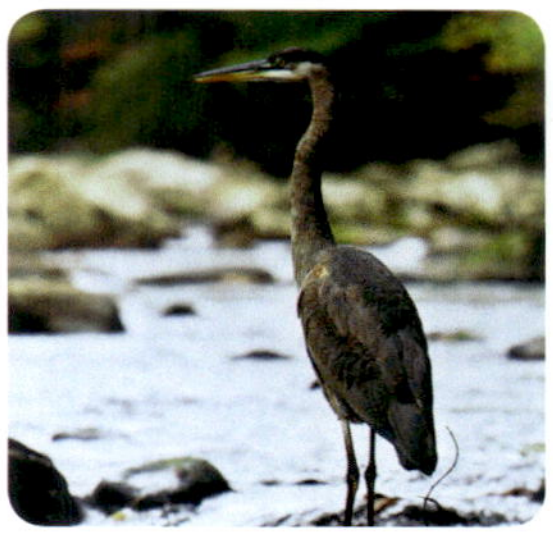

Page 57

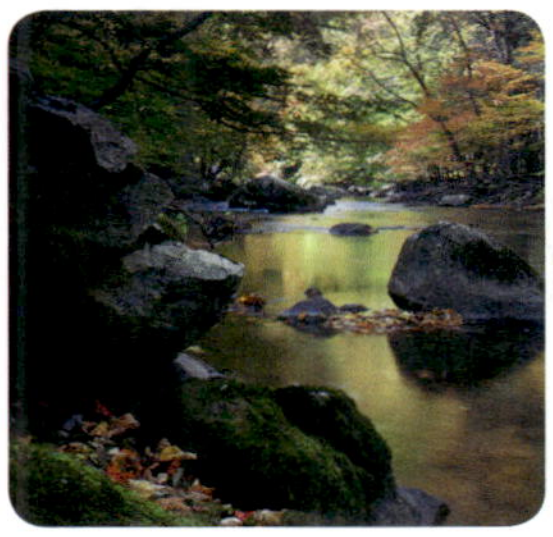

Page 97

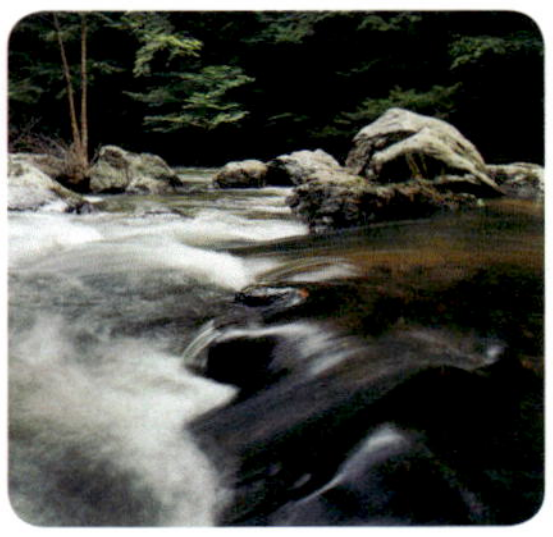

Page 109

Mahlon Dickerson Reservation

The largest park in the Morris County Park system is the Mahlon Dickerson Reservation. The park is named after a former New Jersey Governor and Senator. With 3,200 acres of land set aside for recreational use, including over 20 miles of trails, hiking Mahlon Dickerson will take the walker through multiple forested areas, swamps, ponds, and scenic overlooks. One of the nicest views is from Headly Overlook, complete with outcroppings. It is one of the highest points in the park, with wonderful views of Lake Hopatcong way off in the distance. This spot is especially stunning in the fall.

For more information: ***www.morrisparks.net/aspparks/mahlonmain.asp***

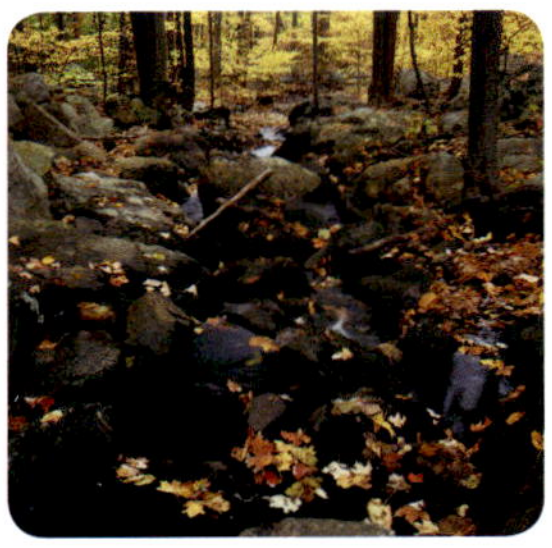

Page 51

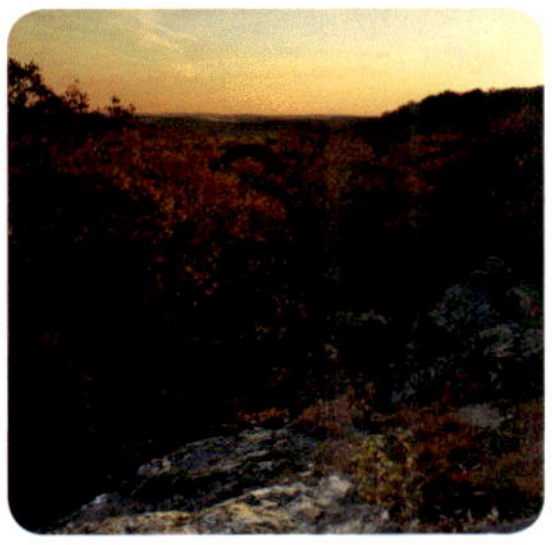

Page 89

Merrill Creek Reservoir

Merrill Creek Reservoir is a 650 acre man-made lake surrounded by 250 acres of wooded property. It was built to control the water flow of the Delaware River and is capable of pumping water to and from the river in times of drought and flooding. Located on the property is a beautiful environmental center overlooking the lake, complete with information about the lake, activities, and the surrounding areas. With its prime location, it is very popular with migrating birds. Depending on the season, hawks, large populations of snow geese, and resident eagles are just part of the variety of birds that can be seen here and make this very popular for birders. Hiking trails surround the lake and adjacent wooded areas, making it fun for everyone.

For more information: ***www.merrillcreek.com***

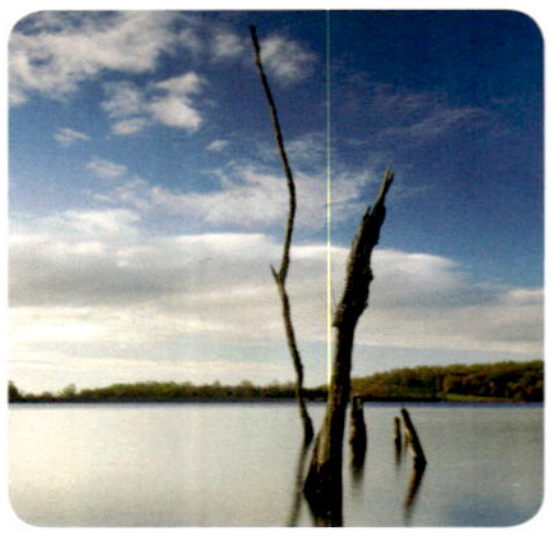

Page 9

Newark-Pequannock Watershed

The Newark-Pequannock Watershed is 100,000 acres owned by the city of Newark to provide water for its residents. The property is opened for hiking, hunting, and fishing, but by permit only. A nominal fee allows access to beautiful lakes, pristine waters, and dense forests. Walking along the shores of its lakes reminds me of Acadia National Park in Maine because of its crystal clear waters and rocky shore lines. As a reminder, your entry pass must be carried at all times when visiting and the purchased sticker posted in your car window needs to be visible.

For more information: ***www.newarkwatershed.com***

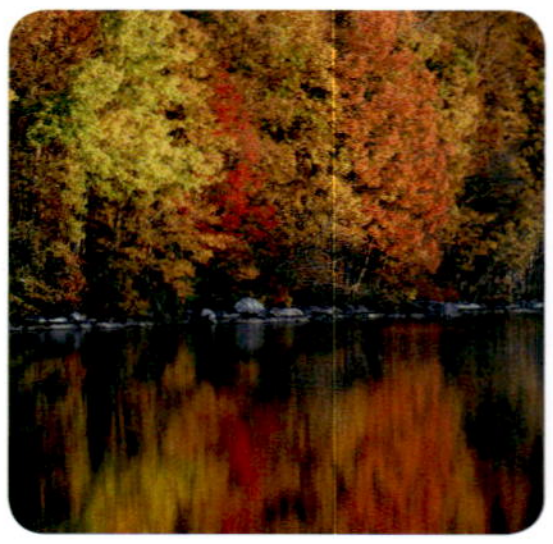

Page 39

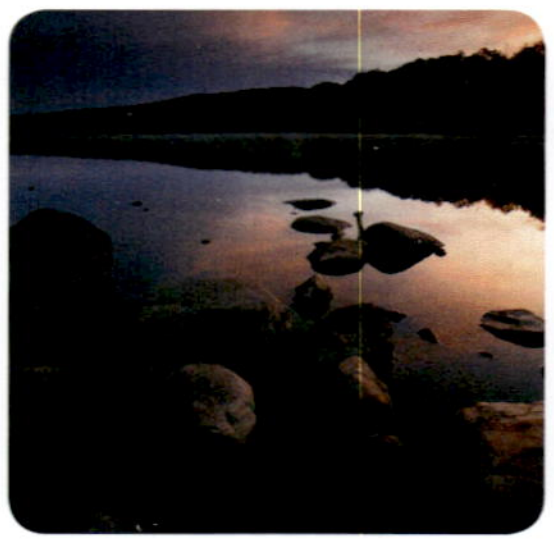

Page 53

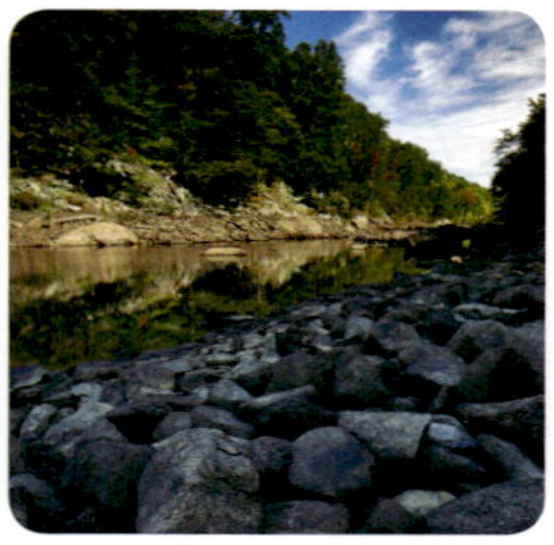

Page 61

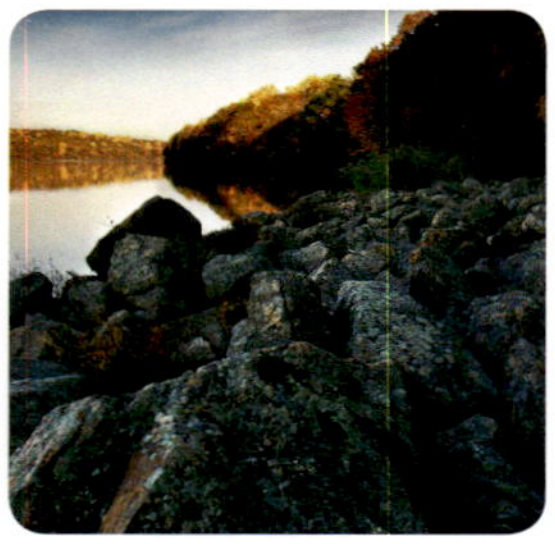

Page 66

Norvin Green State Forest

With over 4,900 acres, Norvin Green State Forest is located in northern New Jersey, part of a region referred to as the Highlands. This mountain range stretches from New York through New Jersey and into Pennsylvania. With peaks topping out at 1,300 feet in Norvin Green, it affords hikers and photographers clear views, some of the best outcroppings in the state. The forest borders Wanaque Reservoir. It is home to the Weis Ecology Center, run by the New Jersey Audubon Society. Adjacent to the Weis Ecology Center is the Highlands Natural Pool, a stream-fed pool carved into the hillside in 1935.

For more information: ***www.state.nj.us/dep/parksandforests/parks/norvin.html***

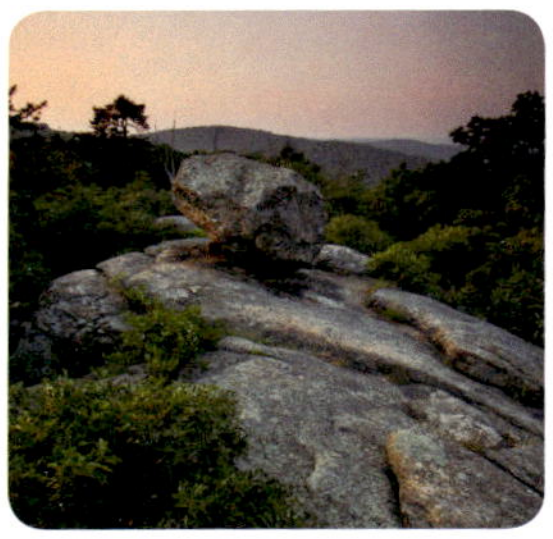

Page 18

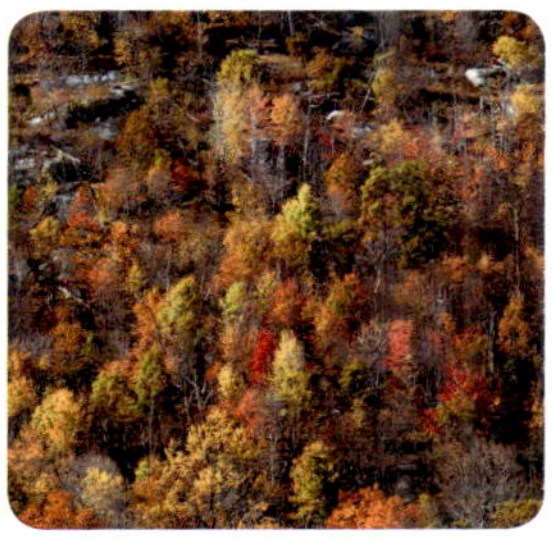

Page 21

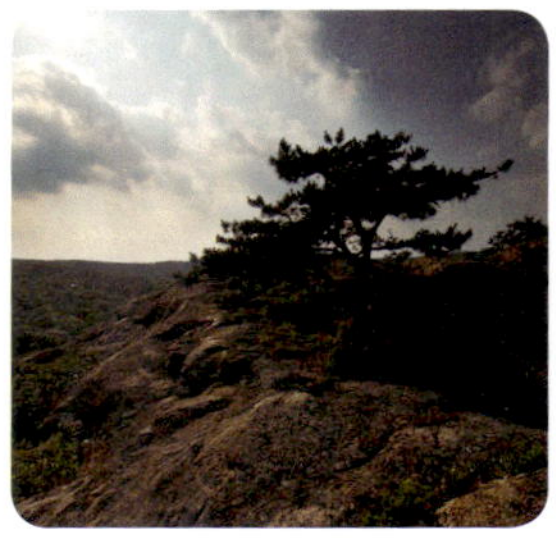

Page 44

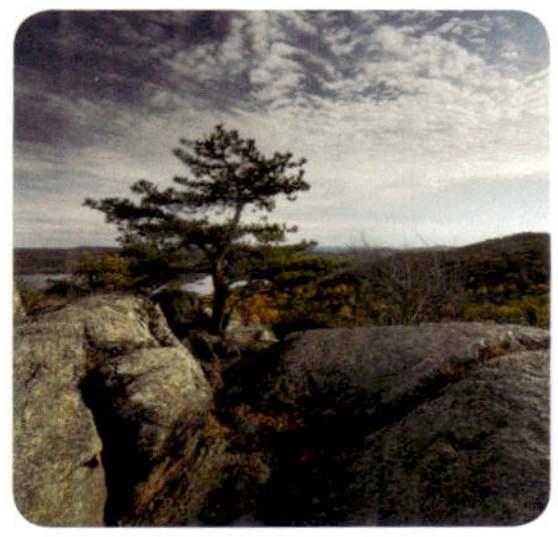

Page 92

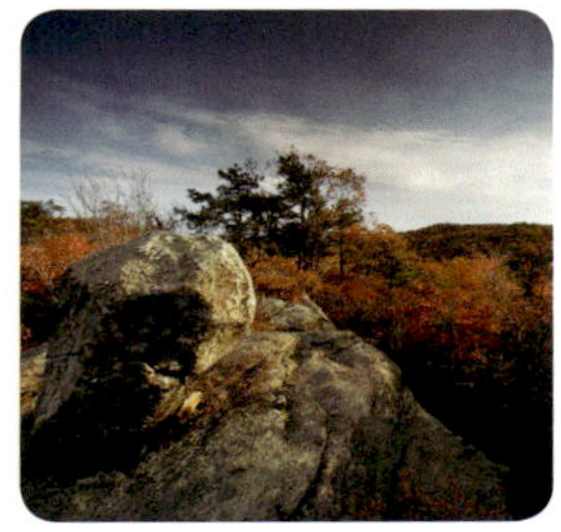

Page 106

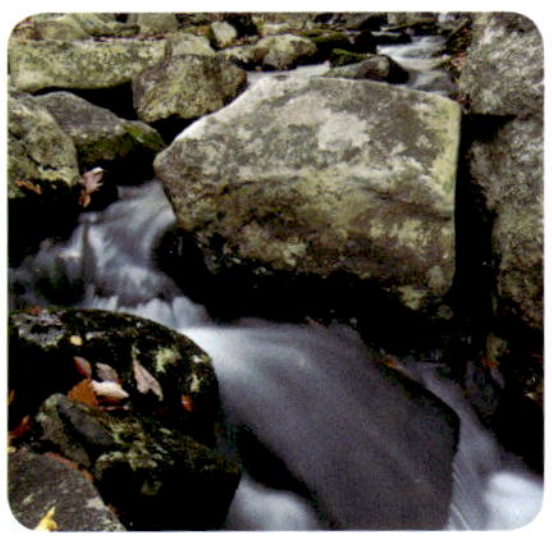

Page 110

Penn State Forest

Within the boundaries of the Pinelands in Burlington County is Penn State Forest. The centerpiece to the park is Oswego Lake, which is easily accessible and very popular with kayakers. As with all of the Pinelands, there is an understated beauty about this region. What may appear as an arid, simple environment is really complex and fascinating. Many of the waters, including Oswego Lake, are tea colored due to the cedar and iron prevalent in the area.

For more information: ***www.state.nj.us/dep/parksandforests/parks/penn.html***

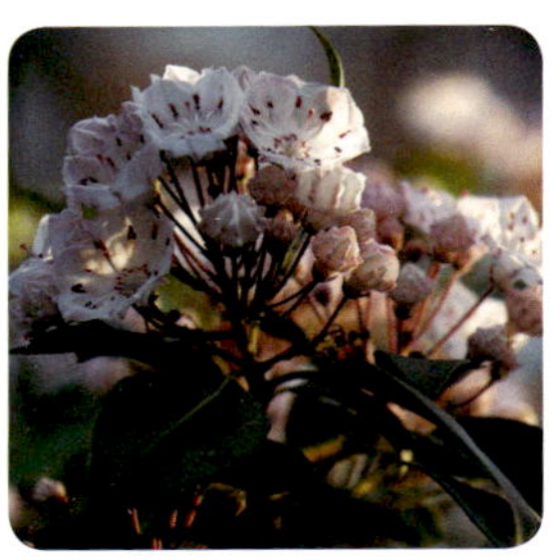

Page 54

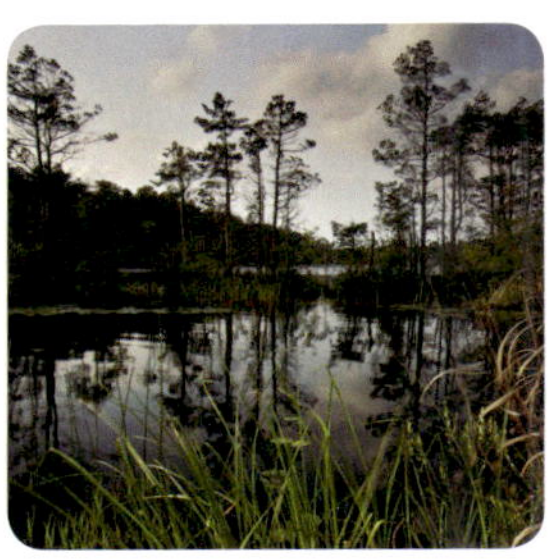

Page 77

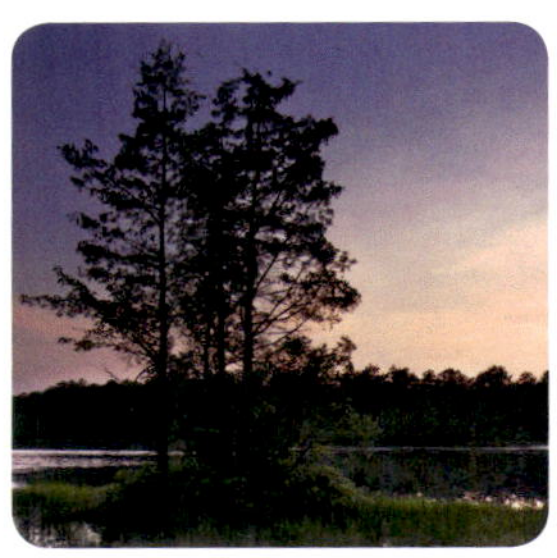

Page 104

Plainsboro Preserve

In the middle of the typical New Jersey suburban sprawl in Middlesex County, is Plainsboro Preserve. It covers 1,000 acres of preserved space with McCormack Lake as its centerpiece. Home to 5 miles of hiking trails, a variety of animals, and 150 species of birds, the Preserve also has a large Environmental Education Center run by the New Jersey Audubon Society. Set on a hill overlooking the lake, it is surrounded by seating with wonderful views of the preserve. The fall season at the preserve offers a variety of trees that yield a rainbow of colors, making for great fall photography and hiking.

For more information: ***www.njaudubon.org/SectionCenters/SectionPlainsboro/AboutPlainsboroPreserve.aspx***

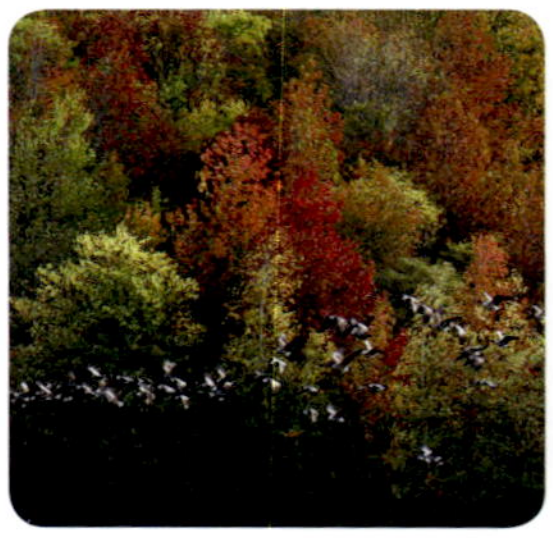

Page 26

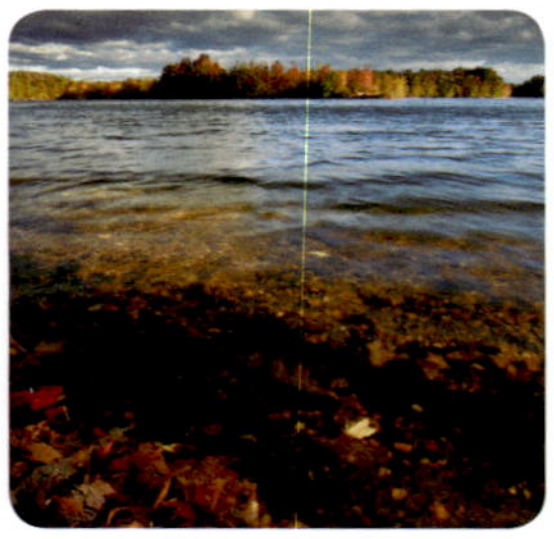

Page 41

Point Mountain Reservation

Point Mountain Reservation is located in Hunterdon County. The park contains over 1,000 acres of forests, rivers, and views. Multiple trails wander through the preserve and up the mountain. The beautiful Musconetcong River cuts through the preserve at the bottom of the gorge and the spectacular views from rock outcroppings at the top of its 935-foot peak are stunning, as they overlook the valley's farmland.

For more information: ***www.nynjtc.org/park/point-mountain***

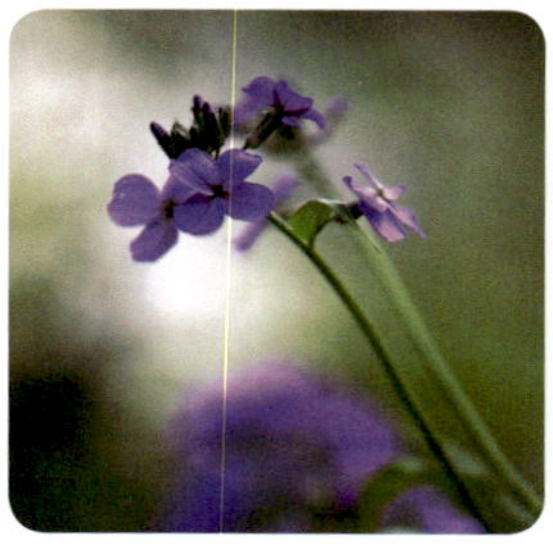

Page 16

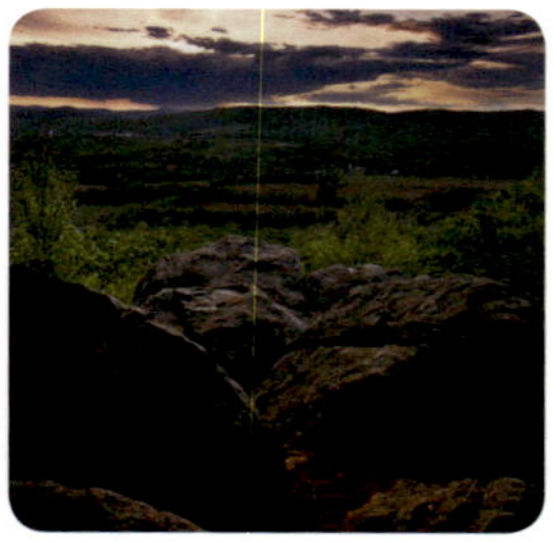

Page 96

Ramapo Mountain State Forest

Ramapo Mountain State Forest encompasses over 4,000 acres in Passaic County, New Jersey. The park offers many outdoor activities including hiking, fishing, and mountain biking. Hiking within the park yields views of New York City, an old estate on a hill, and a beautiful 121-acre lake. The hike around the lake is especially beautiful. Tucked in and around the lake are big outcrops from which to fish or just admire the views. Marsh areas, small streams, and waterfalls add to the overall natural beauty of this park. With its easy location and variety of outdoor activities, this park is very popular year around.

For more information: ***www.nynjtc.org/park/ramapo-mountain-state-forest***

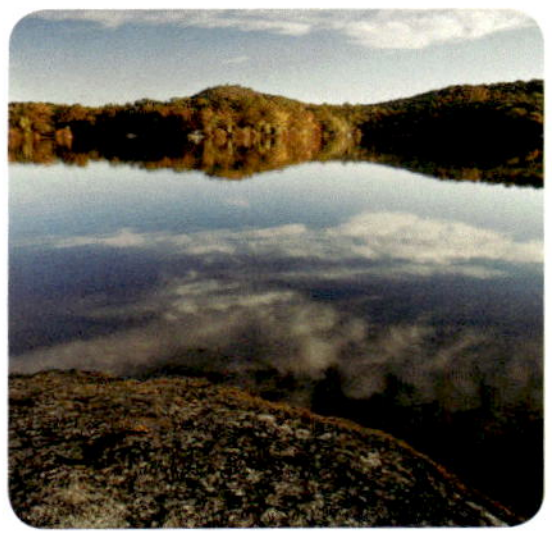

Page 19

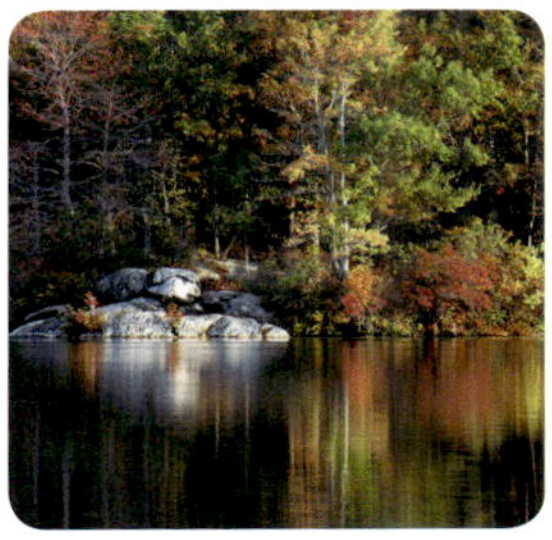

Page 101

Round Valley Recreation Area

The Round Valley Recreation Area, in Clinton, is the second largest lake in New Jersey. A man-made lake created in 1960, it is surrounded by the Cheskunk Mountains and is the deepest lake in the state. It boasts varieties of fish, trails, scuba diving, and, a rarity in New Jersey, wilderness camping. Round Valley is a beautiful lake with soft, rounded hills surrounding it. It offers great opportunities for photography or for just enjoying the beauty while hiking it's hills and shores.

For more information: ***www.state.nj.us/dep/parksandforests/parks/round.html***

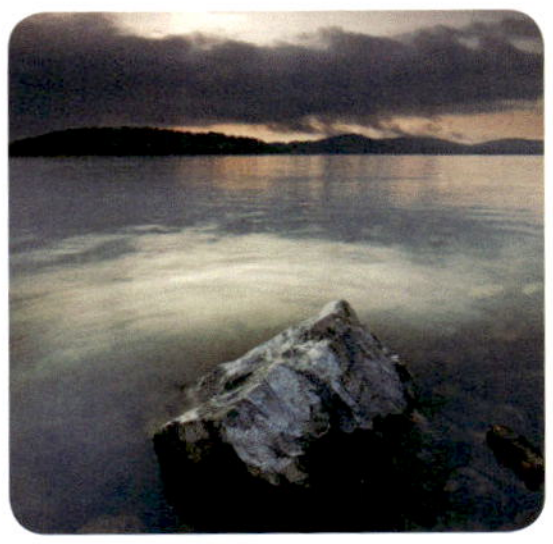

Page 60

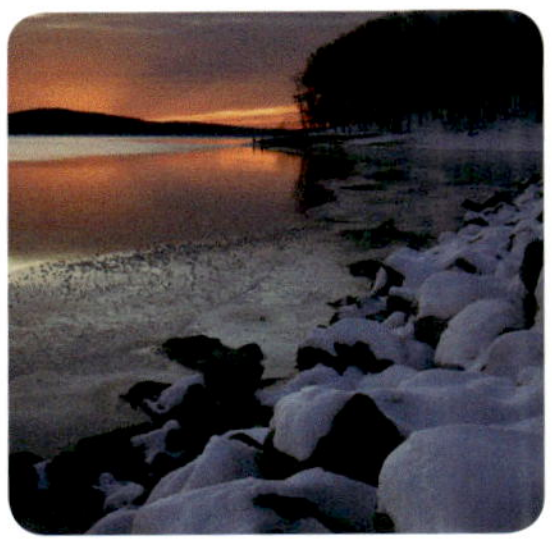

Page 63

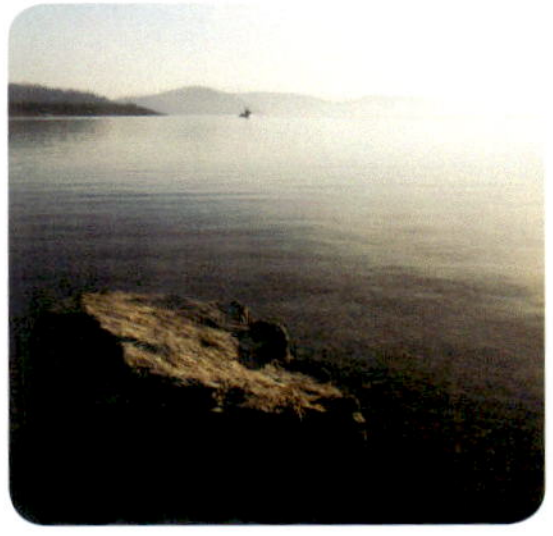

Page 67

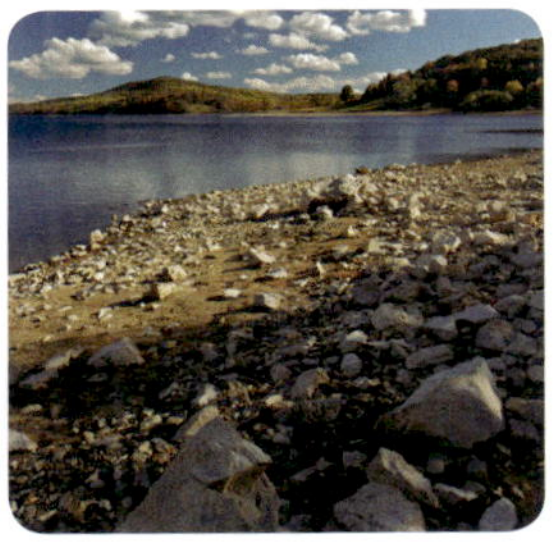

Page 85

Sandy Hook/Gateway National Recreation Area

At the northernmost point of the New Jersey coast line is Sandy Hook/Gateway National Recreation Area. It is a barrier peninsula with seven miles of beach, dunes, and fresh and salt water marshes. With opportunities to hike, fish, swim and watch birds, Sandy Hook has plenty of options for any person who wants to be outside. Sandy Hook also has a long history beginning with the oldest lighthouse in the United States. Reportedly, the beacon was first lit on June 11, 1764, and has had an interesting history ever since. The lighthouse resides within the historic Fort Hancock, a National Historical landmark site.

For more information: ***www.nps.gov/gate/index.htm***

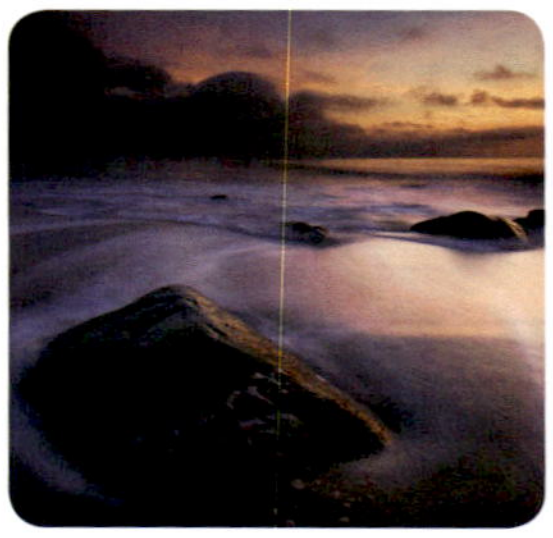
Page 22

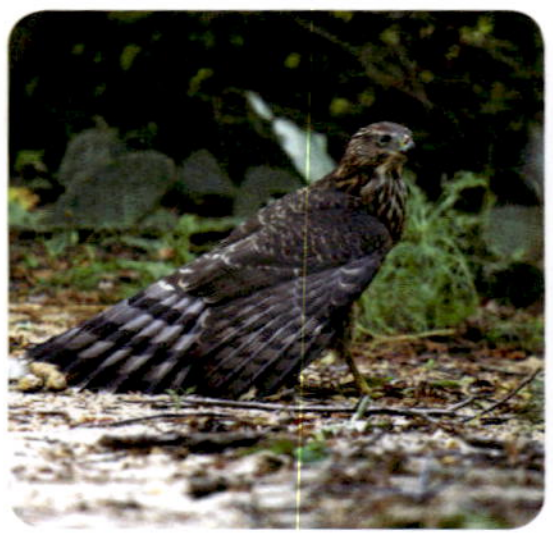
Page 25

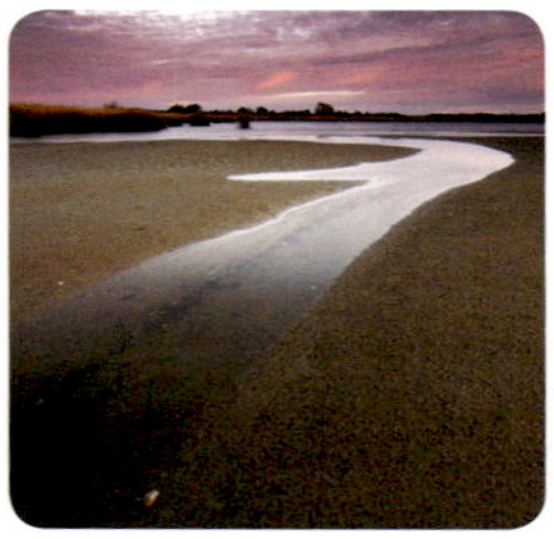
Page 50

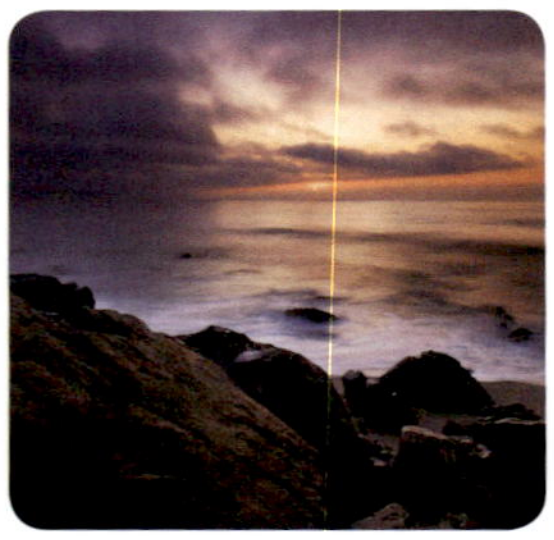
Page 84

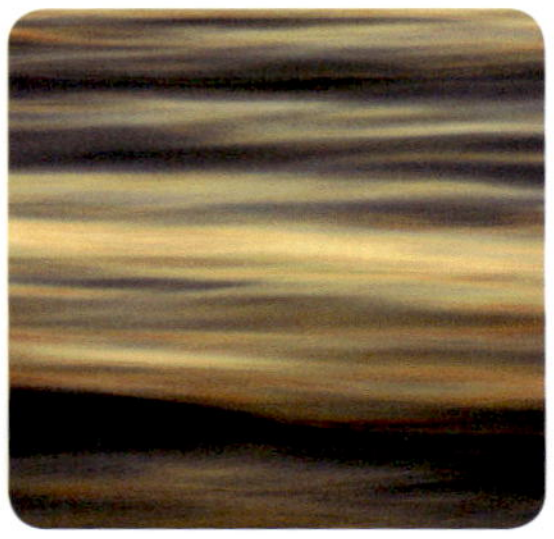
Page 86

South Cape May Meadows

South Cape May Meadows is 200 acres of preserved land that is under the auspices of The Nature Conservatory. In its present state, the area is relatively new. There was once a small town on the land, but it was wiped away in a flood in the early 1950s. The few remaining homes were moved and the land reverted to a meadow, providing pasture for grazing cattle, until the Nature Conservatory took ownership. At that time the dunes were eroding quickly and invasive plants were taking over the wetlands and meadow. Working with the US Army Corp of Engineers a plan was enacted to save the property and have it prosper. The results are beautiful with protected beaches, ponds, and a large variety of birds returning and nesting. It showcases everyone's efforts to save the environment not only for birds to enjoy, but for the residents of New Jersey as well.

For more information: ***www.nature.org***

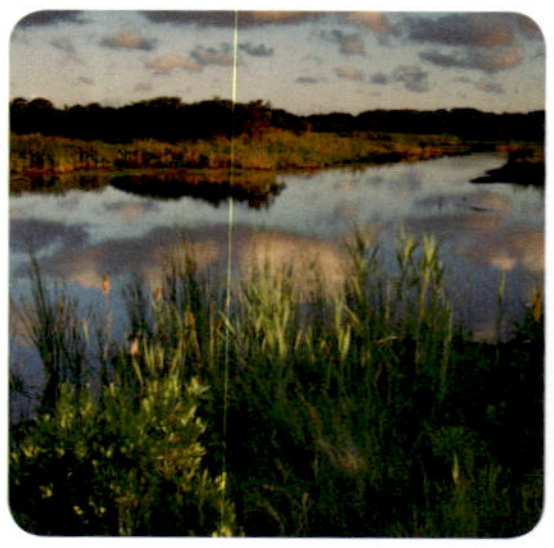
Page 23

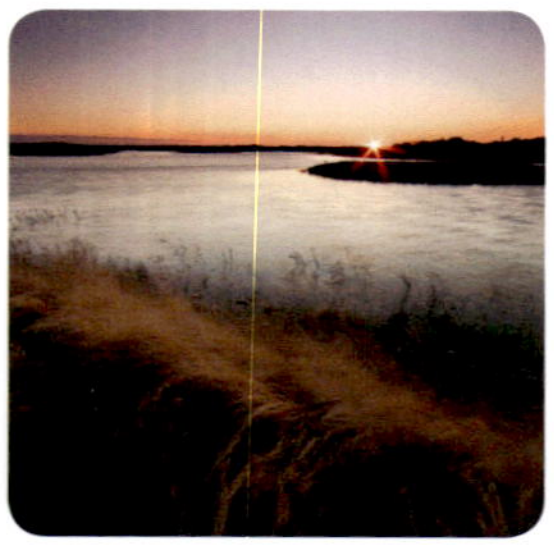
Page 37

Stokes State Forest

A short hike from the parking lot and down into Tillmans Ravine brings you to a beautiful mountain stream cutting through stone walls and bouncing off moss covered rocks. As part of Stokes State Forest Tillmans Ravine is a wonderful area to photograph, hike or have a quiet lunch. As with many areas in northern New Jersey visitors should be wary of black bears that roam the woods. While visiting there in the fall, I encountered a black bear about 40 yards away from where I was shooting. The bear moved on, but it's a reminder that even in the most densely populated state in the country that you share the environment with these large animals.

For more information: ***www.state.nj.us/dep/parksandforests/parks/stokes.html***

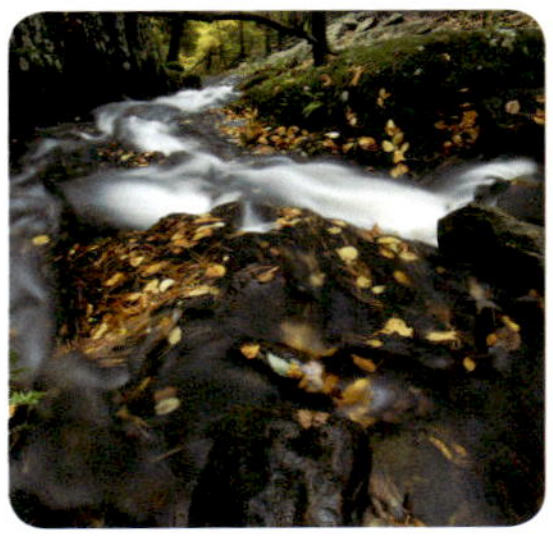

Page 10

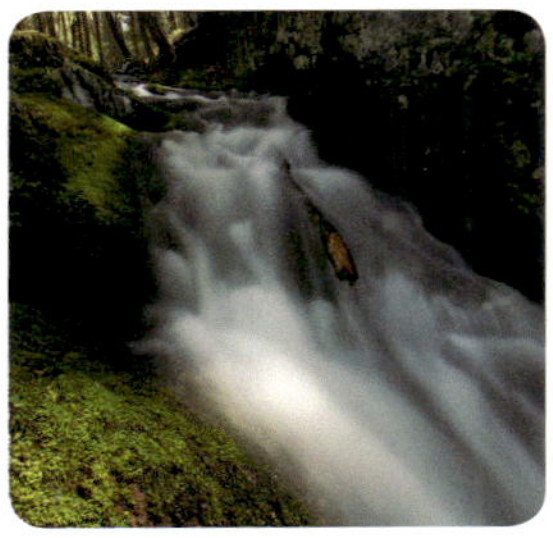

Page 80

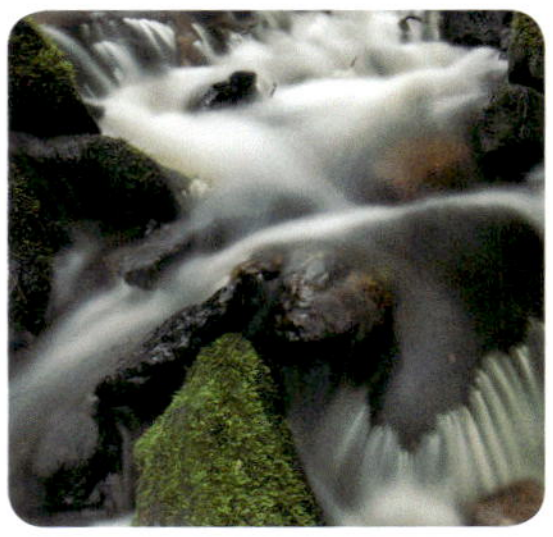

Page 108

Teetertown Preserve

Teetertown Preserve is located in Lebanon Township in Hunterdon County. The Preserve covers more than 500 acres and offers hiking trails and camping. There are multiple connected properties within the preserve, all providing slightly different experiences. During the rainy seasons Hollow Brook begins to swell and becomes a beautiful cascade that runs down the ravine, winding and crashing its way around large beautiful stones. Hiking throughout the preserve showcases the simple beauty of this area of the state, whether it is the open fields or heavy forests. Beautiful ponds to fish in and an abundant variety of birds make this preserve a nice spot to explore.

For more information: ***www.co.hunterdon.nj.us/depts/parks/ParkAreas/Teetertown/info.htm***

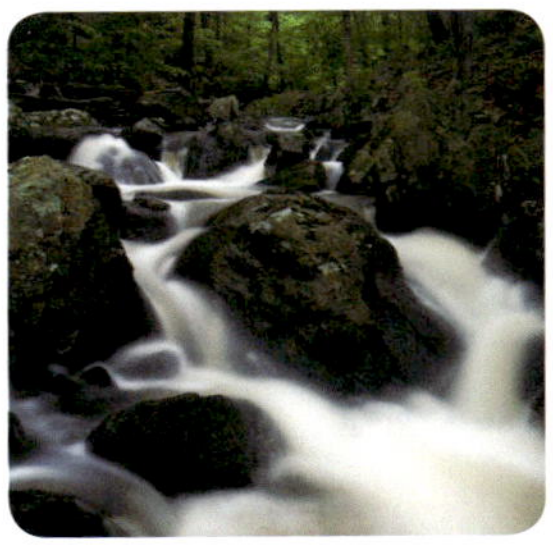

Page 55

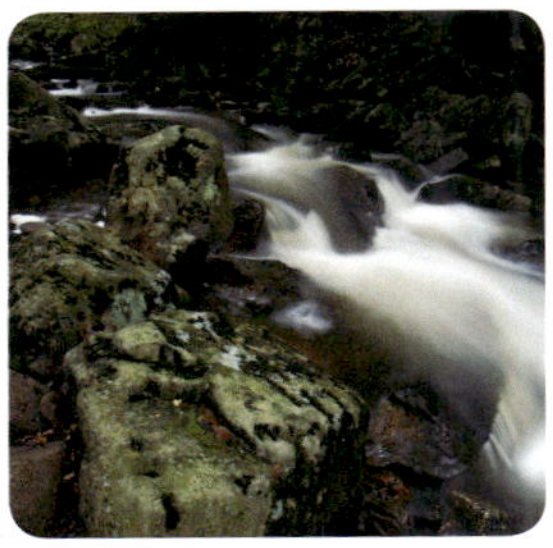

Page 73

Wawayanda State Park

Wawayanda State Park covers more than 16,000 acres, spanning both Sussex and Passaic Counties. The park has facilities for camping and canoeing, 40 miles of hiking trails, and Wawayanda Lake. Whether a seasoned hiker or a beginner, Wawayanda Park offers a variety of options. Twenty miles of the Appalachian Trail cut through the park, offering wonderful views. Bodies of water, such as Terrace Pond, formed thousands of years ago by receding glaciers offer more of a hiking challenge, but with great rewards when the ponds are reached. One of the best views in the state is from Pinwheel Vista off the Appalachian Trail, offering unobstructed, 180-degree vistas from beautiful outcrops. The views and outcrops are some of the best in the state. There are park facilities located by the lake with information and directions for all visitors.

For more information: ***www.state.nj.us/dep/parksandforests/parks/wawayanda.html***

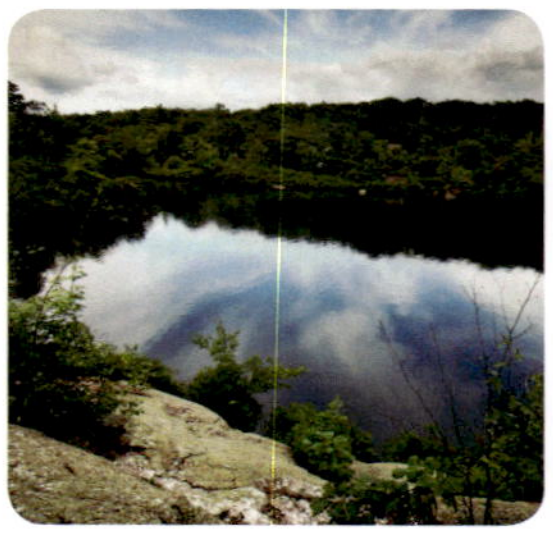

Page 40

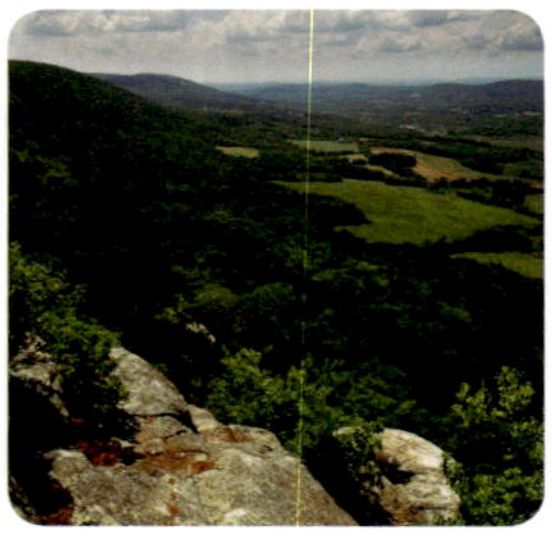

Page 99

Wharton State Forest

The New Jersey Pine Barrens is made up of many state parks and forests set aside to preserve a unique ecosystem. The largest of these parks is the Wharton State Forest. The park is the largest tract of wooded forest in the state, totaling approximately 115,000 acres. It is named after John Wharton, an entrepreneur who purchased most of the land in order to provide clean drinking water to Philadelphia. When the New Jersey State legislature found out about Wharton's plan they outlawed the exporting of water outside of the state. In the 1950s, New Jersey bought the property from Wharton's heirs. These actions taken by the State over many years, preserved one of the largest aquifers on the East Coast, with billions of gallons of pure water. It also saved threatened animals that are present only in the Pinelands and preserved a way of life for the residents in and around this special area.

For more information: ***www.state.nj.us/dep/parksandforests/parks/wharton.html***

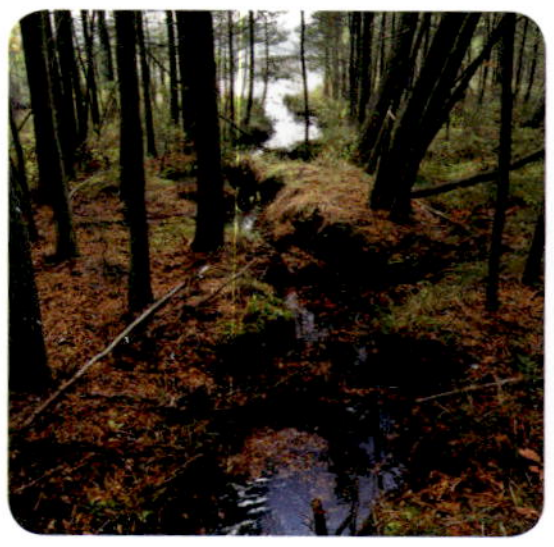

Page 12

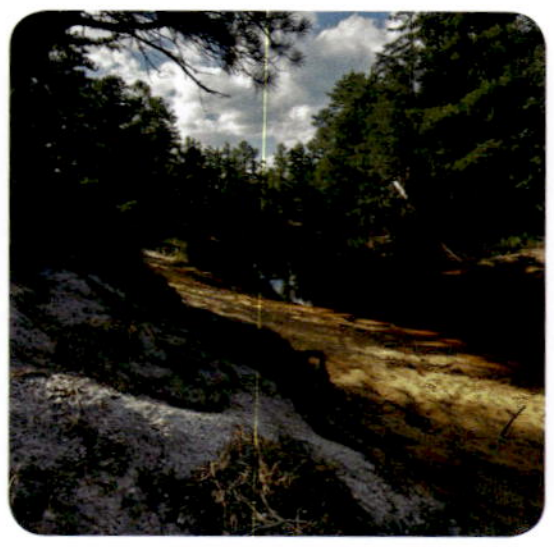

Page 38

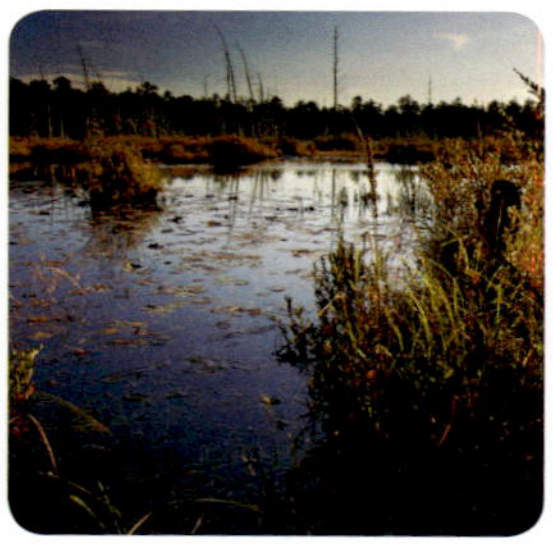

Page 56

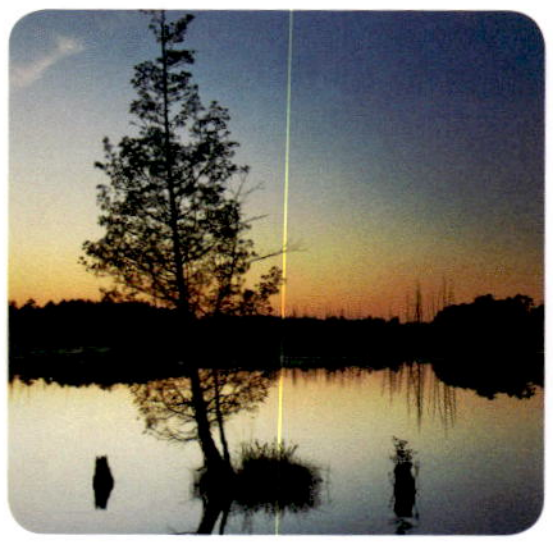

Page 75

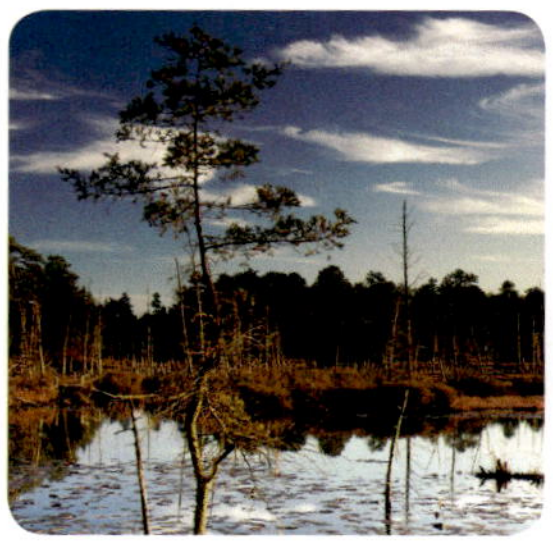

Page 98

Wickecheoke Creek Preserve

Under the auspices of the New Jersey Conservation Foundation this preserve is a series of saved properties bordering the Wickecheoke Creek. Located in Hunterdon County near Stockton, the creek winds thorough beautiful countryside as it makes its way to its final destination, the Delaware Raritan Canal. There are many places to see small cascades and larger waterfalls, especially at times when the creek is saturated. There are plenty of opportunities to get wonderful images in and around the water, often including the wildlife the Preserve supports. Since it contains multiple properties the drive to and from the Wickecheoke Creek Preserve is beautiful. The last covered bridge in New Jersey, Green Sergeant's, is located there as well.

For more information: ***www.njconservation.org/wickecheokepreserve.htm***

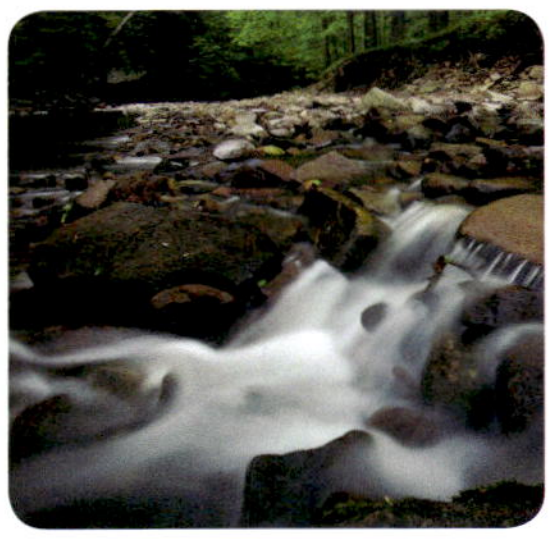

Page 47

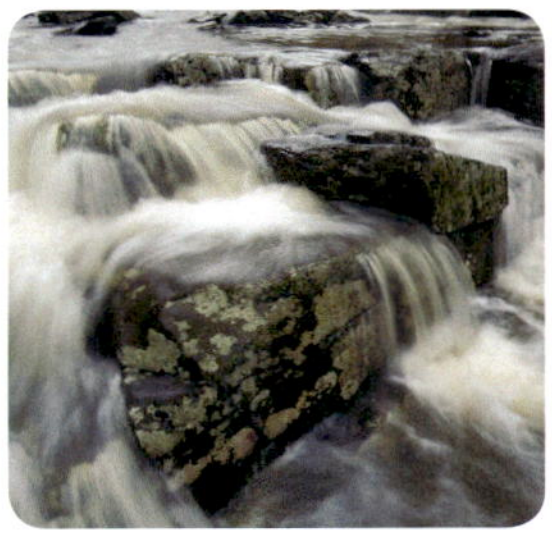

Page 68

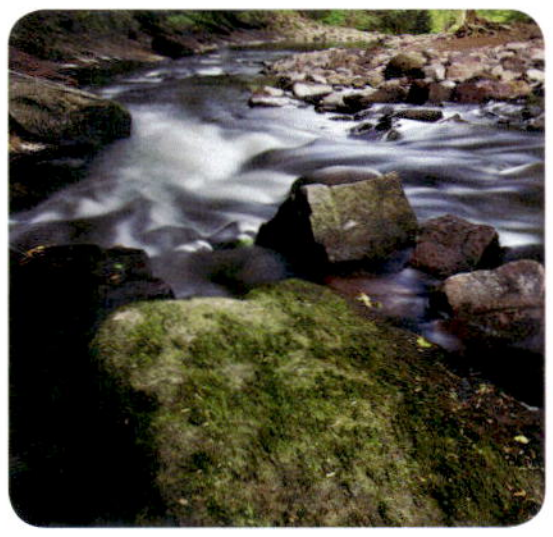

Page 103

Worthington State Forest

Located on the Kittatinny Ridge, Worthington State Forest borders the Delaware River and is situated within the Delaware Gap National Recreation area. It has over 6,000 acres complete with hiking, camping, and boat access to the river. Seven miles of the Appalachian Trail runs along its ridge as it winds its way from Maine to Georgia. There are multiple beautiful destinations within the forest. Dunnfield Creek is a mountain trout stream that makes its way down the mountain by cascading over large boulders. Hikers may want to climb to the top of Mount Tammany for spectacular views up and down the river. Northern New Jersey has many glacier ponds and one of the most popular is Sunfish Pond located on the ridge in this park. This area is a very popular destination because it offers many outdoor opportunities.

For more information: ***www.state.nj.us/dep/parksandforests/parks/worthington.html***

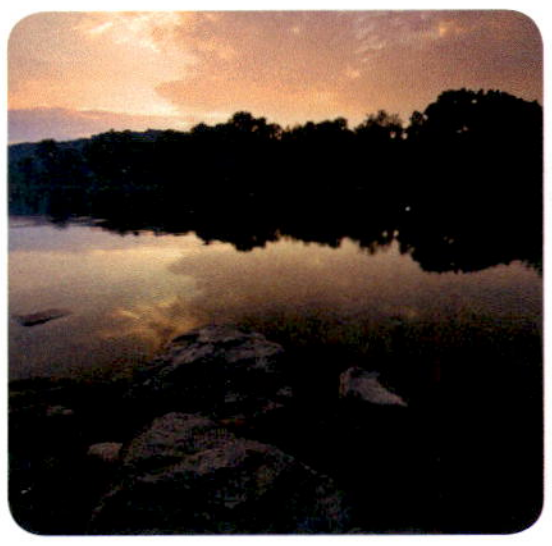

Page 17

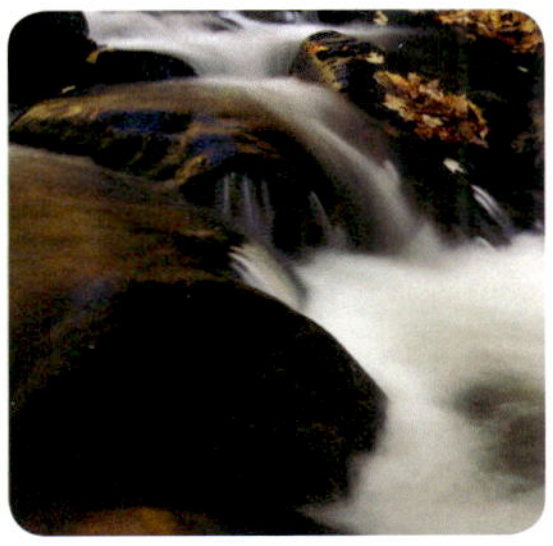

Page 88

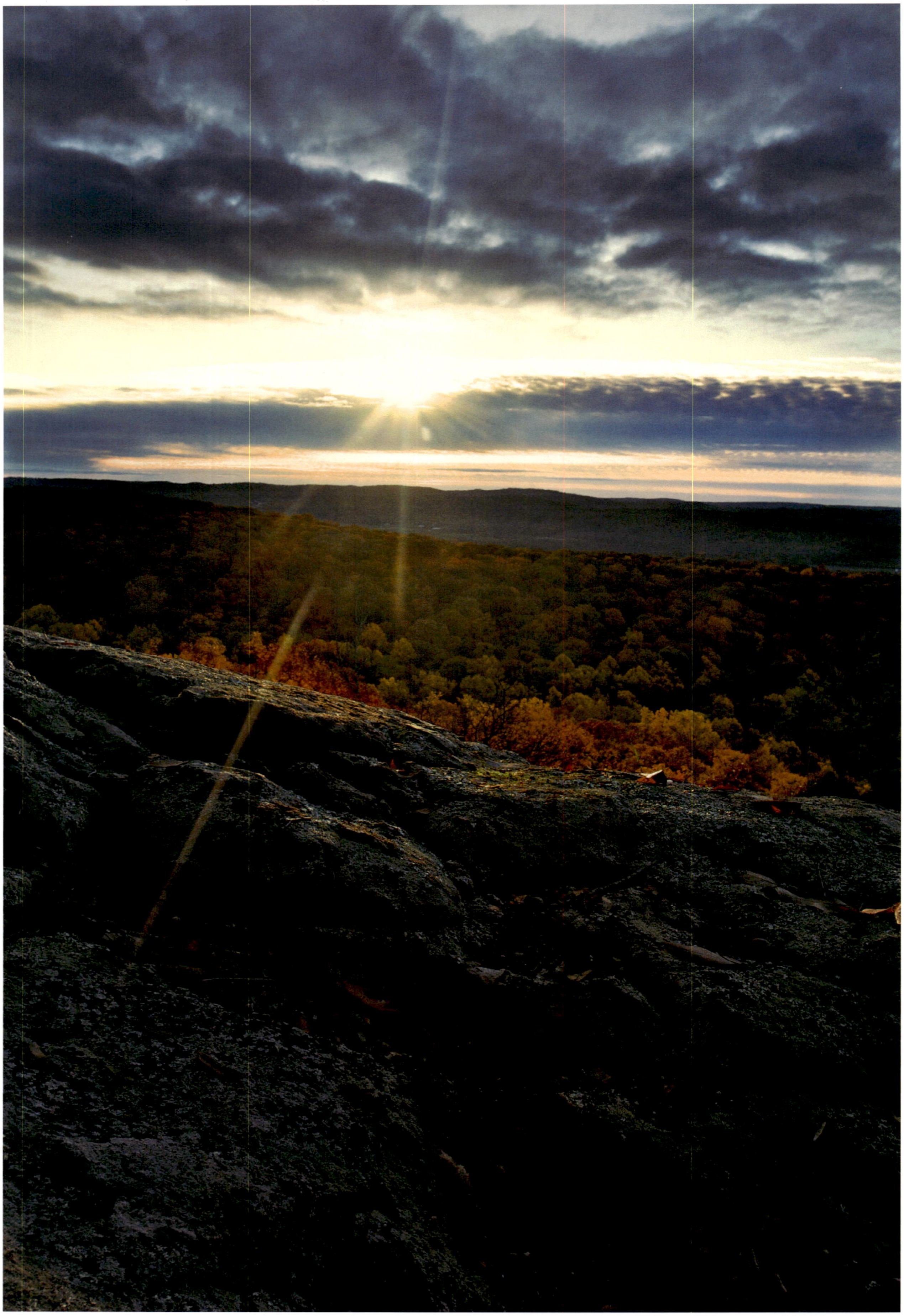

Sunrise at Jenny Jump, Jenny Jump State Forest

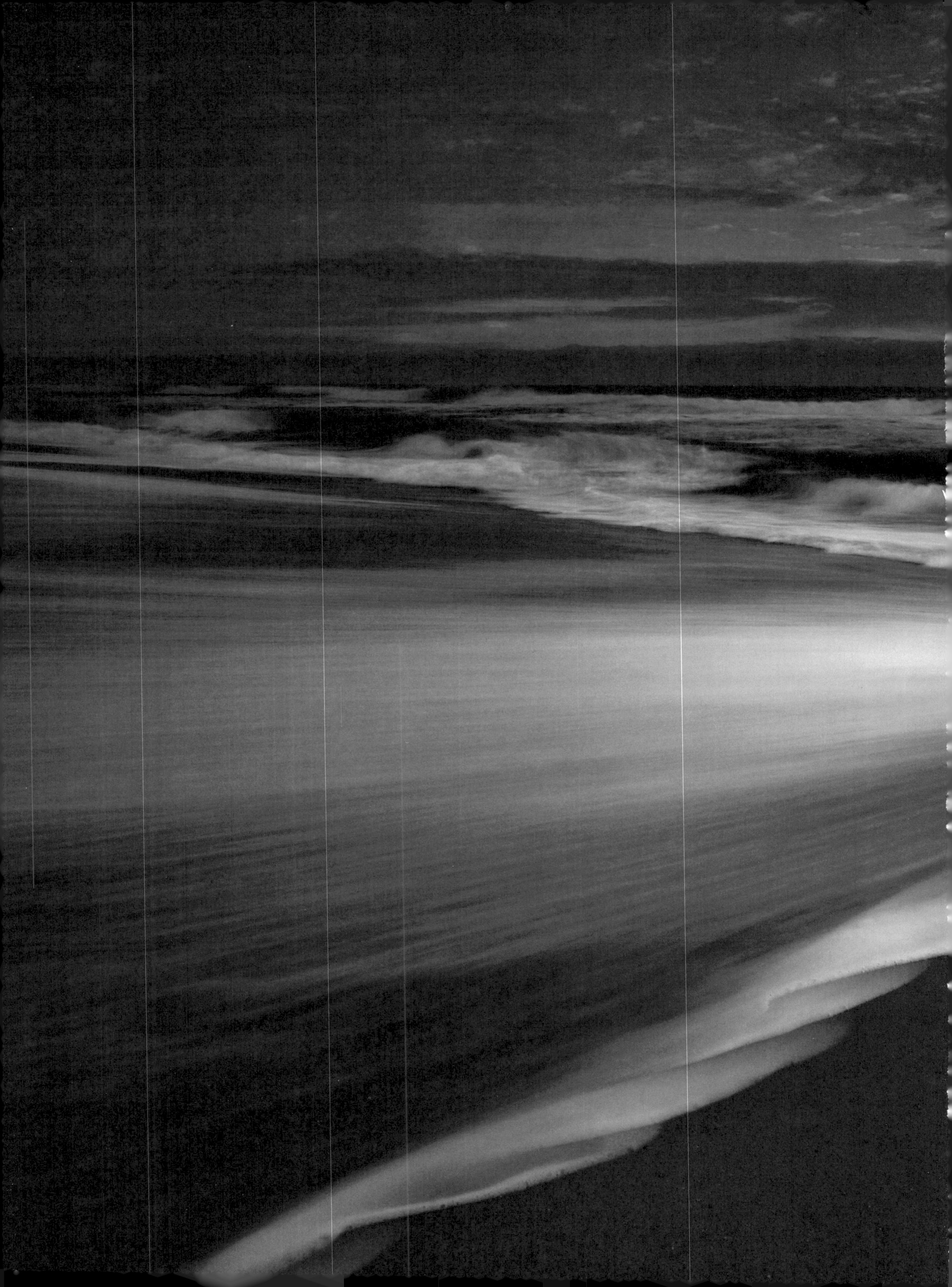